W9-BTE-627

2021 EDITION

MODEL RULES
OF
PROFESSIONAL
CONDUCT

AMERICAN**BAR**ASSOCIATION

Center for Professional
Responsibility

AMERICAN BAR ASSOCIATION
CENTER FOR PROFESSIONAL RESPONSIBILITY

The Center for Professional Responsibility is the American Bar Association's "home" for lawyers who are interested in professionalism, ethics, client protection, legal malpractice, discipline, and regulation. The Center has served as locus for many ABA initiatives, including those of the Commission on Multidisciplinary Practice, the Commission on Multijurisdictional Practice, the Commission on Evaluation of the Rules of Professional Conduct (Ethics 2000), the Joint Commission to Evaluate the Model Code of Judicial Conduct, and the Commission on Ethics 20/20. The Center comprises numerous committees and publishes various works relating to professional responsibility law. In addition, the Center:

- Develops rules of lawyer and judicial ethics, professional discipline, and client protection that serve as the model for jurisdictions throughout the country;
- Produces numerous publications including *Annotated Model Rules of Professional Conduct*, *Annotated Model Code of Judicial Conduct*, *The Paralegal's Guide to Professional Responsibility*, model lawyer, judicial, and client protection rules, and, in partnership with Bloomberg BNA, the *ABA/BNA Lawyers' Manual on Professional Conduct*;
- Issues formal opinions to resolve questions about applying ethics rules;
- Operates the National Lawyer Regulatory Data Bank, the only national repository of information relating to lawyers who have received public disciplinary sanctions;
- Offers on-site consultations to individual jurisdictions reviewing their discipline systems; and
- Presents the National Conference on Professional Responsibility, National Forum on Client Protection, National Legal Malpractice Conference, and numerous CLE webinars.

Center membership is open to ABA lawyer, associate, and law student members in all practice settings. Benefits include steep discounts on publications and CLE events.

Find out more about the Center at http://ambar.org/CPRHome or contact the Center at cpr@americanbar.org.

Dedicated to the memory of
Jeanne P. Gray
Director, ABA Center for Professional Responsibility,
1982–2013

CONTENTS

PUBLIC SERVICE

INFORMATION ABOUT LEGAL SERVICES

MAINTAINING THE INTEGRITY OF THE PROFESSION

APPENDICES

PREFACE

For more than one hundred years, the American Bar Association has provided leadership in legal ethics and professional responsibility through the adoption of professional standards that serve as models of the regulatory law governing the legal profession.

On August 27, 1908, the Association adopted the original Canons of Professional Ethics. These were based principally on the Code of Ethics adopted by the Alabama Bar Association in 1887, which in turn had been borrowed largely from the lectures of Judge George Sharswood, published in 1854 as Professional Ethics, and from the fifty resolutions included in David Hoffman's A Course of Legal Study (2d ed. 1836). Piecemeal amendments to the Canons occasionally followed.

In 1913, the Standing Committee on Professional Ethics of the American Bar Association was established to keep the Association informed about state and local bar activities concerning professional ethics. In 1919 the name of the Committee was changed to the Committee on Professional Ethics and Grievances; its role was expanded in 1922 to include issuing opinions "concerning professional conduct, and particularly concerning the application of the tenets of ethics thereto." In 1958 the Committee on Professional Ethics and Grievances was separated into two committees: a Committee on Professional Grievances, with authority to review issues of professional misconduct, and a Committee on Professional Ethics with responsibility to express its opinion concerning proper professional and judicial conduct. The Committee on Professional Grievances was discontinued in 1971. The name of the Committee on Professional Ethics was changed to the Committee on Ethics and Professional Responsibility in 1971 and remains so.

In 1964, at the request of President Lewis F. Powell Jr., the House of Delegates of the American Bar Association created a Special Committee on Evaluation of Ethical Standards (the "Wright Committee") to assess whether changes should be made in the then-current Canons of Professional Ethics. In response, the Committee produced the Model Code of Professional Responsibility. The Model Code was adopted by the House of Delegates on August 12, 1969, and subsequently by the vast majority of state and federal jurisdictions.

In 1977, the American Bar Association created the Commission on Evaluation of Professional Standards to undertake a comprehensive rethinking of the ethical premises and problems of the legal profession. Upon evaluating the Model Code and determining that amendment of the Code would not achieve a comprehensive statement of the law governing the legal profession, the Commission commenced a six-year study and drafting process that produced the Model Rules of Professional Conduct. The Model Rules were adopted by the House of Delegates of the American Bar Association on August 2, 1983.

Between 1983 and 2002, the House amended the Rules and Comments on fourteen different occasions. In 1997, the American Bar Association created the Commission on Evaluation of the Rules of Professional Conduct ("Ethics 2000 Commission") to comprehensively review the Model Rules and propose amendments as deemed appropriate. On February 5, 2002 the House of Delegates adopted a series of amendments that arose from this process.

In 2000, the American Bar Association created the Commission on Multijurisdictional Practice to research, study and report on the application of current ethics and bar admission rules to the multijurisdictional practice of law. On August 12, 2002 the House of Delegates adopted amendments to Rules 5.5 and 8.5 as a result of the Commission's work and recommendations.

In 2002, the American Bar Association created the Task Force on Corporate Responsibility to examine systemic issues relating to corporate responsibility arising out of the unexpected and traumatic bankruptcy of Enron and other Enron-like situations that had shaken confidence in the effectiveness of the governance and disclosure systems applicable to public companies in the United States. In August 11-12, 2003, the House of Delegates adopted amendments to Rules 1.6 and 1.13 as a result of the Task Force's work and recommendations.

In 2009, the American Bar Association created the Commission on Ethics 20/20 to perform a thorough review of the ABA Model Rules of Professional Conduct and the U.S. system of lawyer regulation in the context of advances in technology and global legal practice developments. On August 6, 2012 and February 11, 2013 the House of Delegates adopted a series of amendments to the Rules and Comments as a result of the Commission's work and recommendations.

In February 2016, the Section on International Law recommended amending Model Rule of Professional Conduct 5.5 and the ABA Model

Rule for Registration of In-House Counsel to include language specifying that the court of highest appellate jurisdiction may, in its discretion, allow foreign in-house lawyers who do not meet the ABA definition of foreign lawyer because they cannot be "members of the bar" to be able to practice as in-house counsel in the United States and to be so registered. On February 8, 2016, the House of Delegates adopted the suggested amendments with further revisions.

In August 2016, the Standing Committee on Ethics and Professional Responsibility brought to the House of Delegates amendments to Model Rule 8.4, Misconduct. Proposed new paragraph (g) prohibited lawyers from discrimination and harassment in conduct related to the practice of law. On August 8, 2016, the House of Delegates adopted the recommended amendments.

In 2018, the Standing Committee on Ethics and Professional Responsibility suggested amendments to the Model Rules regulating lawyer advertising with the goal of simplifying and making those rules more uniform. On August 6, 2018, the House of Delegates adopted the suggested amendments.

In 2020, the Standing Committee on Ethics and Professional Responsibility suggested amendments to Model Rule 1.8(e) to allow lawyers, representing someone on a pro bono basis, to provide limited financial assistance to that client. On August 12, 2020, the House of Delegates adopted the recommended amendments.

The American Bar Association continues to pursue its goal of assuring the highest standards of professional competence and ethical conduct. The Standing Committee on Ethics and Professional Responsibility, charged with interpreting the professional standards of the Association and recommending appropriate amendments and clarifications, issues opinions interpreting the Model Rules of Professional Conduct and the Model Code of Judicial Conduct. The opinions of the Committee are published by the American Bar Association in a series of bound volumes containing opinions from 1924 through 2013 and as individual PDFs starting with the 1984 opinions.

Requests that the Committee issue opinions on particular questions of professional and judicial conduct should be directed to the American Bar Association, Center for Professional Responsibility, 321 N. Clark Street, Chicago, Illinois 60654.

ABA COMMISSION ON
EVALUATION OF PROFESSIONAL STANDARDS
(1977–1983)

COMMISSION ON EVALUATION OF PROFESSIONAL STANDARDS
CHAIR'S INTRODUCTION

The Commission on Evaluation of Professional Standards was appointed in the summer of 1977 by former ABA President William B. Spann, Jr. Chaired by Robert J. Kutak until his death in early 1983, the Commission was charged with evaluating whether existing standards of professional conduct provided comprehensive and consistent guidance for resolving the increasingly complex ethical problems in the practice of law. For the most part, the Commission looked to the former ABA Model Code of Professional Responsibility, which served as a model for the majority of state ethics codes. The Commission also referred to opinions of the ABA Standing Committee on Ethics and Professional Responsibility, as well as to decisions of the United States Supreme Court and of state supreme courts. After thoughtful study, the Commission concluded that piecemeal amendment of the Model Code would not sufficiently clarify the profession's ethical responsibilities in light of changed conditions. The Commission therefore commenced a drafting process that produced numerous drafts, elicited voluminous comment, and launched an unprecedented debate on the ethics of the legal profession.

On January 30, 1980, the Commission presented its initial suggestions to the bar in the form of a Discussion Draft of the proposed Model Rules of Professional Conduct. The Discussion Draft was subject to the widest possible dissemination and interested parties were urged to offer comments and suggestions. Public hearings were held around the country to provide forums for expression of views on the draft.

In the year following the last of these public hearings, the Commission conducted a painstaking analysis of the submitted comments and attempted to integrate into the draft those which seemed consistent with its underlying philosophy. The product of this analysis and integration was presented on May 31, 1981, as the proposed Final Draft of the Model Rules of Professional Conduct. This proposed Final Draft was submitted in two formats. The first format, consisting of blackletter Rules and accompanying Comments in the so-called restatement format, was submitted with the Commission's recommendation that it be adopted. The alternative format was patterned after the Model Code and consisted of Canons, Ethical Considerations, and Disciplinary Rules. In February 1982, the House of Delegates by substantial majority approved the restatement format of the Model Rules.

The proposed Final Draft was submitted to the House of Delegates for debate and approval at the 1982 Annual Meeting of the Association in San Francisco. Many organizations and interested parties offered their comments in the form of proposed amendments to the Final Draft. In the time allotted on its agenda, however, the House debated only proposed amendments to Rule 1.5. Consideration of the remainder of the document was deferred until the 1983 Midyear Meeting in New Orleans. The proposed Final Draft, as amended by the House in San Francisco, was reprinted in the November 1982 issue of the *ABA Journal*.

At the 1983 Midyear Meeting the House resumed consideration of the Final Draft. After two days of often vigorous debate, the House completed its review of the proposed amendments to the blackletter Rules. Many amendments, particularly in the area of confidentiality, were adopted. Debate on a Preamble, Scope, Terminology, and Comments, rewritten to reflect the New Orleans amendments, was deferred until the 1983 Annual Meeting in Atlanta, Georgia.

On March 11, 1983, the text of the blackletter Rules as approved by the House in February, together with the proposed Preamble, Scope, Terminology, and Comments, was circulated to members of the House, Section and Committee chairs, and all other interested parties. The text of the Rules reflected the joint efforts of the Commission and the House Drafting Committee to incorporate the changes approved by the House and to ensure stylistic continuity and uniformity. Recipients of the draft were again urged to submit comments in the form of proposed amendments. The House Committees on Drafting and Rules and Calendar met on May 23, 1983, to consider all of the proposed amendments that had been submitted in response to this draft. In addition, discussions were held among concerned parties in an effort to reach accommodation of the various positions. On July 11, 1983, the final version of the Model Rules was again circulated.

The House of Delegates commenced debate on the proposed Preamble, Scope, Terminology, and Comments on August 2, 1983. After four hours of debate, the House completed its consideration of all the proposed amendments and, upon motion of the Commission, the House voted to adopt the Model Rules of Professional Conduct, together with the ancillary material as amended. The task of the Commission had ended and it was discharged with thanks.

Throughout the drafting process, active participants included not only the members of the Commission but also the Sections and Committees of the American Bar Association and national, state, and local bar organizations. The work of the Commission was subject to virtually continuous scrutiny by academicians, practicing lawyers, members of the press, and the judiciary. Consequently, every provision of the Model Rules reflects the thoughtful consideration and hard work of many dedicated professionals. Because of their input, the Model Rules are truly national in derivation. The Association can take immense pride in its continued demonstration of leadership in the area of professional responsibility.

The Model Rules of Professional Conduct are intended to serve as a national framework for implementation of standards of professional conduct. Although the Commission endeavored to harmonize and accommodate the views of all the participants, no set of national standards that speaks to such a diverse constituency as the legal profession can resolve each issue to the complete satisfaction of every affected party. Undoubtedly there will be those who take issue with one or another of the Rules' provisions. Indeed, such dissent from individual provisions is expected. And the Model Rules, like all model legislation, will be subject to modification at the level of local implementation. Viewed as a whole, however, the Model Rules represent a responsible approach to the ethical practice of law and are consistent with professional obligations imposed by other law, such as constitutional, corporate, tort, fiduciary, and agency law.

I should not end this report without speaking of the Commission's debt to many people who have aided us in our deliberations, and have devoted time, energy, and goodwill to the advancement of our work over the last six years. It would probably be impossible to name each of the particular persons whose help was significant to us, and it surely would be unfortunate if the name of anyone were omitted from the list. We are, and shall remain, deeply grateful to the literally hundreds of people who aided us with welcome and productive suggestions. We think the bar should be grateful to each of them, and to our deceased members, Alan Barth of the District of Columbia, who we hardly had time to know, Bill Spann, who became a member after the conclusion of his presidential term, and our original chair, Bob Kutak.

The long work of the Commission and its resulting new codification of the ethical rules of practice demonstrate, it is submitted, the commitment of the American lawyer to his or her profession and to achievement of the highest standards.

Robert W. Meserve
September 1983

xix

ABA COMMISSION ON EVALUATION OF THE RULES OF PROFESSIONAL CONDUCT (1997–2002)

HON. E. NORMAN VEASEY, *Chair*
Wilmington, Delaware

MARGARET C. LOVE
Washington, D.C.

LAWRENCE J. FOX
Philadelphia, Pennsylvania

SUSAN R. MARTYN
Toledo, Ohio

ALBERT C. HARVEY
Memphis, Tennessee

DAVID T. MCLAUGHLIN
New London, New Hampshire

GEOFFREY C. HAZARD, JR.
Swarthmore, Pennsylvania

RICHARD E. MULROY
Ridgewood, New Jersey

HON. PATRICK E. HIGGINBOTHAM
Dallas, Texas

LUCIAN T. PERA
Memphis, Tennessee

W. LOEBER LANDAU
New York, New York

HON. HENRY RAMSEY, JR. (Ret.)
Berkeley, California

HON. LAURIE D. ZELON
Los Angeles, California

LIAISONS

JAMES B. LEE
Salt Lake City, Utah
Board of Governors

SETH ROSNER
Greenfield Center, New York
Board of Governors

REPORTERS

NANCY J. MOORE
Boston, Massachusetts
Chief Reporter

THOMAS D. MORGAN (1998–1999)
Washington, D.C.

CARL A. PIERCE
Knoxville, Tennessee

CENTER FOR PROFESSIONAL RESPONSIBILITY

JEANNE P. GRAY
Chicago, Illinois
Director

CHARLOTTE K. STRETCH, *Counsel*
Chicago, Illinois

SUSAN M. CAMPBELL, *Paralegal*
Chicago, Illinois

COMMISSION ON EVALUATION OF THE
RULES OF PROFESSIONAL CONDUCT ("ETHICS 2000")
CHAIR'S INTRODUCTION

In mid-1997, ABA President Jerome J. Shestack, his immediate predecessor, N. Lee Cooper, and his successor, Philip S. Anderson had the vision to establish the "Ethics 2000" Commission. These three leaders persuaded the ABA Board of Governors that the Model Rules adopted by the ABA House of Delegates in 1983 needed comprehensive review and some revision, and this project was launched. Though some might have thought it premature to reopen the Model Rules to such a rigorous general reassessment after only fourteen years, the evaluation process has proven that the ABA leadership was correct.

One of the primary reasons behind the decision to revisit the Model Rules was the growing disparity in state ethics codes. While a large majority of states and the District of Columbia had adopted some version of the Model Rules (then thirty-nine, now forty-two), there were many significant differences among the state versions that resulted in an undesirable lack of uniformity—a problem that had been exacerbated by the approximately thirty amendments to the Model Rules between 1983 and 1997. A few states had elected to retain some version of the 1969 Model Code of Professional Responsibility, and California remained committed to an entirely separate system of lawyer regulation.

But it was not only the patchwork pattern of state regulation that motivated the ABA leaders of 1997 to take this action. There were also new issues and questions raised by the influence that technological developments were having on the delivery of legal services. The explosive dynamics of modern law practice and the anticipated developments in the future of the legal profession lent a sense of urgency as well as a substantive dimension to the project. These developments were underscored by the work then underway on the American Law Institute's *Restatement of the Law Governing Lawyers*.

There was also a strong countervailing sense that there was much to be valued in the existing concepts and articulation of the Model Rules. The Commission concluded early on that these valuable aspects of the Rules should not be lost or put at risk in our revision effort. As a result, the Commission set about to be comprehensive, but at the same time conservative, and to recommend change only where necessary. In balancing the need to preserve the good with the need for improvement, we were mindful of Thomas Jefferson's words of nearly 185 years ago, in a letter concerning the Virginia Constitution, that "moderate imperfections had better be borne with; because, when once known, we accommodate ourselves to them, and find practical means of correcting their ill effects."

Thus, we retained the basic architecture of the Model Rules. We also retained the primary disciplinary function of the Rules, resisting the temptation to preach aspirationally about "best practices" or professionalism concepts. Valuable as the profession might find such guidance, it would not have—and should not be misperceived as having—a regulatory dimension. We were, however, always conscious of the educational role of the Model Rules. Finally, we tried to keep our changes to a minimum: when a particular provision was found not to be "broken" we did not try to "fix" it. Even so, as the reader will note, the Commission ended up making a large number of changes: some are relatively innocuous and nonsubstantive, in the nature of editorial or stylistic changes; others are substantive but not particularly controversial; and a few are both substantive and controversial.

The deliberations of the Commission did not take place in a vacuum and our determinations are not being pronounced *ex cathedra*. Rather, they are products of thorough research, scholarly analysis, and thoughtful consideration. Of equal importance, they have been influenced by the views of practitioners, scholars, other members of the legal profession, and the public. All these constituencies have had continual access to and considerable—and proper—influence upon the deliberations of the Commission throughout this process.

I must pause to underscore the openness of our process. We held over fifty days of meetings, all of which were open, and ten public hearings at regular intervals over a four-and-a-half-year period. There were a large number of interested observers at our meetings, many of whom were members of our Advisory Council of 250-plus persons, to offer comments and suggestions. Those observations were very helpful and influential in shaping the Report. Our public discussion drafts, minutes, and Report were available on our website for the world to see and comment upon. As a consequence, we received an enormous number of excellent comments and suggestions, many of which were adopted in the formulation of our Report.

Moreover, we encouraged state and local bar associations, ABA sections and divisions, other professional organizations, and the judiciary to appoint specially designated committees to work with and counsel the Commission. This effort was successful, and the Commission benefitted significantly from the considered views of these groups.

In heeding the counsel of these advisors, we were constantly mindful of substantial and high-velocity changes in the legal profession, particularly over the past decade. These changes have been highlighted by increased public scrutiny of lawyers and an awareness of their influential role in the formation and implementation of public policy; persistent concerns about lawyer honesty, candor, and civility; external competitive and technological pressures on the legal profession; internal pressures on law firm organization and management raised by sheer size, as well as specialization and lawyer mobility; jurisdictional and governance issues, such as multidisciplinary and multijurisdictional practice; special concerns of lawyers in nontraditional practice settings, such as government lawyers and in-house counsel; and the need to enhance public trust and confidence in the legal profession.

At the end of the day, our goal was to develop Rules that are comprehensible to the public and provide clear guidance to the practitioner. Our desire was to preserve all that is valuable and enduring about the existing Model Rules, while at the same time adapting them to the realities of modern law practice and the limits of professional discipline. We believe our product is a balanced blend of traditional precepts and forward-looking provisions that are responsive to modern developments. Our process has been thorough, painstaking, open, scholarly, objective, and collegial.

It is impossible here to go into detail about the changes proposed by the Commission. The changes recommended by the Commission clarified and strengthened a lawyer's duty to communicate with the client; clarified and strengthened a lawyer's duty to clients in certain specific problem areas; responded to the changing organization and structure of modern law practice; responded to new issues and questions raised by the influence that technological developments are having on the delivery of legal services; clarified existing Rules to provide better guidance and explanation to lawyers; clarified and strengthened a lawyer's obligations to the tribunal and to the justice system; responded to the need for changes in the delivery of legal services to low- and middle-income persons; and increased protection of third parties.

The ABA House of Delegates began consideration of the Commission's Report at the August 2001 Annual Meeting in Chicago and completed its review at the February 2002 Midyear Meeting in Philadelphia.

At the August 2002 Annual Meeting in Washington, D.C., the ABA House of Delegates considered and adopted additional amendments to the Model Rules sponsored by the ABA Commission on Multijurisdictional Practice and the ABA Standing Committee on Ethics and Professional Responsibility. As state supreme courts consider implementation of these newly revised Rules, it is our fervent hope that the goal of uniformity will be the guiding beacon.

In closing, the Commission expresses its gratitude to the law firm of Drinker Biddle & Reath, whose generous contribution helped make possible the continued, invaluable support of the Commission's Chief Reporter. I also want to express personally my gratitude to and admiration for my colleagues. The chemistry, goodwill, good humor, serious purpose, collegiality, and hard work of the Commission members, Reporters, and ABA staff have been extraordinary. The profession and the public have been enriched beyond measure by their efforts. It has been a pleasure and a privilege for me to work with all of them.

Hon. E. Norman Veasey
August 2002

PREAMBLE AND SCOPE

PREAMBLE:
A LAWYER'S RESPONSIBILITIES

[1] A lawyer, as a member of the legal profession, is a representative of clients, an officer of the legal system and a public citizen having special responsibility for the quality of justice.

[2] As a representative of clients, a lawyer performs various functions. As advisor, a lawyer provides a client with an informed understanding of the client's legal rights and obligations and explains their practical implications. As advocate, a lawyer zealously asserts the client's position under the rules of the adversary system. As negotiator, a lawyer seeks a result advantageous to the client but consistent with requirements of honest dealings with others. As an evaluator, a lawyer acts by examining a client's legal affairs and reporting about them to the client or to others.

[3] In addition to these representational functions, a lawyer may serve as a third-party neutral, a nonrepresentational role helping the parties to resolve a dispute or other matter. Some of these Rules apply directly to lawyers who are or have served as third-party neutrals. See, e.g., Rules 1.12 and 2.4. In addition, there are Rules that apply to lawyers who are not active in the practice of law or to practicing lawyers even when they are acting in a nonprofessional capacity. For example, a lawyer who commits fraud in the conduct of a business is subject to discipline for engaging in conduct involving dishonesty, fraud, deceit or misrepresentation. See Rule 8.4.

[4] In all professional functions a lawyer should be competent, prompt and diligent. A lawyer should maintain communication with a client concerning the representation. A lawyer should keep in confidence information relating to representation of a client except so far as disclosure is required or permitted by the Rules of Professional Conduct or other law.

[5] A lawyer's conduct should conform to the requirements of the law, both in professional service to clients and in the lawyer's business and personal affairs. A lawyer should use the law's procedures only for legitimate purposes and not to harass or intimidate others. A lawyer should demonstrate respect for the legal system and for those who serve it, including judges, other lawyers and public officials. While it is a law-

yer's duty, when necessary, to challenge the rectitude of official action, it is also a lawyer's duty to uphold legal process.

[6] As a public citizen, a lawyer should seek improvement of the law, access to the legal system, the administration of justice and the quality of service rendered by the legal profession. As a member of a learned profession, a lawyer should cultivate knowledge of the law beyond its use for clients, employ that knowledge in reform of the law and work to strengthen legal education. In addition, a lawyer should further the public's understanding of and confidence in the rule of law and the justice system because legal institutions in a constitutional democracy depend on popular participation and support to maintain their authority. A lawyer should be mindful of deficiencies in the administration of justice and of the fact that the poor, and sometimes persons who are not poor, cannot afford adequate legal assistance. Therefore, all lawyers should devote professional time and resources and use civic influence to ensure equal access to our system of justice for all those who because of economic or social barriers cannot afford or secure adequate legal counsel. A lawyer should aid the legal profession in pursuing these objectives and should help the bar regulate itself in the public interest.

[7] Many of a lawyer's professional responsibilities are prescribed in the Rules of Professional Conduct, as well as substantive and procedural law. However, a lawyer is also guided by personal conscience and the approbation of professional peers. A lawyer should strive to attain the highest level of skill, to improve the law and the legal profession and to exemplify the legal profession's ideals of public service.

[8] A lawyer's responsibilities as a representative of clients, an officer of the legal system and a public citizen are usually harmonious. Thus, when an opposing party is well represented, a lawyer can be a zealous advocate on behalf of a client and at the same time assume that justice is being done. So also, a lawyer can be sure that preserving client confidences ordinarily serves the public interest because people are more likely to seek legal advice, and thereby heed their legal obligations, when they know their communications will be private.

[9] In the nature of law practice, however, conflicting responsibilities are encountered. Virtually all difficult ethical problems arise from conflict between a lawyer's responsibilities to clients, to the legal system and to the lawyer's own interest in remaining an ethical person while earning a satisfactory living. The Rules of Professional Conduct often prescribe terms for resolving such conflicts. Within the framework of these Rules,

however, many difficult issues of professional discretion can arise. Such issues must be resolved through the exercise of sensitive professional and moral judgment guided by the basic principles underlying the Rules. These principles include the lawyer's obligation zealously to protect and pursue a client's legitimate interests, within the bounds of the law, while maintaining a professional, courteous and civil attitude toward all persons involved in the legal system.

[10] The legal profession is largely self-governing. Although other professions also have been granted powers of self-government, the legal profession is unique in this respect because of the close relationship between the profession and the processes of government and law enforcement. This connection is manifested in the fact that ultimate authority over the legal profession is vested largely in the courts.

[11] To the extent that lawyers meet the obligations of their professional calling, the occasion for government regulation is obviated. Self-regulation also helps maintain the legal profession's independence from government domination. An independent legal profession is an important force in preserving government under law, for abuse of legal authority is more readily challenged by a profession whose members are not dependent on government for the right to practice.

[12] The legal profession's relative autonomy carries with it special responsibilities of self-government. The profession has a responsibility to assure that its regulations are conceived in the public interest and not in furtherance of parochial or self-interested concerns of the bar. Every lawyer is responsible for observance of the Rules of Professional Conduct. A lawyer should also aid in securing their observance by other lawyers. Neglect of these responsibilities compromises the independence of the profession and the public interest which it serves.

[13] Lawyers play a vital role in the preservation of society. The fulfillment of this role requires an understanding by lawyers of their relationship to our legal system. The Rules of Professional Conduct, when properly applied, serve to define that relationship.

SCOPE

[14] The Rules of Professional Conduct are rules of reason. They should be interpreted with reference to the purposes of legal representation and of the law itself. Some of the Rules are imperatives, cast in the terms "shall" or "shall not." These define proper conduct for purposes of professional discipline. Others, generally cast in the term "may," are

permissive and define areas under the Rules in which the lawyer has discretion to exercise professional judgment. No disciplinary action should be taken when the lawyer chooses not to act or acts within the bounds of such discretion. Other Rules define the nature of relationships between the lawyer and others. The Rules are thus partly obligatory and disciplinary and partly constitutive and descriptive in that they define a lawyer's professional role. Many of the Comments use the term "should." Comments do not add obligations to the Rules but provide guidance for practicing in compliance with the Rules.

[15] The Rules presuppose a larger legal context shaping the lawyer's role. That context includes court rules and statutes relating to matters of licensure, laws defining specific obligations of lawyers and substantive and procedural law in general. The Comments are sometimes used to alert lawyers to their responsibilities under such other law.

[16] Compliance with the Rules, as with all law in an open society, depends primarily upon understanding and voluntary compliance, secondarily upon reinforcement by peer and public opinion and finally, when necessary, upon enforcement through disciplinary proceedings. The Rules do not, however, exhaust the moral and ethical considerations that should inform a lawyer, for no worthwhile human activity can be completely defined by legal rules. The Rules simply provide a framework for the ethical practice of law.

[17] Furthermore, for purposes of determining the lawyer's authority and responsibility, principles of substantive law external to these Rules determine whether a client-lawyer relationship exists. Most of the duties flowing from the client-lawyer relationship attach only after the client has requested the lawyer to render legal services and the lawyer has agreed to do so. But there are some duties, such as that of confidentiality under Rule 1.6, that attach when the lawyer agrees to consider whether a client-lawyer relationship shall be established. See Rule 1.18. Whether a client-lawyer relationship exists for any specific purpose can depend on the circumstances and may be a question of fact.

[18] Under various legal provisions, including constitutional, statutory and common law, the responsibilities of government lawyers may include authority concerning legal matters that ordinarily reposes in the client in private client-lawyer relationships. For example, a lawyer for a government agency may have authority on behalf of the government to decide upon settlement or whether to appeal from an adverse judgment. Such authority in various respects is generally vested in the attorney

general and the state's attorney in state government, and their federal counterparts, and the same may be true of other government law officers. Also, lawyers under the supervision of these officers may be authorized to represent several government agencies in intragovernmental legal controversies in circumstances where a private lawyer could not represent multiple private clients. These Rules do not abrogate any such authority.

[19] Failure to comply with an obligation or prohibition imposed by a Rule is a basis for invoking the disciplinary process. The Rules presuppose that disciplinary assessment of a lawyer's conduct will be made on the basis of the facts and circumstances as they existed at the time of the conduct in question and in recognition of the fact that a lawyer often has to act upon uncertain or incomplete evidence of the situation. Moreover, the Rules presuppose that whether or not discipline should be imposed for a violation, and the severity of a sanction, depend on all the circumstances, such as the willfulness and seriousness of the violation, extenuating factors and whether there have been previous violations.

[20] Violation of a Rule should not itself give rise to a cause of action against a lawyer nor should it create any presumption in such a case that a legal duty has been breached. In addition, violation of a Rule does not necessarily warrant any other nondisciplinary remedy, such as disqualification of a lawyer in pending litigation. The Rules are designed to provide guidance to lawyers and to provide a structure for regulating conduct through disciplinary agencies. They are not designed to be a basis for civil liability. Furthermore, the purpose of the Rules can be subverted when they are invoked by opposing parties as procedural weapons. The fact that a Rule is a just basis for a lawyer's self-assessment, or for sanctioning a lawyer under the administration of a disciplinary authority, does not imply that an antagonist in a collateral proceeding or transaction has standing to seek enforcement of the Rule. Nevertheless, since the Rules do establish standards of conduct by lawyers, a lawyer's violation of a Rule may be evidence of breach of the applicable standard of conduct.

[21] The Comment accompanying each Rule explains and illustrates the meaning and purpose of the Rule. The Preamble and this note on Scope provide general orientation. The Comments are intended as guides to interpretation, but the text of each Rule is authoritative.

RULE 1.0: TERMINOLOGY

(a) "Belief" or "believes" denotes that the person involved actually supposed the fact in question to be true. A person's belief may be inferred from circumstances.

(b) "Confirmed in writing," when used in reference to the informed consent of a person, denotes informed consent that is given in writing by the person or a writing that a lawyer promptly transmits to the person confirming an oral informed consent. See paragraph (e) for the definition of "informed consent." If it is not feasible to obtain or transmit the writing at the time the person gives informed consent, then the lawyer must obtain or transmit it within a reasonable time thereafter.

(c) "Firm" or "law firm" denotes a lawyer or lawyers in a law partnership, professional corporation, sole proprietorship or other association authorized to practice law; or lawyers employed in a legal services organization or the legal department of a corporation or other organization.

(d) "Fraud" or "fraudulent" denotes conduct that is fraudulent under the substantive or procedural law of the applicable jurisdiction and has a purpose to deceive.

(e) "Informed consent" denotes the agreement by a person to a proposed course of conduct after the lawyer has communicated adequate information and explanation about the material risks of and reasonably available alternatives to the proposed course of conduct.

(f) "Knowingly," "known," or "knows" denotes actual knowledge of the fact in question. A person's knowledge may be inferred from circumstances.

(g) "Partner" denotes a member of a partnership, a shareholder in a law firm organized as a professional corporation, or a member of an association authorized to practice law.

(h) "Reasonable" or "reasonably" when used in relation to conduct by a lawyer denotes the conduct of a reasonably prudent and competent lawyer.

(i) "Reasonable belief" or "reasonably believes" when used in reference to a lawyer denotes that the lawyer believes the matter in question and that the circumstances are such that the belief is reasonable.

(j) "Reasonably should know" when used in reference to a lawyer denotes that a lawyer of reasonable prudence and competence would ascertain the matter in question.

(k) "Screened" denotes the isolation of a lawyer from any participation in a matter through the timely imposition of procedures within a firm that are reasonably adequate under the circumstances to protect information that the isolated lawyer is obligated to protect under these Rules or other law.

(l) "Substantial" when used in reference to degree or extent denotes a material matter of clear and weighty importance.

(m) "Tribunal" denotes a court, an arbitrator in a binding arbitration proceeding or a legislative body, administrative agency or other body acting in an adjudicative capacity. A legislative body, administrative agency or other body acts in an adjudicative capacity when a neutral official, after the presentation of evidence or legal argument by a party or parties, will render a binding legal judgment directly affecting a party's interests in a particular matter.

(n) "Writing" or "written" denotes a tangible or electronic record of a communication or representation, including handwriting, typewriting, printing, photostating, photography, audio or videorecording, and electronic communications. A "signed" writing includes an electronic sound, symbol or process attached to or logically associated with a writing and executed or adopted by a person with the intent to sign the writing.

Comment

Confirmed in Writing

[1] If it is not feasible to obtain or transmit a written confirmation at the time the client gives informed consent, then the lawyer must obtain or transmit it within a reasonable time thereafter. If a lawyer has obtained a client's informed consent, the lawyer may act in reliance on that consent so long as it is confirmed in writing within a reasonable time thereafter.

Firm

[2] Whether two or more lawyers constitute a firm within paragraph (c) can depend on the specific facts. For example, two practitioners who share office space and occasionally consult or assist each other ordinarily would not be regarded as constituting a firm. However, if they present themselves to the public in a way that suggests that they are a firm or conduct themselves as a firm, they should be regarded as a firm for purposes of the Rules. The terms of any formal agreement between associated lawyers are relevant in determining whether they are a firm, as

is the fact that they have mutual access to information concerning the clients they serve. Furthermore, it is relevant in doubtful cases to consider the underlying purpose of the Rule that is involved. A group of lawyers could be regarded as a firm for purposes of the Rule that the same lawyer should not represent opposing parties in litigation, while it might not be so regarded for purposes of the Rule that information acquired by one lawyer is attributed to another.

[3] With respect to the law department of an organization, including the government, there is ordinarily no question that the members of the department constitute a firm within the meaning of the Rules of Professional Conduct. There can be uncertainty, however, as to the identity of the client. For example, it may not be clear whether the law department of a corporation represents a subsidiary or an affiliated corporation, as well as the corporation by which the members of the department are directly employed. A similar question can arise concerning an unincorporated association and its local affiliates.

[4] Similar questions can also arise with respect to lawyers in legal aid and legal services organizations. Depending upon the structure of the organization, the entire organization or different components of it may constitute a firm or firms for purposes of these Rules.

Fraud

[5] When used in these Rules, the terms "fraud" or "fraudulent" refer to conduct that is characterized as such under the substantive or procedural law of the applicable jurisdiction and has a purpose to deceive. This does not include merely negligent misrepresentation or negligent failure to apprise another of relevant information. For purposes of these Rules, it is not necessary that anyone has suffered damages or relied on the misrepresentation or failure to inform.

Informed Consent

[6] Many of the Rules of Professional Conduct require the lawyer to obtain the informed consent of a client or other person (e.g., a former client or, under certain circumstances, a prospective client) before accepting or continuing representation or pursuing a course of conduct. See, e.g., Rules 1.2(c), 1.6(a) and 1.7(b). The communication necessary to obtain such consent will vary according to the Rule involved and the circumstances giving rise to the need to obtain informed consent. The lawyer must make reasonable efforts to ensure that the client or other person

possesses information reasonably adequate to make an informed decision. Ordinarily, this will require communication that includes a disclosure of the facts and circumstances giving rise to the situation, any explanation reasonably necessary to inform the client or other person of the material advantages and disadvantages of the proposed course of conduct and a discussion of the client's or other person's options and alternatives. In some circumstances it may be appropriate for a lawyer to advise a client or other person to seek the advice of other counsel. A lawyer need not inform a client or other person of facts or implications already known to the client or other person; nevertheless, a lawyer who does not personally inform the client or other person assumes the risk that the client or other person is inadequately informed and the consent is invalid. In determining whether the information and explanation provided are reasonably adequate, relevant factors include whether the client or other person is experienced in legal matters generally and in making decisions of the type involved, and whether the client or other person is independently represented by other counsel in giving the consent. Normally, such persons need less information and explanation than others, and generally a client or other person who is independently represented by other counsel in giving the consent should be assumed to have given informed consent.

[7] Obtaining informed consent will usually require an affirmative response by the client or other person. In general, a lawyer may not assume consent from a client's or other person's silence. Consent may be inferred, however, from the conduct of a client or other person who has reasonably adequate information about the matter. A number of Rules require that a person's consent be confirmed in writing. See Rules 1.7(b) and 1.9(a). For a definition of "writing" and "confirmed in writing," see paragraphs (n) and (b). Other Rules require that a client's consent be obtained in a writing signed by the client. See, e.g., Rules 1.8(a) and (g). For a definition of "signed," see paragraph (n).

Screened

[8] This definition applies to situations where screening of a personally disqualified lawyer is permitted to remove imputation of a conflict of interest under Rules 1.10, 1.11, 1.12 or 1.18.

[9] The purpose of screening is to assure the affected parties that confidential information known by the personally disqualified lawyer remains protected. The personally disqualified lawyer should acknowledge

the obligation not to communicate with any of the other lawyers in the firm with respect to the matter. Similarly, other lawyers in the firm who are working on the matter should be informed that the screening is in place and that they may not communicate with the personally disqualified lawyer with respect to the matter. Additional screening measures that are appropriate for the particular matter will depend on the circumstances. To implement, reinforce and remind all affected lawyers of the presence of the screening, it may be appropriate for the firm to undertake such procedures as a written undertaking by the screened lawyer to avoid any communication with other firm personnel and any contact with any firm files or other information, including information in electronic form, relating to the matter, written notice and instructions to all other firm personnel forbidding any communication with the screened lawyer relating to the matter, denial of access by the screened lawyer to firm files or other information, including information in electronic form, relating to the matter and periodic reminders of the screen to the screened lawyer and all other firm personnel.

[10] In order to be effective, screening measures must be implemented as soon as practical after a lawyer or law firm knows or reasonably should know that there is a need for screening.

CLIENT-LAWYER RELATIONSHIP

RULE 1.1: COMPETENCE

A lawyer shall provide competent representation to a client. Competent representation requires the legal knowledge, skill, thoroughness and preparation reasonably necessary for the representation.

Comment
Legal Knowledge and Skill

[1] In determining whether a lawyer employs the requisite knowledge and skill in a particular matter, relevant factors include the relative complexity and specialized nature of the matter, the lawyer's general experience, the lawyer's training and experience in the field in question, the preparation and study the lawyer is able to give the matter and whether it is feasible to refer the matter to, or associate or consult with, a lawyer of established competence in the field in question. In many instances, the

required proficiency is that of a general practitioner. Expertise in a particular field of law may be required in some circumstances.

[2] A lawyer need not necessarily have special training or prior experience to handle legal problems of a type with which the lawyer is unfamiliar. A newly admitted lawyer can be as competent as a practitioner with long experience. Some important legal skills, such as the analysis of precedent, the evaluation of evidence and legal drafting, are required in all legal problems. Perhaps the most fundamental legal skill consists of determining what kind of legal problems a situation may involve, a skill that necessarily transcends any particular specialized knowledge. A lawyer can provide adequate representation in a wholly novel field through necessary study. Competent representation can also be provided through the association of a lawyer of established competence in the field in question.

[3] In an emergency a lawyer may give advice or assistance in a matter in which the lawyer does not have the skill ordinarily required where referral to or consultation or association with another lawyer would be impractical. Even in an emergency, however, assistance should be limited to that reasonably necessary in the circumstances, for ill-considered action under emergency conditions can jeopardize the client's interest.

[4] A lawyer may accept representation where the requisite level of competence can be achieved by reasonable preparation. This applies as well to a lawyer who is appointed as counsel for an unrepresented person. See also Rule 6.2.

Thoroughness and Preparation

[5] Competent handling of a particular matter includes inquiry into and analysis of the factual and legal elements of the problem, and use of methods and procedures meeting the standards of competent practitioners. It also includes adequate preparation. The required attention and preparation are determined in part by what is at stake; major litigation and complex transactions ordinarily require more extensive treatment than matters of lesser complexity and consequence. An agreement between the lawyer and the client regarding the scope of the representation may limit the matters for which the lawyer is responsible. See Rule 1.2(c).

Retaining or Contracting With Other Lawyers

[6] Before a lawyer retains or contracts with other lawyers outside the lawyer's own firm to provide or assist in the provision of legal services to a client, the lawyer should ordinarily obtain informed consent

from the client and must reasonably believe that the other lawyers' services will contribute to the competent and ethical representation of the client. See also Rules 1.2 (allocation of authority), 1.4 (communication with client), 1.5(e) (fee sharing), 1.6 (confidentiality), and 5.5(a) (unauthorized practice of law). The reasonableness of the decision to retain or contract with other lawyers outside the lawyer's own firm will depend upon the circumstances, including the education, experience and reputation of the nonfirm lawyers; the nature of the services assigned to the nonfirm lawyers; and the legal protections, professional conduct rules, and ethical environments of the jurisdictions in which the services will be performed, particularly relating to confidential information.

[7] When lawyers from more than one law firm are providing legal services to the client on a particular matter, the lawyers ordinarily should consult with each other and the client about the scope of their respective representations and the allocation of responsibility among them. See Rule 1.2. When making allocations of responsibility in a matter pending before a tribunal, lawyers and parties may have additional obligations that are a matter of law beyond the scope of these Rules.

Maintaining Competence

[8] To maintain the requisite knowledge and skill, a lawyer should keep abreast of changes in the law and its practice, including the benefits and risks associated with relevant technology, engage in continuing study and education and comply with all continuing legal education requirements to which the lawyer is subject.

Definitional Cross-References

"Reasonably" *See* Rule 1.0(h)

RULE 1.2: SCOPE OF REPRESENTATION AND ALLOCATION OF AUTHORITY BETWEEN CLIENT AND LAWYER

(a) Subject to paragraphs (c) and (d), a lawyer shall abide by a client's decisions concerning the objectives of representation and, as required by Rule 1.4, shall consult with the client as to the means by which they are to be pursued. A lawyer may take such action on behalf of the client as is impliedly authorized to carry out the representation. A lawyer shall abide by a client's decision

"purpose"
for example

whether to settle a matter. In a criminal case, the lawyer shall abide by the client's decision, after consultation with the lawyer, as to a plea to be entered, whether to waive jury trial and whether the client will testify.

(b) A lawyer's representation of a client, including representation by appointment, does not constitute an endorsement of the client's political, economic, social or moral views or activities.

(c) A lawyer may limit the scope of the representation if the limitation is reasonable under the circumstances and the client gives informed consent.

(d) A lawyer shall not counsel a client to engage, or assist a client, in conduct that the lawyer knows is criminal or fraudulent, but a lawyer may discuss the legal consequences of any proposed course of conduct with a client and may counsel or assist a client to make a good faith effort to determine the validity, scope, meaning or application of the law.

Comment

Allocation of Authority between Client and Lawyer

[1] Paragraph (a) confers upon the client the ultimate authority to determine the purposes to be served by legal representation, within the limits imposed by law and the lawyer's professional obligations. The decisions specified in paragraph (a), such as whether to settle a civil matter, must also be made by the client. See Rule 1.4(a)(1) for the lawyer's duty to communicate with the client about such decisions. With respect to the means by which the client's objectives are to be pursued, the lawyer shall consult with the client as required by Rule 1.4(a)(2) and may take such action as is impliedly authorized to carry out the representation.

[2] On occasion, however, a lawyer and a client may disagree about the means to be used to accomplish the client's objectives. Clients normally defer to the special knowledge and skill of their lawyer with respect to the means to be used to accomplish their objectives, particularly with respect to technical, legal and tactical matters. Conversely, lawyers usually defer to the client regarding such questions as the expense to be incurred and concern for third persons who might be adversely affected. Because of the varied nature of the matters about which a lawyer and client might disagree and because the actions in question may implicate the interests of a tribunal or other persons, this Rule does not prescribe how

such disagreements are to be resolved. Other law, however, may be applicable and should be consulted by the lawyer. The lawyer should also consult with the client and seek a mutually acceptable resolution of the disagreement. If such efforts are unavailing and the lawyer has a fundamental disagreement with the client, the lawyer may withdraw from the representation. See Rule 1.16(b)(4). Conversely, the client may resolve the disagreement by discharging the lawyer. See Rule 1.16(a)(3).

[3] At the outset of a representation, the client may authorize the lawyer to take specific action on the client's behalf without further consultation. Absent a material change in circumstances and subject to Rule 1.4, a lawyer may rely on such an advance authorization. The client may, however, revoke such authority at any time.

[4] In a case in which the client appears to be suffering diminished capacity, the lawyer's duty to abide by the client's decisions is to be guided by reference to Rule 1.14.

Independence from Client's Views or Activities

[5] Legal representation should not be denied to people who are unable to afford legal services, or whose cause is controversial or the subject of popular disapproval. By the same token, representing a client does not constitute approval of the client's views or activities.

Agreements Limiting Scope of Representation

[6] The scope of services to be provided by a lawyer may be limited by agreement with the client or by the terms under which the lawyer's services are made available to the client. When a lawyer has been retained by an insurer to represent an insured, for example, the representation may be limited to matters related to the insurance coverage. A limited representation may be appropriate because the client has limited objectives for the representation. In addition, the terms upon which representation is undertaken may exclude specific means that might otherwise be used to accomplish the client's objectives. Such limitations may exclude actions that the client thinks are too costly or that the lawyer regards as repugnant or imprudent.

[7] Although this Rule affords the lawyer and client substantial latitude to limit the representation, the limitation must be reasonable under the circumstances. If, for example, a client's objective is limited to securing general information about the law the client needs in order to handle a common and typically uncomplicated legal problem, the lawyer and

client may agree that the lawyer's services will be limited to a brief telephone consultation. Such a limitation, however, would not be reasonable if the time allotted was not sufficient to yield advice upon which the client could rely. Although an agreement for a limited representation does not exempt a lawyer from the duty to provide competent representation, the limitation is a factor to be considered when determining the legal knowledge, skill, thoroughness and preparation reasonably necessary for the representation. See Rule 1.1.

[8] All agreements concerning a lawyer's representation of a client must accord with the Rules of Professional Conduct and other law. See, e.g., Rules 1.1, 1.8 and 5.6.

Criminal, Fraudulent and Prohibited Transactions

[9] Paragraph (d) prohibits a lawyer from knowingly counseling or assisting a client to commit a crime or fraud. This prohibition, however, does not preclude the lawyer from giving an honest opinion about the actual consequences that appear likely to result from a client's conduct. Nor does the fact that a client uses advice in a course of action that is criminal or fraudulent of itself make a lawyer a party to the course of action. There is a critical distinction between presenting an analysis of legal aspects of questionable conduct and recommending the means by which a crime or fraud might be committed with impunity.

[10] When the client's course of action has already begun and is continuing, the lawyer's responsibility is especially delicate. The lawyer is required to avoid assisting the client, for example, by drafting or delivering documents that the lawyer knows are fraudulent or by suggesting how the wrongdoing might be concealed. A lawyer may not continue assisting a client in conduct that the lawyer originally supposed was legally proper but then discovers is criminal or fraudulent. The lawyer must, therefore, withdraw from the representation of the client in the matter. See Rule 1.16(a). In some cases, withdrawal alone might be insufficient. It may be necessary for the lawyer to give notice of the fact of withdrawal and to disaffirm any opinion, document, affirmation or the like. See Rule 4.1.

[11] Where the client is a fiduciary, the lawyer may be charged with special obligations in dealings with a beneficiary.

[12] Paragraph (d) applies whether or not the defrauded party is a party to the transaction. Hence, a lawyer must not participate in a transaction to effectuate criminal or fraudulent avoidance of tax liability. Paragraph (d) does not preclude undertaking a criminal defense incident to a

general retainer for legal services to a lawful enterprise. The last clause of paragraph (d) recognizes that determining the validity or interpretation of a statute or regulation may require a course of action involving disobedience of the statute or regulation or of the interpretation placed upon it by governmental authorities.

[13] If a lawyer comes to know or reasonably should know that a client expects assistance not permitted by the Rules of Professional Conduct or other law or if the lawyer intends to act contrary to the client's instructions, the lawyer must consult with the client regarding the limitations on the lawyer's conduct. See Rule 1.4(a)(5).

Definitional Cross-References
"Fraudulent" *See* Rule 1.0(d)
"Informed consent" *See* Rule 1.0(e)
"Knows" *See* Rule 1.0(f)
"Reasonable" *See* Rule 1.0(h)

RULE 1.3: DILIGENCE

A lawyer shall act with reasonable diligence and promptness in representing a client.

Comment

[1] A lawyer should pursue a matter on behalf of a client despite opposition, obstruction or personal inconvenience to the lawyer, and take whatever lawful and ethical measures are required to vindicate a client's cause or endeavor. A lawyer must also act with commitment and dedication to the interests of the client and with zeal in advocacy upon the client's behalf. A lawyer is not bound, however, to press for every advantage that might be realized for a client. For example, a lawyer may have authority to exercise professional discretion in determining the means by which a matter should be pursued. See Rule 1.2. The lawyer's duty to act with reasonable diligence does not require the use of offensive tactics or preclude the treating of all persons involved in the legal process with courtesy and respect.

[2] A lawyer's work load must be controlled so that each matter can be handled competently. -> Don't take on to many cues!

[3] Perhaps no professional shortcoming is more widely resented than procrastination. A client's interests often can be adversely affected

by the passage of time or the change of conditions; in extreme instances, as when a lawyer overlooks a statute of limitations, the client's legal position may be destroyed. Even when the client's interests are not affected in substance, however, unreasonable delay can cause a client needless anxiety and undermine confidence in the lawyer's trustworthiness. A lawyer's duty to act with reasonable promptness, however, does not preclude the lawyer from agreeing to a reasonable request for a postponement that will not prejudice the lawyer's client.

[4] Unless the relationship is terminated as provided in Rule 1.16, a lawyer should carry through to conclusion all matters undertaken for a client. If a lawyer's employment is limited to a specific matter, the relationship terminates when the matter has been resolved. If a lawyer has served a client over a substantial period in a variety of matters, the client sometimes may assume that the lawyer will continue to serve on a continuing basis unless the lawyer gives notice of withdrawal. Doubt about whether a client-lawyer relationship still exists should be clarified by the lawyer, preferably in writing, so that the client will not mistakenly suppose the lawyer is looking after the client's affairs when the lawyer has ceased to do so. For example, if a lawyer has handled a judicial or administrative proceeding that produced a result adverse to the client and the lawyer and the client have not agreed that the lawyer will handle the matter on appeal, the lawyer must consult with the client about the possibility of appeal before relinquishing responsibility for the matter. See Rule 1.4(a)(2). Whether the lawyer is obligated to prosecute the appeal for the client depends on the scope of the representation the lawyer has agreed to provide to the client. See Rule 1.2.

[5] To prevent neglect of client matters in the event of a sole practitioner's death or disability, the duty of diligence may require that each sole practitioner prepare a plan, in conformity with applicable rules, that designates another competent lawyer to review client files, notify each client of the lawyer's death or disability, and determine whether there is a need for immediate protective action. Cf. Rule 28 of the American Bar Association Model Rules for Lawyer Disciplinary Enforcement (providing for court appointment of a lawyer to inventory files and take other protective action in absence of a plan providing for another lawyer to protect the interests of the clients of a deceased or disabled lawyer).

Definitional Cross-References

"Reasonable" *See* Rule 1.0(h)

RULE 1.4: COMMUNICATION

(a) A lawyer shall:

(1) promptly inform the client of any decision or circumstance with respect to which the client's informed consent, as defined in Rule 1.0(e), is required by these Rules;

(2) reasonably consult with the client about the means by which the client's objectives are to be accomplished;

(3) keep the client reasonably informed about the status of the matter;

(4) promptly comply with reasonable requests for information; and

(5) consult with the client about any relevant limitation on the lawyer's conduct when the lawyer knows that the client expects assistance not permitted by the Rules of Professional Conduct or other law.

(b) A lawyer shall explain a matter to the extent reasonably necessary to permit the client to make informed decisions regarding the representation.

Comment

[1] Reasonable communication between the lawyer and the client is necessary for the client effectively to participate in the representation.

Communicating with Client

[2] If these Rules require that a particular decision about the representation be made by the client, paragraph (a)(1) requires that the lawyer promptly consult with and secure the client's consent prior to taking action unless prior discussions with the client have resolved what action the client wants the lawyer to take. For example, a lawyer who receives from opposing counsel an offer of settlement in a civil controversy or a proffered plea bargain in a criminal case must promptly inform the client of its substance unless the client has previously indicated that the proposal will be acceptable or unacceptable or has authorized the lawyer to accept or to reject the offer. See Rule 1.2(a).

[3] Paragraph (a)(2) requires the lawyer to reasonably consult with the client about the means to be used to accomplish the client's objectives. In some situations—depending on both the importance of the action under consideration and the feasibility of consulting with the client —this duty will require consultation prior to taking action. In other cir-

cumstances, such as during a trial when an immediate decision must be made, the exigency of the situation may require the lawyer to act without prior consultation. In such cases the lawyer must nonetheless act reasonably to inform the client of actions the lawyer has taken on the client's behalf. Additionally, paragraph (a)(3) requires that the lawyer keep the client reasonably informed about the status of the matter, such as significant developments affecting the timing or the substance of the representation.

[4] A lawyer's regular communication with clients will minimize the occasions on which a client will need to request information concerning the representation. When a client makes a reasonable request for information, however, paragraph (a)(4) requires prompt compliance with the request, or if a prompt response is not feasible, that the lawyer, or a member of the lawyer's staff, acknowledge receipt of the request and advise the client when a response may be expected. A lawyer should promptly respond to or acknowledge client communications.

Explaining Matters

[5] The client should have sufficient information to participate intelligently in decisions concerning the objectives of the representation and the means by which they are to be pursued, to the extent the client is willing and able to do so. Adequacy of communication depends in part on the kind of advice or assistance that is involved. For example, when there is time to explain a proposal made in a negotiation, the lawyer should review all important provisions with the client before proceeding to an agreement. In litigation a lawyer should explain the general strategy and prospects of success and ordinarily should consult the client on tactics that are likely to result in significant expense or to injure or coerce others. On the other hand, a lawyer ordinarily will not be expected to describe trial or negotiation strategy in detail. The guiding principle is that the lawyer should fulfill reasonable client expectations for information consistent with the duty to act in the client's best interests, and the client's overall requirements as to the character of representation. In certain circumstances, such as when a lawyer asks a client to consent to a representation affected by a conflict of interest, the client must give informed consent, as defined in Rule 1.0(e).

[6] Ordinarily, the information to be provided is that appropriate for a client who is a comprehending and responsible adult. However, fully informing the client according to this standard may be impracticable, for example, where the client is a child or suffers from diminished capacity.

See Rule 1.14. When the client is an organization or group, it is often impossible or inappropriate to inform every one of its members about its legal affairs; ordinarily, the lawyer should address communications to the appropriate officials of the organization. See Rule 1.13. Where many routine matters are involved, a system of limited or occasional reporting may be arranged with the client.

Withholding Information

[7] In some circumstances, a lawyer may be justified in delaying transmission of information when the client would be likely to react imprudently to an immediate communication. Thus, a lawyer might withhold a psychiatric diagnosis of a client when the examining psychiatrist indicates that disclosure would harm the client. A lawyer may not withhold information to serve the lawyer's own interest or convenience or the interests or convenience of another person. Rules or court orders governing litigation may provide that information supplied to a lawyer may not be disclosed to the client. Rule 3.4(c) directs compliance with such rules or orders.

Definitional Cross-References

"Informed consent" *See* Rule 1.0(e)
"Knows" *See* Rule 1.0(f)
"Reasonably" *See* Rule 1.0(h)

RULE 1.5: FEES

(a) A lawyer shall not make an agreement for, charge, or collect an unreasonable fee or an unreasonable amount for expenses. The factors to be considered in determining the reasonableness of a fee include the following:

(1) the time and labor required, the novelty and difficulty of the questions involved, and the skill requisite to perform the legal service properly;

(2) the likelihood, if apparent to the client, that the acceptance of the particular employment will preclude other employment by the lawyer;

(3) the fee customarily charged in the locality for similar legal services;

(4) the amount involved and the results obtained;

(5) the time limitations imposed by the client or by the circumstances;

(6) the nature and length of the professional relationship with the client;

(7) the experience, reputation, and ability of the lawyer or lawyers performing the services; and

(8) whether the fee is fixed or contingent.

(b) The scope of the representation and the basis or rate of the fee and expenses for which the client will be responsible shall be communicated to the client, preferably in writing, before or within a reasonable time after commencing the representation, except when the lawyer will charge a regularly represented client on the same basis or rate. Any changes in the basis or rate of the fee or expenses shall also be communicated to the client.

(c) A fee may be contingent on the outcome of the matter for which the service is rendered, except in a matter in which a contingent fee is prohibited by paragraph (d) or other law. A contingent fee agreement shall be in a writing signed by the client and shall state the method by which the fee is to be determined, including the percentage or percentages that shall accrue to the lawyer in the event of settlement, trial or appeal; litigation and other expenses to be deducted from the recovery; and whether such expenses are to be deducted before or after the contingent fee is calculated. The agreement must clearly notify the client of any expenses for which the client will be liable whether or not the client is the prevailing party. Upon conclusion of a contingent fee matter, the lawyer shall provide the client with a written statement stating the outcome of the matter and, if there is a recovery, showing the remittance to the client and the method of its determination.

(d) A lawyer shall not enter into an arrangement for, charge, or collect:

(1) any fee in a domestic relations matter, the payment or amount of which is contingent upon the securing of a divorce or upon the amount of alimony or support, or property settlement in lieu thereof; or

(2) a contingent fee for representing a defendant in a criminal case.

(e) A division of a fee between lawyers who are not in the same firm may be made only if:

(1) the division is in proportion to the services performed by each lawyer or each lawyer assumes joint responsibility for the representation;

(2) the client agrees to the arrangement, including the share each lawyer will receive, and the agreement is confirmed in writing; and

(3) the total fee is reasonable.

Comment

Reasonableness of Fee and Expenses

[1] Paragraph (a) requires that lawyers charge fees that are reasonable under the circumstances. The factors specified in (1) through (8) are not exclusive. Nor will each factor be relevant in each instance. Paragraph (a) also requires that expenses for which the client will be charged must be reasonable. A lawyer may seek reimbursement for the cost of services performed in-house, such as copying, or for other expenses incurred in-house, such as telephone charges, either by charging a reasonable amount to which the client has agreed in advance or by charging an amount that reasonably reflects the cost incurred by the lawyer.

Basis or Rate of Fee

[2] When the lawyer has regularly represented a client, they ordinarily will have evolved an understanding concerning the basis or rate of the fee and the expenses for which the client will be responsible. In a new client-lawyer relationship, however, an understanding as to fees and expenses must be promptly established. Generally, it is desirable to furnish the client with at least a simple memorandum or copy of the lawyer's customary fee arrangements that states the general nature of the legal services to be provided, the basis, rate or total amount of the fee and whether and to what extent the client will be responsible for any costs, expenses or disbursements in the course of the representation. A written statement concerning the terms of the engagement reduces the possibility of misunderstanding.

[3] Contingent fees, like any other fees, are subject to the reasonableness standard of paragraph (a) of this Rule. In determining whether a particular contingent fee is reasonable, or whether it is reasonable to charge any form of contingent fee, a lawyer must consider the factors that are relevant under the circumstances. Applicable law may impose limitations on contingent fees, such as a ceiling on the percentage allowable, or

may require a lawyer to offer clients an alternative basis for the fee. Applicable law also may apply to situations other than a contingent fee, for example, government regulations regarding fees in certain tax matters.

Terms of Payment

[4] A lawyer may require advance payment of a fee, but is obliged to return any unearned portion. See Rule 1.16(d). A lawyer may accept property in payment for services, such as an ownership interest in an enterprise, providing this does not involve acquisition of a proprietary interest in the cause of action or subject matter of the litigation contrary to Rule 1.8 (i). However, a fee paid in property instead of money may be subject to the requirements of Rule 1.8(a) because such fees often have the essential qualities of a business transaction with the client.

[5] An agreement may not be made whose terms might induce the lawyer improperly to curtail services for the client or perform them in a way contrary to the client's interest. For example, a lawyer should not enter into an agreement whereby services are to be provided only up to a stated amount when it is foreseeable that more extensive services probably will be required, unless the situation is adequately explained to the client. Otherwise, the client might have to bargain for further assistance in the midst of a proceeding or transaction. However, it is proper to define the extent of services in light of the client's ability to pay. A lawyer should not exploit a fee arrangement based primarily on hourly charges by using wasteful procedures.

Prohibited Contingent Fees

[6] Paragraph (d) prohibits a lawyer from charging a contingent fee in a domestic relations matter when payment is contingent upon the securing of a divorce or upon the amount of alimony or support or property settlement to be obtained. This provision does not preclude a contract for a contingent fee for legal representation in connection with the recovery of post-judgment balances due under support, alimony or other financial orders because such contracts do not implicate the same policy concerns.

Division of Fee

[7] A division of fee is a single billing to a client covering the fee of two or more lawyers who are not in the same firm. A division of fee facilitates association of more than one lawyer in a matter in which neither alone could serve the client as well, and most often is used when the fee

is contingent and the division is between a referring lawyer and a trial specialist. Paragraph (e) permits the lawyers to divide a fee either on the basis of the proportion of services they render or if each lawyer assumes responsibility for the representation as a whole. In addition, the client must agree to the arrangement, including the share that each lawyer is to receive, and the agreement must be confirmed in writing. Contingent fee agreements must be in a writing signed by the client and must otherwise comply with paragraph (c) of this Rule. Joint responsibility for the representation entails financial and ethical responsibility for the representation as if the lawyers were associated in a partnership. A lawyer should only refer a matter to a lawyer whom the referring lawyer reasonably believes is competent to handle the matter. See Rule 1.1.

[8] Paragraph (e) does not prohibit or regulate division of fees to be received in the future for work done when lawyers were previously associated in a law firm.

Disputes over Fees

[9] If a procedure has been established for resolution of fee disputes, such as an arbitration or mediation procedure established by the bar, the lawyer must comply with the procedure when it is mandatory, and, even when it is voluntary, the lawyer should conscientiously consider submitting to it. Law may prescribe a procedure for determining a lawyer's fee, for example, in representation of an executor or administrator, a class or a person entitled to a reasonable fee as part of the measure of damages. The lawyer entitled to such a fee and a lawyer representing another party concerned with the fee should comply with the prescribed procedure.

Definitional Cross-References

"Confirmed in writing" *See* Rule 1.0(b)
"Firm" *See* Rule 1.0(c)
"Writing" and "Written" and "Signed" *See* Rule 1.0(n)

RULE 1.6: CONFIDENTIALITY OF INFORMATION

(a) A lawyer shall not reveal information relating to the representation of a client unless the client gives informed consent, the disclosure is impliedly authorized in order to carry out the representation or the disclosure is permitted by paragraph (b).

(b) A lawyer may reveal information relating to the

25

representation of a client to the extent the lawyer reasonably believes necessary:

(1) to prevent reasonably certain death or substantial bodily harm;

(2) to prevent the client from committing a crime or fraud that is reasonably certain to result in substantial injury to the financial interests or property of another and in furtherance of which the client has used or is using the lawyer's services;

(3) to prevent, mitigate or rectify substantial injury to the financial interests or property of another that is reasonably certain to result or has resulted from the client's commission of a crime or fraud in furtherance of which the client has used the lawyer's services;

(4) to secure legal advice about the lawyer's compliance with these Rules;

(5) to establish a claim or defense on behalf of the lawyer in a controversy between the lawyer and the client, to establish a defense to a criminal charge or civil claim against the lawyer based upon conduct in which the client was involved, or to respond to allegations in any proceeding concerning the lawyer's representation of the client;

(6) to comply with other law or a court order; or

(7) to detect and resolve conflicts of interest arising from the lawyer's change of employment or from changes in the composition or ownership of a firm, but only if the revealed information would not compromise the attorney-client privilege or otherwise prejudice the client.

(c) A lawyer shall make reasonable efforts to prevent the inadvertent or unauthorized disclosure of, or unauthorized access to, information relating to the representation of a client.

Comment

[1] This Rule governs the disclosure by a lawyer of information relating to the representation of a client during the lawyer's representation of the client. See Rule 1.18 for the lawyer's duties with respect to information provided to the lawyer by a prospective client, Rule 1.9(c)(2) for the lawyer's duty not to reveal information relating to the lawyer's prior representation of a former client and Rules 1.8(b) and 1.9(c)(1) for the lawyer's duties with respect to the use of such information to the disadvantage of clients and former clients.

[2] A fundamental principle in the client-lawyer relationship is that, in the absence of the client's informed consent, the lawyer must not reveal information relating to the representation. See Rule 1.0(e) for the definition of informed consent. This contributes to the trust that is the hallmark of the client-lawyer relationship. The client is thereby encouraged to seek legal assistance and to communicate fully and frankly with the lawyer even as to embarrassing or legally damaging subject matter. The lawyer needs this information to represent the client effectively and, if necessary, to advise the client to refrain from wrongful conduct. Almost without exception, clients come to lawyers in order to determine their rights and what is, in the complex of laws and regulations, deemed to be legal and correct. Based upon experience, lawyers know that almost all clients follow the advice given, and the law is upheld.

[3] The principle of client-lawyer confidentiality is given effect by related bodies of law: the attorney-client privilege, the work product doctrine and the rule of confidentiality established in professional ethics. The attorney-client privilege and work product doctrine apply in judicial and other proceedings in which a lawyer may be called as a witness or otherwise required to produce evidence concerning a client. The rule of client-lawyer confidentiality applies in situations other than those where evidence is sought from the lawyer through compulsion of law. The confidentiality rule, for example, applies not only to matters communicated in confidence by the client but also to all information relating to the representation, whatever its source. A lawyer may not disclose such information except as authorized or required by the Rules of Professional Conduct or other law. See also Scope.

[4] Paragraph (a) prohibits a lawyer from revealing information relating to the representation of a client. This prohibition also applies to disclosures by a lawyer that do not in themselves reveal protected information but could reasonably lead to the discovery of such information by a third person. A lawyer's use of a hypothetical to discuss issues relating to the representation is permissible so long as there is no reasonable likelihood that the listener will be able to ascertain the identity of the client or the situation involved.

Authorized Disclosure

[5] Except to the extent that the client's instructions or special circumstances limit that authority, a lawyer is impliedly authorized to make disclosures about a client when appropriate in carrying out the represen-

tation. In some situations, for example, a lawyer may be impliedly authorized to admit a fact that cannot properly be disputed or to make a disclosure that facilitates a satisfactory conclusion to a matter. Lawyers in a firm may, in the course of the firm's practice, disclose to each other information relating to a client of the firm, unless the client has instructed that particular information be confined to specified lawyers.

Disclosure Adverse to Client

[6] Although the public interest is usually best served by a strict rule requiring lawyers to preserve the confidentiality of information relating to the representation of their clients, the confidentiality rule is subject to limited exceptions. Paragraph (b)(1) recognizes the overriding value of life and physical integrity and permits disclosure reasonably necessary to prevent reasonably certain death or substantial bodily harm. Such harm is reasonably certain to occur if it will be suffered imminently or if there is a present and substantial threat that a person will suffer such harm at a later date if the lawyer fails to take action necessary to eliminate the threat. Thus, a lawyer who knows that a client has accidentally discharged toxic waste into a town's water supply may reveal this information to the authorities if there is a present and substantial risk that a person who drinks the water will contract a life-threatening or debilitating disease and the lawyer's disclosure is necessary to eliminate the threat or reduce the number of victims.

[7] Paragraph (b)(2) is a limited exception to the rule of confidentiality that permits the lawyer to reveal information to the extent necessary to enable affected persons or appropriate authorities to prevent the client from committing a crime or fraud, as defined in Rule 1.0(d), that is reasonably certain to result in substantial injury to the financial or property interests of another and in furtherance of which the client has used or is using the lawyer's services. Such a serious abuse of the client-lawyer relationship by the client forfeits the protection of this Rule. The client can, of course, prevent such disclosure by refraining from the wrongful conduct. Although paragraph (b)(2) does not require the lawyer to reveal the client's misconduct, the lawyer may not counsel or assist the client in conduct the lawyer knows is criminal or fraudulent. See Rule 1.2(d). See also Rule 1.16 with respect to the lawyer's obligation or right to withdraw from the representation of the client in such circumstances, and Rule 1.13(c), which permits the lawyer, where the client is an organization, to reveal information relating to the representation in limited circumstances.

[8] Paragraph (b)(3) addresses the situation in which the lawyer does not learn of the client's crime or fraud until after it has been consummated. Although the client no longer has the option of preventing disclosure by refraining from the wrongful conduct, there will be situations in which the loss suffered by the affected person can be prevented, rectified or mitigated. In such situations, the lawyer may disclose information relating to the representation to the extent necessary to enable the affected persons to prevent or mitigate reasonably certain losses or to attempt to recoup their losses. Paragraph (b)(3) does not apply when a person who has committed a crime or fraud thereafter employs a lawyer for representation concerning that offense.

[9] A lawyer's confidentiality obligations do not preclude a lawyer from securing confidential legal advice about the lawyer's personal responsibility to comply with these Rules. In most situations, disclosing information to secure such advice will be impliedly authorized for the lawyer to carry out the representation. Even when the disclosure is not impliedly authorized, paragraph (b)(4) permits such disclosure because of the importance of a lawyer's compliance with the Rules of Professional Conduct.

[10] Where a legal claim or disciplinary charge alleges complicity of the lawyer in a client's conduct or other misconduct of the lawyer involving representation of the client, the lawyer may respond to the extent the lawyer reasonably believes necessary to establish a defense. The same is true with respect to a claim involving the conduct or representation of a former client. Such a charge can arise in a civil, criminal, disciplinary or other proceeding and can be based on a wrong allegedly committed by the lawyer against the client or on a wrong alleged by a third person, for example, a person claiming to have been defrauded by the lawyer and client acting together. The lawyer's right to respond arises when an assertion of such complicity has been made. Paragraph (b)(5) does not require the lawyer to await the commencement of an action or proceeding that charges such complicity, so that the defense may be established by responding directly to a third party who has made such an assertion. The right to defend also applies, of course, where a proceeding has been commenced.

[11] A lawyer entitled to a fee is permitted by paragraph (b)(5) to prove the services rendered in an action to collect it. This aspect of the rule expresses the principle that the beneficiary of a fiduciary relationship may not exploit it to the detriment of the fiduciary.

[12] Other law may require that a lawyer disclose information about a client. Whether such a law supersedes Rule 1.6 is a question of law beyond the scope of these Rules. When disclosure of information relating to the representation appears to be required by other law, the lawyer must discuss the matter with the client to the extent required by Rule 1.4. If, however, the other law supersedes this Rule and requires disclosure, paragraph (b)(6) permits the lawyer to make such disclosures as are necessary to comply with the law.

Detection of Conflicts of Interest

[13] Paragraph (b)(7) recognizes that lawyers in different firms may need to disclose limited information to each other to detect and resolve conflicts of interest, such as when a lawyer is considering an association with another firm, two or more firms are considering a merger, or a lawyer is considering the purchase of a law practice. See Rule 1.17, Comment [7]. Under these circumstances, lawyers and law firms are permitted to disclose limited information, but only once substantive discussions regarding the new relationship have occurred. Any such disclosure should ordinarily include no more than the identity of the persons and entities involved in a matter, a brief summary of the general issues involved, and information about whether the matter has terminated. Even this limited information, however, should be disclosed only to the extent reasonably necessary to detect and resolve conflicts of interest that might arise from the possible new relationship. Moreover, the disclosure of any information is prohibited if it would compromise the attorney-client privilege or otherwise prejudice the client (e.g., the fact that a corporate client is seeking advice on a corporate takeover that has not been publicly announced; that a person has consulted a lawyer about the possibility of divorce before the person's intentions are known to the person's spouse; or that a person has consulted a lawyer about a criminal investigation that has not led to a public charge). Under those circumstances, paragraph (a) prohibits disclosure unless the client or former client gives informed consent. A lawyer's fiduciary duty to the lawyer's firm may also govern a lawyer's conduct when exploring an association with another firm and is beyond the scope of these Rules.

[14] Any information disclosed pursuant to paragraph (b)(7) may be used or further disclosed only to the extent necessary to detect and resolve conflicts of interest. Paragraph (b)(7) does not restrict the use of information acquired by means independent of any disclosure pursu-

ant to paragraph (b)(7). Paragraph (b)(7) also does not affect the disclosure of information within a law firm when the disclosure is otherwise authorized, see Comment [5], such as when a lawyer in a firm discloses information to another lawyer in the same firm to detect and resolve conflicts of interest that could arise in connection with undertaking a new representation.

[15] A lawyer may be ordered to reveal information relating to the representation of a client by a court or by another tribunal or governmental entity claiming authority pursuant to other law to compel the disclosure. Absent informed consent of the client to do otherwise, the lawyer should assert on behalf of the client all nonfrivolous claims that the order is not authorized by other law or that the information sought is protected against disclosure by the attorney-client privilege or other applicable law. In the event of an adverse ruling, the lawyer must consult with the client about the possibility of appeal to the extent required by Rule 1.4. Unless review is sought, however, paragraph (b)(6) permits the lawyer to comply with the court's order.

[16] Paragraph (b) permits disclosure only to the extent the lawyer reasonably believes the disclosure is necessary to accomplish one of the purposes specified. Where practicable, the lawyer should first seek to persuade the client to take suitable action to obviate the need for disclosure. In any case, a disclosure adverse to the client's interest should be no greater than the lawyer reasonably believes necessary to accomplish the purpose. If the disclosure will be made in connection with a judicial proceeding, the disclosure should be made in a manner that limits access to the information to the tribunal or other persons having a need to know it and appropriate protective orders or other arrangements should be sought by the lawyer to the fullest extent practicable.

[17] Paragraph (b) permits but does not require the disclosure of information relating to a client's representation to accomplish the purposes specified in paragraphs (b)(1) through (b)(6). In exercising the discretion conferred by this Rule, the lawyer may consider such factors as the nature of the lawyer's relationship with the client and with those who might be injured by the client, the lawyer's own involvement in the transaction and factors that may extenuate the conduct in question. A lawyer's decision not to disclose as permitted by paragraph (b) does not violate this Rule. Disclosure may be required, however, by other Rules. Some Rules require disclosure only if such disclosure would be permitted by paragraph (b). See Rules 1.2(d), 4.1(b), 8.1 and 8.3. Rule 3.3, on the other hand,

requires disclosure in some circumstances regardless of whether such disclosure is permitted by this Rule. See Rule 3.3(c).

Acting Competently to Preserve Confidentiality

[18] Paragraph (c) requires a lawyer to act competently to safeguard information relating to the representation of a client against unauthorized access by third parties and against inadvertent or unauthorized disclosure by the lawyer or other persons who are participating in the representation of the client or who are subject to the lawyer's supervision. See Rules 1.1, 5.1 and 5.3. The unauthorized access to, or the inadvertent or unauthorized disclosure of, information relating to the representation of a client does not constitute a violation of paragraph (c) if the lawyer has made reasonable efforts to prevent the access or disclosure. Factors to be considered in determining the reasonableness of the lawyer's efforts include, but are not limited to, the sensitivity of the information, the likelihood of disclosure if additional safeguards are not employed, the cost of employing additional safeguards, the difficulty of implementing the safeguards, and the extent to which the safeguards adversely affect the lawyer's ability to represent clients (e.g., by making a device or important piece of software excessively difficult to use). A client may require the lawyer to implement special security measures not required by this Rule or may give informed consent to forgo security measures that would otherwise be required by this Rule. Whether a lawyer may be required to take additional steps to safeguard a client's information in order to comply with other law, such as state and federal laws that govern data privacy or that impose notification requirements upon the loss of, or unauthorized access to, electronic information, is beyond the scope of these Rules. For a lawyer's duties when sharing information with nonlawyers outside the lawyer's own firm, see Rule 5.3, Comments [3]-[4].

[19] When transmitting a communication that includes information relating to the representation of a client, the lawyer must take reasonable precautions to prevent the information from coming into the hands of unintended recipients. This duty, however, does not require that the lawyer use special security measures if the method of communication affords a reasonable expectation of privacy. Special circumstances, however, may warrant special precautions. Factors to be considered in determining the reasonableness of the lawyer's expectation of confidentiality include the sensitivity of the information and the extent to which the privacy of the communication is protected by law or by a confidentiality agreement. A client may require the lawyer to implement special security measures

not required by this Rule or may give informed consent to the use of a means of communication that would otherwise be prohibited by this Rule. Whether a lawyer may be required to take additional steps in order to comply with other law, such as state and federal laws that govern data privacy, is beyond the scope of these Rules.

Former Client

[20] The duty of confidentiality continues after the client-lawyer relationship has terminated. See Rule 1.9(c)(2). See Rule 1.9(c)(1) for the prohibition against using such information to the disadvantage of the former client.

Definitional Cross-References

"Firm" *See* Rule 1.0(c)
"Fraud" *See* Rule 1.0(d)
"Informed consent" *See* Rule 1.0(e)
"Reasonable" and "Reasonably" *See* Rule 1.0(h)
"Reasonably believes" *See* Rule 1.0(i)
"Substantial" *See* Rule 1.0(l)

RULE 1.7: CONFLICT OF INTEREST: CURRENT CLIENTS

(a) Except as provided in paragraph (b), a lawyer shall not represent a client if the representation involves a concurrent conflict of interest. A concurrent conflict of interest exists if:

(1) the representation of one client will be directly adverse to another client; or

(2) there is a significant risk that the representation of one or more clients will be materially limited by the lawyer's responsibilities to another client, a former client or a third person or by a personal interest of the lawyer.

(b) Notwithstanding the existence of a concurrent conflict of interest under paragraph (a), a lawyer may represent a client if:

(1) the lawyer reasonably believes that the lawyer will be able to provide competent and diligent representation to each affected client;

(2) the representation is not prohibited by law;

(3) the representation does not involve the assertion of a claim by one client against another client represented by

[handwritten margin notes: "even if not directly adverse, still may be conflict of interest"; "may represent concurrent interest in certain instances"]

the lawyer in the same litigation or other proceeding before a tribunal; and

(4) each affected client gives informed consent, confirmed in writing. *Must give written consent*

Comment

General Principles

[1] Loyalty and independent judgment are essential elements in the lawyer's relationship to a client. Concurrent conflicts of interest can arise from the lawyer's responsibilities to another client, a former client or a third person or from the lawyer's own interests. For specific Rules regarding certain concurrent conflicts of interest, see Rule 1.8. For former client conflicts of interest, see Rule 1.9. For conflicts of interest involving prospective clients, see Rule 1.18. For definitions of "informed consent" and "confirmed in writing," see Rule 1.0(e) and (b).

[2] Resolution of a conflict of interest problem under this Rule requires the lawyer to: 1) clearly identify the client or clients; 2) determine whether a conflict of interest exists; 3) decide whether the representation may be undertaken despite the existence of a conflict, i.e., whether the conflict is consentable; and 4) if so, consult with the clients affected under paragraph (a) and obtain their informed consent, confirmed in writing. The clients affected under paragraph (a) include both of the clients referred to in paragraph (a)(1) and the one or more clients whose representation might be materially limited under paragraph (a)(2).

[3] A conflict of interest may exist before representation is undertaken, in which event the representation must be declined, unless the lawyer obtains the informed consent of each client under the conditions of paragraph (b). To determine whether a conflict of interest exists, a lawyer should adopt reasonable procedures, appropriate for the size and type of firm and practice, to determine in both litigation and non-litigation matters the persons and issues involved. See also Comment to Rule 5.1. Ignorance caused by a failure to institute such procedures will not excuse a lawyer's violation of this Rule. As to whether a client-lawyer relationship exists or, having once been established, is continuing, see Comment to Rule 1.3 and Scope.

[4] If a conflict arises after representation has been undertaken, the lawyer ordinarily must withdraw from the representation, unless the lawyer has obtained the informed consent of the client under the conditions of paragraph (b). See Rule 1.16. Where more than one client is in-

volved, whether the lawyer may continue to represent any of the clients is determined both by the lawyer's ability to comply with duties owed to the former client and by the lawyer's ability to represent adequately the remaining client or clients, given the lawyer's duties to the former client. See Rule 1.9. See also Comments [5] and [29].

[5] Unforeseeable developments, such as changes in corporate and other organizational affiliations or the addition or realignment of parties in litigation, might create conflicts in the midst of a representation, as when a company sued by the lawyer on behalf of one client is bought by another client represented by the lawyer in an unrelated matter. Depending on the circumstances, the lawyer may have the option to withdraw from one of the representations in order to avoid the conflict. The lawyer must seek court approval where necessary and take steps to minimize harm to the clients. See Rule 1.16. The lawyer must continue to protect the confidences of the client from whose representation the lawyer has withdrawn. See Rule 1.9(c). — exception to the 'hot potato' rule

Identifying Conflicts of Interest:
Directly Adverse

[6] Loyalty to a current client prohibits undertaking representation directly adverse to that client without that client's informed consent. Thus, absent consent, a lawyer may not act as an advocate in one matter against a person the lawyer represents in some other matter, even when the matters are wholly unrelated. The client as to whom the representation is directly adverse is likely to feel betrayed, and the resulting damage to the client-lawyer relationship is likely to impair the lawyer's ability to represent the client effectively. In addition, the client on whose behalf the adverse representation is undertaken reasonably may fear that the lawyer will pursue that client's case less effectively out of deference to the other client, i.e., that the representation may be materially limited by the lawyer's interest in retaining the current client. Similarly, a directly adverse conflict may arise when a lawyer is required to cross-examine a client who appears as a witness in a lawsuit involving another client, as when the testimony will be damaging to the client who is represented in the lawsuit. On the other hand, simultaneous representation in unrelated matters of clients whose interests are only economically adverse, such as representation of competing economic enterprises in unrelated litigation, does not ordinarily constitute a conflict of interest and thus may not require consent of the respective clients.

Another example

[7] Underlined: Directly adverse conflicts can also arise in transactional matters. For example, if a lawyer is asked to represent the seller of a business in negotiations with a buyer represented by the lawyer, not in the same transaction but in another, unrelated matter, the lawyer could not undertake the representation without the informed consent of each client.

Identifying Conflicts of Interest: Material Limitation

[8] Even where there is no direct adverseness, a conflict of interest exists if there is a significant risk that a lawyer's ability to consider, recommend or carry out an appropriate course of action for the client will be materially limited as a result of the lawyer's other responsibilities or interests. For example, a lawyer asked to represent several individuals seeking to form a joint venture is likely to be materially limited in the lawyer's ability to recommend or advocate all possible positions that each might take because of the lawyer's duty of loyalty to the others. The conflict in effect forecloses alternatives that would otherwise be available to the client. The mere possibility of subsequent harm does not itself require disclosure and consent. The critical questions are the likelihood that a difference in interests will eventuate and, if it does, whether it will materially interfere with the lawyer's independent professional judgment in considering alternatives or foreclose courses of action that reasonably should be pursued on behalf of the client.

Lawyer's Responsibilities to Former Clients and Other Third Persons

[9] In addition to conflicts with other current clients, a lawyer's duties of loyalty and independence may be materially limited by responsibilities to former clients under Rule 1.9 or by the lawyer's responsibilities to other persons, such as fiduciary duties arising from a lawyer's service as a trustee, executor or corporate director.

Personal Interest Conflicts

[10] The lawyer's own interests should not be permitted to have an adverse effect on representation of a client. For example, if the probity of a lawyer's own conduct in a transaction is in serious question, it may be difficult or impossible for the lawyer to give a client detached advice. Similarly, when a lawyer has discussions concerning possible employment with an opponent of the lawyer's client, or with a law firm repre-

senting the opponent, such discussions could materially limit the lawyer's representation of the client. In addition, a lawyer may not allow related business interests to affect representation, for example, by referring clients to an enterprise in which the lawyer has an undisclosed financial interest. See Rule 1.8 for specific Rules pertaining to a number of personal interest conflicts, including business transactions with clients. See also Rule 1.10 (personal interest conflicts under Rule 1.7 ordinarily are not imputed to other lawyers in a law firm).

[11] When lawyers representing different clients in the same matter or in substantially related matters are closely related by blood or marriage, there may be a significant risk that client confidences will be revealed and that the lawyer's family relationship will interfere with both loyalty and independent professional judgment. As a result, each client is entitled to know of the existence and implications of the relationship between the lawyers before the lawyer agrees to undertake the representation. Thus, a lawyer related to another lawyer, e.g., as parent, child, sibling or spouse, ordinarily may not represent a client in a matter where that lawyer is representing another party, unless each client gives informed consent. The disqualification arising from a close family relationship is personal and ordinarily is not imputed to members of firms with whom the lawyers are associated. See Rule 1.10.

[12] A lawyer is prohibited from engaging in sexual relationships with a client unless the sexual relationship predates the formation of the client-lawyer relationship. See Rule 1.8(j).

Interest of Person Paying for a Lawyer's Service

[13] A lawyer may be paid from a source other than the client, including a co-client, if the client is informed of that fact and consents and the arrangement does not compromise the lawyer's duty of loyalty or independent judgment to the client. See Rule 1.8(f). If acceptance of the payment from any other source presents a significant risk that the lawyer's representation of the client will be materially limited by the lawyer's own interest in accommodating the person paying the lawyer's fee or by the lawyer's responsibilities to a payer who is also a co-client, then the lawyer must comply with the requirements of paragraph (b) before accepting the representation, including determining whether the conflict is consentable and, if so, that the client has adequate information about the material risks of the representation.

Prohibited Representations

[14] Ordinarily, clients may consent to representation notwithstanding a conflict. However, as indicated in paragraph (b), some conflicts are nonconsentable, meaning that the lawyer involved cannot properly ask for such agreement or provide representation on the basis of the client's consent. When the lawyer is representing more than one client, the question of consentability must be resolved as to each client.

[15] Consentability is typically determined by considering whether the interests of the clients will be adequately protected if the clients are permitted to give their informed consent to representation burdened by a conflict of interest. Thus, under paragraph (b)(1), representation is prohibited if in the circumstances the lawyer cannot reasonably conclude that the lawyer will be able to provide competent and diligent representation. See Rule 1.1 (competence) and Rule 1.3 (diligence).

[16] Paragraph (b)(2) describes conflicts that are nonconsentable because the representation is prohibited by applicable law. For example, in some states substantive law provides that the same lawyer may not represent more than one defendant in a capital case, even with the consent of the clients, and under federal criminal statutes certain representations by a former government lawyer are prohibited, despite the informed consent of the former client. In addition, decisional law in some states limits the ability of a governmental client, such as a municipality, to consent to a conflict of interest.

[17] Paragraph (b)(3) describes conflicts that are nonconsentable because of the institutional interest in vigorous development of each client's position when the clients are aligned directly against each other in the same litigation or other proceeding before a tribunal. Whether clients are aligned directly against each other within the meaning of this paragraph requires examination of the context of the proceeding. Although this paragraph does not preclude a lawyer's multiple representation of adverse parties to a mediation (because mediation is not a proceeding before a "tribunal" under Rule 1.0(m)), such representation may be precluded by paragraph (b)(1).

Informed Consent

[18] Informed consent requires that each affected client be aware of the relevant circumstances and of the material and reasonably foreseeable ways that the conflict could have adverse effects on the interests of that client. See Rule 1.0(e) (informed consent). The information required

38

depends on the nature of the conflict and the nature of the risks involved. When representation of multiple clients in a single matter is undertaken, the information must include the implications of the common representation, including possible effects on loyalty, confidentiality and the attorney-client privilege and the advantages and risks involved. See Comments [30] and [31] (effect of common representation on confidentiality).

[19] Under some circumstances it may be impossible to make the disclosure necessary to obtain consent. For example, when the lawyer represents different clients in related matters and one of the clients refuses to consent to the disclosure necessary to permit the other client to make an informed decision, the lawyer cannot properly ask the latter to consent. In some cases the alternative to common representation can be that each party may have to obtain separate representation with the possibility of incurring additional costs. These costs, along with the benefits of securing separate representation, are factors that may be considered by the affected client in determining whether common representation is in the client's interests.

Consent Confirmed in Writing

[20] Paragraph (b) requires the lawyer to obtain the informed consent of the client, confirmed in writing. Such a writing may consist of a document executed by the client or one that the lawyer promptly records and transmits to the client following an oral consent. See Rule 1.0(b). See also Rule 1.0(n) (writing includes electronic transmission). If it is not feasible to obtain or transmit the writing at the time the client gives informed consent, then the lawyer must obtain or transmit it within a reasonable time thereafter. See Rule 1.0(b). The requirement of a writing does not supplant the need in most cases for the lawyer to talk with the client, to explain the risks and advantages, if any, of representation burdened with a conflict of interest, as well as reasonably available alternatives, and to afford the client a reasonable opportunity to consider the risks and alternatives and to raise questions and concerns. Rather, the writing is required in order to impress upon clients the seriousness of the decision the client is being asked to make and to avoid disputes or ambiguities that might later occur in the absence of a writing.

Revoking Consent

[21] A client who has given consent to a conflict may revoke the consent and, like any other client, may terminate the lawyer's representation

at any time. Whether revoking consent to the client's own representation precludes the lawyer from continuing to represent other clients depends on the circumstances, including the nature of the conflict, whether the client revoked consent because of a material change in circumstances, the reasonable expectations of the other clients and whether material detriment to the other clients or the lawyer would result.

—> - waiving future conflicts

Consent to Future Conflict

[22] Whether a lawyer may properly request a client to waive conflicts that might arise in the future is subject to the test of paragraph (b). The effectiveness of such waivers is generally determined by the extent to which the client reasonably understands the material risks that the waiver entails. The more comprehensive the explanation of the types of future representations that might arise and the actual and reasonably foreseeable adverse consequences of those representations, the greater the likelihood that the client will have the requisite understanding. Thus, if the client agrees to consent to a particular type of conflict with which the client is already familiar, then the consent ordinarily will be effective with regard to that type of conflict. If the consent is general and open-ended, then the consent ordinarily will be ineffective, because it is not reasonably likely that the client will have understood the material risks involved. On the other hand, if the client is an experienced user of the legal services involved and is reasonably informed regarding the risk that a conflict may arise, such consent is more likely to be effective, particularly if, e.g., the client is independently represented by other counsel in giving consent and the consent is limited to future conflicts unrelated to the subject of the representation. In any case, advance consent cannot be effective if the circumstances that materialize in the future are such as would make the conflict nonconsentable under paragraph (b).

important

Conflicts in Litigation

[23] Paragraph (b)(3) prohibits representation of opposing parties in the same litigation, regardless of the clients' consent. On the other hand, simultaneous representation of parties whose interests in litigation may conflict, such as coplaintiffs or codefendants, is governed by paragraph (a)(2). A conflict may exist by reason of substantial discrepancy in the parties' testimony, incompatibility in positions in relation to an opposing party or the fact that there are substantially different possibilities of settlement of the claims or liabilities in question. Such conflicts can arise in

criminal cases as well as civil. The potential for conflict of interest in representing multiple defendants in a criminal case is so grave that ordinarily a lawyer should decline to represent more than one codefendant. On the other hand, common representation of persons having similar interests in civil litigation is proper if the requirements of paragraph (b) are met.

[24] Ordinarily a lawyer may take inconsistent legal positions in different tribunals at different times on behalf of different clients. The mere fact that advocating a legal position on behalf of one client might create precedent adverse to the interests of a client represented by the lawyer in an unrelated matter does not create a conflict of interest. A conflict of interest exists, however, if there is a significant risk that a lawyer's action on behalf of one client will materially limit the lawyer's effectiveness in representing another client in a different case; for example, when a decision favoring one client will create a precedent likely to seriously weaken the position taken on behalf of the other client. Factors relevant in determining whether the clients need to be advised of the risk include: where the cases are pending, whether the issue is substantive or procedural, the temporal relationship between the matters, the significance of the issue to the immediate and long-term interests of the clients involved and the clients' reasonable expectations in retaining the lawyer. If there is significant risk of material limitation, then absent informed consent of the affected clients, the lawyer must refuse one of the representations or withdraw from one or both matters.

[25] When a lawyer represents or seeks to represent a class of plaintiffs or defendants in a class-action lawsuit, unnamed members of the class are ordinarily not considered to be clients of the lawyer for purposes of applying paragraph (a)(1) of this Rule. Thus, the lawyer does not typically need to get the consent of such a person before representing a client suing the person in an unrelated matter. Similarly, a lawyer seeking to represent an opponent in a class action does not typically need the consent of an unnamed member of the class whom the lawyer represents in an unrelated matter.

Nonlitigation Conflicts

[26] Conflicts of interest under paragraphs (a)(1) and (a)(2) arise in contexts other than litigation. For a discussion of directly adverse conflicts in transactional matters, see Comment [7]. Relevant factors in determining whether there is significant potential for material limitation include the duration and intimacy of the lawyer's relationship with the

client or clients involved, the functions being performed by the lawyer, the likelihood that disagreements will arise and the likely prejudice to the client from the conflict. The question is often one of proximity and degree. See Comment [8].

[27] For example, conflict questions may arise in estate planning and estate administration. A lawyer may be called upon to prepare wills for several family members, such as husband and wife, and, depending upon the circumstances, a conflict of interest may be present. In estate administration the identity of the client may be unclear under the law of a particular jurisdiction. Under one view, the client is the fiduciary; under another view the client is the estate or trust, including its beneficiaries. In order to comply with conflict of interest rules, the lawyer should make clear the lawyer's relationship to the parties involved.

[28] Whether a conflict is consentable depends on the circumstances. For example, a lawyer may not represent multiple parties to a negotiation whose interests are fundamentally antagonistic to each other, but common representation is permissible where the clients are generally aligned in interest even though there is some difference in interest among them. Thus, a lawyer may seek to establish or adjust a relationship between clients on an amicable and mutually advantageous basis; for example, in helping to organize a business in which two or more clients are entrepreneurs, working out the financial reorganization of an enterprise in which two or more clients have an interest or arranging a property distribution in settlement of an estate. The lawyer seeks to resolve potentially adverse interests by developing the parties' mutual interests. Otherwise, each party might have to obtain separate representation, with the possibility of incurring additional cost, complication or even litigation. Given these and other relevant factors, the clients may prefer that the lawyer act for all of them.

Special Considerations in Common Representation

[29] In considering whether to represent multiple clients in the same matter, a lawyer should be mindful that if the common representation fails because the potentially adverse interests cannot be reconciled, the result can be additional cost, embarrassment and recrimination. Ordinarily, the lawyer will be forced to withdraw from representing all of the clients if the common representation fails. In some situations, the risk of failure is so great that multiple representation is plainly impossible. For example, a lawyer cannot undertake common representation of clients where

contentious litigation or negotiations between them are imminent or contemplated. Moreover, because the lawyer is required to be impartial between commonly represented clients, representation of multiple clients is improper when it is unlikely that impartiality can be maintained. Generally, if the relationship between the parties has already assumed antagonism, the possibility that the clients' interests can be adequately served by common representation is not very good. Other relevant factors are whether the lawyer subsequently will represent both parties on a continuing basis and whether the situation involves creating or terminating a relationship between the parties.

[30] A particularly important factor in determining the appropriateness of common representation is the effect on client-lawyer confidentiality and the attorney-client privilege. With regard to the attorney-client privilege, the prevailing rule is that, as between commonly represented clients, the privilege does not attach. Hence, it must be assumed that if litigation eventuates between the clients, the privilege will not protect any such communications, and the clients should be so advised.

[31] As to the duty of confidentiality, continued common representation will almost certainly be inadequate if one client asks the lawyer not to disclose to the other client information relevant to the common representation. This is so because the lawyer has an equal duty of loyalty to each client, and each client has the right to be informed of anything bearing on the representation that might affect that client's interests and the right to expect that the lawyer will use that information to that client's benefit. See Rule 1.4. The lawyer should, at the outset of the common representation and as part of the process of obtaining each client's informed consent, advise each client that information will be shared and that the lawyer will have to withdraw if one client decides that some matter material to the representation should be kept from the other. In limited circumstances, it may be appropriate for the lawyer to proceed with the representation when the clients have agreed, after being properly informed, that the lawyer will keep certain information confidential. For example, the lawyer may reasonably conclude that failure to disclose one client's trade secrets to another client will not adversely affect representation involving a joint venture between the clients and agree to keep that information confidential with the informed consent of both clients.

[32] When seeking to establish or adjust a relationship between clients, the lawyer should make clear that the lawyer's role is not that of partisanship normally expected in other circumstances and, thus, that

the clients may be required to assume greater responsibility for decisions than when each client is separately represented. Any limitations on the scope of the representation made necessary as a result of the common representation should be fully explained to the clients at the outset of the representation. See Rule 1.2(c).

[33] Subject to the above limitations, each client in the common representation has the right to loyal and diligent representation and the protection of Rule 1.9 concerning the obligations to a former client. The client also has the right to discharge the lawyer as stated in Rule 1.16.

Organizational Clients

[34] A lawyer who represents a corporation or other organization does not, by virtue of that representation, necessarily represent any constituent or affiliated organization, such as a parent or subsidiary. See Rule 1.13(a). Thus, the lawyer for an organization is not barred from accepting representation adverse to an affiliate in an unrelated matter, unless the circumstances are such that the affiliate should also be considered a client of the lawyer, there is an understanding between the lawyer and the organizational client that the lawyer will avoid representation adverse to the client's affiliates, or the lawyer's obligations to either the organizational client or the new client are likely to limit materially the lawyer's representation of the other client.

[35] A lawyer for a corporation or other organization who is also a member of its board of directors should determine whether the responsibilities of the two roles may conflict. The lawyer may be called on to advise the corporation in matters involving actions of the directors. Consideration should be given to the frequency with which such situations may arise, the potential intensity of the conflict, the effect of the lawyer's resignation from the board and the possibility of the corporation's obtaining legal advice from another lawyer in such situations. If there is material risk that the dual role will compromise the lawyer's independence of professional judgment, the lawyer should not serve as a director or should cease to act as the corporation's lawyer when conflicts of interest arise. The lawyer should advise the other members of the board that in some circumstances matters discussed at board meetings while the lawyer is present in the capacity of director might not be protected by the attorney-client privilege and that conflict of interest considerations might require the lawyer's recusal as a director or might require the lawyer and the lawyer's firm to decline representation of the corporation in a matter.

Definitional Cross-References

"Confirmed in writing" *See* Rule 1.0(b)
"Informed consent" *See* Rule 1.0(e)
"Reasonably believes" *See* Rule 1.0(i)
"Tribunal" *See* Rule 1.0(m)

RULE 1.8: CONFLICT OF INTEREST: CURRENT CLIENTS: SPECIFIC RULES

(a) A lawyer shall not enter into a business transaction with a client or knowingly acquire an ownership, possessory, security or other pecuniary interest adverse to a client unless:

(1) the transaction and terms on which the lawyer acquires the interest are fair and reasonable to the client and are fully disclosed and transmitted in writing in a manner that can be reasonably understood by the client;

(2) the client is advised in writing of the desirability of seeking and is given a reasonable opportunity to seek the advice of independent legal counsel on the transaction; and

(3) the client gives informed consent, in a writing signed by the client, to the essential terms of the transaction and the lawyer's role in the transaction, including whether the lawyer is representing the client in the transaction.

(b) A lawyer shall not use information relating to representation of a client to the disadvantage of the client unless the client gives informed consent, except as permitted or required by these Rules.

(c) A lawyer shall not solicit any substantial gift from a client, including a testamentary gift, or prepare on behalf of a client an instrument giving the lawyer or a person related to the lawyer any substantial gift unless the lawyer or other recipient of the gift is related to the client. For purposes of this paragraph, related persons include a spouse, child, grandchild, parent, grandparent or other relative or individual with whom the lawyer or the client maintains a close, familial relationship.

(d) Prior to the conclusion of representation of a client, a lawyer shall not make or negotiate an agreement giving the lawyer literary or media rights to a portrayal or account based in substantial part on information relating to the representation.

(e) A lawyer shall not provide financial assistance to a client in connection with pending or contemplated litigation, except that:

(1) a lawyer may advance court costs and expenses of litigation, the repayment of which may be contingent on the outcome of the matter; and

(2) a lawyer representing an indigent client may pay court costs and expenses of litigation on behalf of the client; and

(3) a lawyer representing an indigent client pro bono, a lawyer representing an indigent client pro bono through a nonprofit legal services or public interest organization and a lawyer representing an indigent client pro bono through a law school clinical or pro bono program may provide modest gifts to the client for food, rent, transportation, medicine and other basic living expenses. The lawyer:

(i) may not promise, assure or imply the availability of such gifts prior to retention or as an inducement to continue the client-lawyer relationship after retention;

(ii) may not seek or accept reimbursement from the client, a relative of the client or anyone affiliated with the client; and

(iii) may not publicize or advertise a willingness to provide such gifts to prospective clients.

Financial assistance under this Rule may be provided even if the representation is eligible for fees under a fee-shifting statute.

(f) A lawyer shall not accept compensation for representing a client from one other than the client unless:

(1) the client gives informed consent;

(2) there is no interference with the lawyer's independence of professional judgment or with the client-lawyer relationship; and

(3) information relating to representation of a client is protected as required by Rule 1.6..

(g) A lawyer who represents two or more clients shall not participate in making an aggregate settlement of the claims of or against the clients, or in a criminal case an aggregated agreement as to guilty or nolo contendere pleas, unless each client gives informed consent, in a writing signed by the client. The lawyer's disclosure shall include the existence and nature of all the claims or pleas involved and of the participation of each person in the settlement.

(h) A lawyer shall not:

(1) make an agreement prospectively limiting the lawyer's liability to a client for malpractice unless the client is independently represented in making the agreement; or

(2) settle a claim or potential claim for such liability with an unrepresented client or former client unless that person is advised in writing of the desirability of seeking and is given a reasonable opportunity to seek the advice of independent legal counsel in connection therewith.

(i) A lawyer shall not acquire a proprietary interest in the cause of action or subject matter of litigation the lawyer is conducting for a client, except that the lawyer may:

(1) acquire a lien authorized by law to secure the lawyer's fee or expenses; and

(2) contract with a client for a reasonable contingent fee in a civil case.

(j) A lawyer shall not have sexual relations with a client unless a consensual sexual relationship existed between them when the client-lawyer relationship commenced.

(k) While lawyers are associated in a firm, a prohibition in the foregoing paragraphs (a) through (i) that applies to any one of them shall apply to all of them.

Comment

Business Transactions between Client and Lawyer

[1] A lawyer's legal skill and training, together with the relationship of trust and confidence between lawyer and client, create the possibility of overreaching when the lawyer participates in a business, property or financial transaction with a client, for example, a loan or sales transaction or a lawyer investment on behalf of a client. The requirements of paragraph (a) must be met even when the transaction is not closely related to the subject matter of the representation, as when a lawyer drafting a will for a client learns that the client needs money for unrelated expenses and offers to make a loan to the client. The Rule applies to lawyers engaged in the sale of goods or services related to the practice of law, for example, the sale of title insurance or investment services to existing clients of the lawyer's legal practice. See Rule 5.7. It also applies to lawyers purchasing property from estates they represent. It does not apply to ordinary fee arrangements between client and lawyer, which are governed by Rule 1.5, although its requirements must be met when the lawyer accepts an in-

terest in the client's business or other nonmonetary property as payment of all or part of a fee. In addition, the Rule does not apply to standard commercial transactions between the lawyer and the client for products or services that the client generally markets to others, for example, banking or brokerage services, medical services, products manufactured or distributed by the client, and utilities' services. In such transactions, the lawyer has no advantage in dealing with the client, and the restrictions in paragraph (a) are unnecessary and impracticable.

[2] Paragraph (a)(1) requires that the transaction itself be fair to the client and that its essential terms be communicated to the client, in writing, in a manner that can be reasonably understood. Paragraph (a)(2) requires that the client also be advised, in writing, of the desirability of seeking the advice of independent legal counsel. It also requires that the client be given a reasonable opportunity to obtain such advice. Paragraph (a)(3) requires that the lawyer obtain the client's informed consent, in a writing signed by the client, both to the essential terms of the transaction and to the lawyer's role. When necessary, the lawyer should discuss both the material risks of the proposed transaction, including any risk presented by the lawyer's involvement, and the existence of reasonably available alternatives and should explain why the advice of independent legal counsel is desirable. See Rule 1.0(e) (definition of informed consent).

[3] The risk to a client is greatest when the client expects the lawyer to represent the client in the transaction itself or when the lawyer's financial interest otherwise poses a significant risk that the lawyer's representation of the client will be materially limited by the lawyer's financial interest in the transaction. Here the lawyer's role requires that the lawyer must comply, not only with the requirements of paragraph (a), but also with the requirements of Rule 1.7. Under that Rule, the lawyer must disclose the risks associated with the lawyer's dual role as both legal adviser and participant in the transaction, such as the risk that the lawyer will structure the transaction or give legal advice in a way that favors the lawyer's interests at the expense of the client. Moreover, the lawyer must obtain the client's informed consent. In some cases, the lawyer's interest may be such that Rule 1.7 will preclude the lawyer from seeking the client's consent to the transaction.

[4] If the client is independently represented in the transaction, paragraph (a)(2) of this Rule is inapplicable, and the paragraph (a)(1) requirement for full disclosure is satisfied either by a written disclosure by the lawyer involved in the transaction or by the client's independent counsel. The fact that the client was independently represented in the transaction

is relevant in determining whether the agreement was fair and reasonable to the client as paragraph (a)(1) further requires.

Use of Information Related to Representation

[5] Use of information relating to the representation to the disadvantage of the client violates the lawyer's duty of loyalty. Paragraph (b) applies when the information is used to benefit either the lawyer or a third person, such as another client or business associate of the lawyer. For example, if a lawyer learns that a client intends to purchase and develop several parcels of land, the lawyer may not use that information to purchase one of the parcels in competition with the client or to recommend that another client make such a purchase. The Rule does not prohibit uses that do not disadvantage the client. For example, a lawyer who learns a government agency's interpretation of trade legislation during the representation of one client may properly use that information to benefit other clients. Paragraph (b) prohibits disadvantageous use of client information unless the client gives informed consent, except as permitted or required by these Rules. See Rules 1.2(d), 1.6, 1.9(c), 3.3, 4.1(b), 8.1 and 8.3.

Gifts to Lawyers

[6] A lawyer may accept a gift from a client, if the transaction meets general standards of fairness. For example, a simple gift such as a present given at a holiday or as a token of appreciation is permitted. If a client offers the lawyer a more substantial gift, paragraph (c) does not prohibit the lawyer from accepting it, although such a gift may be voidable by the client under the doctrine of undue influence, which treats client gifts as presumptively fraudulent. In any event, due to concerns about overreaching and imposition on clients, a lawyer may not suggest that a substantial gift be made to the lawyer or for the lawyer's benefit, except where the lawyer is related to the client as set forth in paragraph (c).

[7] If effectuation of a substantial gift requires preparing a legal instrument such as a will or conveyance, the client should have the detached advice that another lawyer can provide. The sole exception to this Rule is where the client is a relative of the donee.

[8] This Rule does not prohibit a lawyer from seeking to have the lawyer or a partner or associate of the lawyer named as executor of the client's estate or to another potentially lucrative fiduciary position. Nevertheless, such appointments will be subject to the general conflict of interest provision in Rule 1.7 when there is a significant risk that the lawyer's interest in obtaining the appointment will materially limit the lawyer's independent

professional judgment in advising the client concerning the choice of an executor or other fiduciary. In obtaining the client's informed consent to the conflict, the lawyer should advise the client concerning the nature and extent of the lawyer's financial interest in the appointment, as well as the availability of alternative candidates for the position.

Literary Rights

[9] An agreement by which a lawyer acquires literary or media rights concerning the conduct of the representation creates a conflict between the interests of the client and the personal interests of the lawyer. Measures suitable in the representation of the client may detract from the publication value of an account of the representation. Paragraph (d) does not prohibit a lawyer representing a client in a transaction concerning literary property from agreeing that the lawyer's fee shall consist of a share in ownership in the property, if the arrangement conforms to Rule 1.5 and paragraphs (a) and (i).

Financial Assistance

[10] Lawyers may not subsidize lawsuits or administrative proceedings brought on behalf of their clients, including making or guaranteeing loans to their clients for living expenses, because to do so would encourage clients to pursue lawsuits that might not otherwise be brought and because such assistance gives lawyers too great a financial stake in the litigation. These dangers do not warrant a prohibition on a lawyer lending a client court costs and litigation expenses, including the expenses of medical examination and the costs of obtaining and presenting evidence, because these advances are virtually indistinguishable from contingent fees and help ensure access to the courts. Similarly, an exception allowing lawyers representing indigent clients to pay court costs and litigation expenses regardless of whether these funds will be repaid is warranted.

[11] Paragraph (e)(3) provides another exception. A lawyer representing an indigent client without fee, a lawyer representing an indigent client pro bono through a nonprofit legal services or public interest organization and a lawyer representing an indigent client pro bono through a law school clinical or pro bono program may give the client modest gifts Gifts permitted under paragraph (e)(3) include modest contributions for food, rent, transportation, medicine and similar basic necessities of life. If the gift may have consequences for the client, including, e.g., for receipt of government benefits, social services, or tax liability, the lawyer should consult with the client about these. See Rule 1.4.

50

[12] The paragraph (e)(3) exception is narrow. Modest gifts are allowed in specific circumstances where it is unlikely to create conflicts of interest or invite abuse. Paragraph (e)(3) prohibits the lawyer from (i) promising, assuring or implying the availability of financial assistance prior to retention or as an inducement to continue the client-lawyer relationship after retention; (ii) seeking or accepting reimbursement from the client, a relative of the client or anyone affiliated with the client; and (iii) publicizing or advertising a willingness to provide gifts to prospective to clients beyond court costs and expenses of litigation in connection with contemplated or pending litigation or administrative proceedings.

[13] Financial assistance, including modest gifts pursuant to paragraph (e)(3), may be provided even if the representation is eligible for fees under a fee-shifting statute. However, paragraph (e)(3) does not permit lawyers to provide assistance in other contemplated or pending litigation in which the lawyer may eventually recover a fee, such as contingent-fee personal injury cases or cases in which fees may be available under a contractual fee-shifting provision, even if the lawyer does not eventually receive a fee.

Person Paying for a Lawyer's Services

[14] Lawyers are frequently asked to represent a client under circumstances in which a third person will compensate the lawyer, in whole or in part. The third person might be a relative or friend, an indemnitor (such as a liability insurance company) or a co-client (such as a corporation sued along with one or more of its employees). Because third-party payers frequently have interests that differ from those of the client, including interests in minimizing the amount spent on the representation and in learning how the representation is progressing, lawyers are prohibited from accepting or continuing such representations unless the lawyer determines that there will be no interference with the lawyer's independent professional judgment and there is informed consent from the client. See also Rule 5.4(c) (prohibiting interference with a lawyer's professional judgment by one who recommends, employs or pays the lawyer to render legal services for another).

[15] Sometimes, it will be sufficient for the lawyer to obtain the client's informed consent regarding the fact of the payment and the identity of the third-party payer. If, however, the fee arrangement creates a conflict of interest for the lawyer, then the lawyer must comply with Rule 1.7. The lawyer must also conform to the requirements of Rule 1.6 concerning confidentiality. Under Rule 1.7(a), a conflict of interest exists if there

is significant risk that the lawyer's representation of the client will be materially limited by the lawyer's own interest in the fee arrangement or by the lawyer's responsibilities to the third-party payer (for example, when the third-party payer is a co-client). Under Rule 1.7(b), the lawyer may accept or continue the representation with the informed consent of each affected client, unless the conflict is nonconsentable under that paragraph. Under Rule 1.7(b), the informed consent must be confirmed in writing..

Aggregate Settlements

—[16] Differences in willingness to make or accept an offer of settlement are among the risks of common representation of multiple clients by a single lawyer. Under Rule 1.7, this is one of the risks that should be discussed before undertaking the representation, as part of the process of obtaining the clients' informed consent. In addition, Rule 1.2(a) protects each client's right to have the final say in deciding whether to accept or reject an offer of settlement and in deciding whether to enter a guilty or nolo contendere plea in a criminal case. The rule stated in this paragraph is a corollary of both these Rules and provides that, before any settlement offer or plea bargain is made or accepted on behalf of multiple clients, the lawyer must inform each of them about all the material terms of the settlement, including what the other clients will receive or pay if the settlement or plea offer is accepted. See also Rule 1.0(e) (definition of informed consent). Lawyers representing a class of plaintiffs or defendants, or those proceeding derivatively, may not have a full client-lawyer relationship with each member of the class; nevertheless, such lawyers must comply with applicable rules regulating notification of class members and other procedural requirements designed to ensure adequate protection of the entire class.

Limiting Liability and Settling Malpractice Claims

[17] Agreements prospectively limiting a lawyer's liability for malpractice are prohibited unless the client is independently represented in making the agreement because they are likely to undermine competent and diligent representation. Also, many clients are unable to evaluate the desirability of making such an agreement before a dispute has arisen, particularly if they are then represented by the lawyer seeking the agreement. This paragraph does not, however, prohibit a lawyer from entering into an agreement with the client to arbitrate legal malpractice claims, provided such agreements are enforceable and the client is fully informed of the scope and effect of the agreement. Nor does this paragraph limit

the ability of lawyers to practice in the form of a limited-liability entity, where permitted by law, provided that each lawyer remains personally liable to the client for his or her own conduct and the firm complies with any conditions required by law, such as provisions requiring client notification or maintenance of adequate liability insurance. Nor does it prohibit an agreement in accordance with Rule 1.2 that defines the scope of the representation, although a definition of scope that makes the obligations of representation illusory will amount to an attempt to limit liability.

[18] Agreements settling a claim or a potential claim for malpractice are not prohibited by this Rule. Nevertheless, in view of the danger that a lawyer will take unfair advantage of an unrepresented client or former client, the lawyer must first advise such a person in writing of the appropriateness of independent representation in connection with such a settlement. In addition, the lawyer must give the client or former client a reasonable opportunity to find and consult independent counsel.

Acquiring Proprietary Interest in Litigation

[19] Paragraph (i) states the traditional general rule that lawyers are prohibited from acquiring a proprietary interest in litigation. Like paragraph (e), the general rule has its basis in common law champerty and maintenance and is designed to avoid giving the lawyer too great an interest in the representation. In addition, when the lawyer acquires an ownership interest in the subject of the representation, it will be more difficult for a client to discharge the lawyer if the client so desires. The Rule is subject to specific exceptions developed in decisional law and continued in these Rules. The exception for certain advances of the costs of litigation is set forth in paragraph (e). In addition, paragraph (i) sets forth exceptions for liens authorized by law to secure the lawyer's fees or expenses and contracts for reasonable contingent fees. The law of each jurisdiction determines which liens are authorized by law. These may include liens granted by statute, liens originating in common law and liens acquired by contract with the client. When a lawyer acquires by contract a security interest in property other than that recovered through the lawyer's efforts in the litigation, such an acquisition is a business or financial transaction with a client and is governed by the requirements of paragraph (a). Contracts for contingent fees in civil cases are governed by Rule 1.5.

Client-Lawyer Sexual Relationships

[20] The relationship between lawyer and client is a fiduciary one in which the lawyer occupies the highest position of trust and confidence.

The relationship is almost always unequal; thus, a sexual relationship between lawyer and client can involve unfair exploitation of the lawyer's fiduciary role, in violation of the lawyer's basic ethical obligation not to use the trust of the client to the client's disadvantage. In addition, such a relationship presents a significant danger that, because of the lawyer's emotional involvement, the lawyer will be unable to represent the client without impairment of the exercise of independent professional judgment. Moreover, a blurred line between the professional and personal relationships may make it difficult to predict to what extent client confidences will be protected by the attorney-client evidentiary privilege, since client confidences are protected by privilege only when they are imparted in the context of the client-lawyer relationship. Because of the significant danger of harm to client interests and because the client's own emotional involvement renders it unlikely that the client could give adequate informed consent, this Rule prohibits the lawyer from having sexual relations with a client regardless of whether the relationship is consensual and regardless of the absence of prejudice to the client.

[21] Sexual relationships that predate the client-lawyer relationship are not prohibited. Issues relating to the exploitation of the fiduciary relationship and client dependency are diminished when the sexual relationship existed prior to the commencement of the client-lawyer relationship. However, before proceeding with the representation in these circumstances, the lawyer should consider whether the lawyer's ability to represent the client will be materially limited by the relationship. See Rule 1.7(a)(2).

[22] When the client is an organization, paragraph (j) of this Rule prohibits a lawyer for the organization (whether inside counsel or outside counsel) from having a sexual relationship with a constituent of the organization who supervises, directs or regularly consults with that lawyer concerning the organization's legal matters.

Imputation of Prohibitions

[23] Under paragraph (k), a prohibition on conduct by an individual lawyer in paragraphs (a) through (i) also applies to all lawyers associated in a firm with the personally prohibited lawyer. For example, one lawyer in a firm may not enter into a business transaction with a client of another member of the firm without complying with paragraph (a), even if the first lawyer is not personally involved in the representation of the client. The prohibition set forth in paragraph (j) is personal and is not applied to associated lawyers.

Definitional Cross-References

"Firm" *See* Rule 1.0(c)

"Informed consent" *See* Rule 1.0(e)

"Knowingly" *See* Rule 1.0(f)

"Substantial" *See* Rule 1.0(l)

"Writing" and "Signed" *See* Rule 1.0(n)

RULE 1.9: DUTIES TO FORMER CLIENTS

(a) A lawyer who has formerly represented a client in a matter shall not thereafter represent another person in the same or a substantially related matter in which that person's interests are materially adverse to the interests of the former client unless the former client gives informed consent, confirmed in writing.

(b) A lawyer shall not knowingly represent a person in the same or a substantially related matter in which a firm with which the lawyer formerly was associated had previously represented a client

(1) whose interests are materially adverse to that person; and

(2) about whom the lawyer had acquired information protected by Rules 1.6 and 1.9(c) that is material to the matter; unless the former client gives informed consent, confirmed in writing.

(c) A lawyer who has formerly represented a client in a matter or whose present or former firm has formerly represented a client in a matter shall not thereafter:

(1) use information relating to the representation to the disadvantage of the former client except as these Rules would permit or require with respect to a client, or when the information has become generally known; or

(2) reveal information relating to the representation except as these Rules would permit or require with respect to a client.

Comment

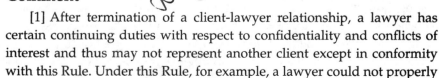

[1] After termination of a client-lawyer relationship, a lawyer has certain continuing duties with respect to confidentiality and conflicts of interest and thus may not represent another client except in conformity with this Rule. Under this Rule, for example, a lawyer could not properly

seek to rescind on behalf of a new client a contract drafted on behalf of the former client. So also a lawyer who has prosecuted an accused person could not properly represent the accused in a subsequent civil action against the government concerning the same transaction. Nor could a lawyer who has represented multiple clients in a matter represent one of the clients against the others in the same or a substantially related matter after a dispute arose among the clients in that matter, unless all affected clients give informed consent. See Comment [9]. Current and former government lawyers must comply with this Rule to the extent required by Rule 1.11.

[2] The scope of a "matter" for purposes of this Rule depends on the facts of a particular situation or transaction. The lawyer's involvement in a matter can also be a question of degree. When a lawyer has been directly involved in a specific transaction, subsequent representation of other clients with materially adverse interests in that transaction clearly is prohibited. On the other hand, a lawyer who recurrently handled a type of problem for a former client is not precluded from later representing another client in a factually distinct problem of that type even though the subsequent representation involves a position adverse to the prior client. Similar considerations can apply to the reassignment of military lawyers between defense and prosecution functions within the same military jurisdictions. The underlying question is whether the lawyer was so involved in the matter that the subsequent representation can be justly regarded as a changing of sides in the matter in question.

[3] Matters are "substantially related" for purposes of this Rule if they involve the same transaction or legal dispute or if there otherwise is a substantial risk that confidential factual information as would normally have been obtained in the prior representation would materially advance the client's position in the subsequent matter. For example, a lawyer who has represented a businessperson and learned extensive private financial information about that person may not then represent that person's spouse in seeking a divorce. Similarly, a lawyer who has previously represented a client in securing environmental permits to build a shopping center would be precluded from representing neighbors seeking to oppose rezoning of the property on the basis of environmental considerations; however, the lawyer would not be precluded, on the grounds of substantial relationship, from defending a tenant of the completed shopping center in resisting eviction for nonpayment of rent. Information that has been disclosed to the public or to other parties adverse to the former

client ordinarily will not be disqualifying. Information acquired in a prior representation may have been rendered obsolete by the passage of time, a circumstance that may be relevant in determining whether two representations are substantially related. In the case of an organizational client, general knowledge of the client's policies and practices ordinarily will not preclude a subsequent representation; on the other hand, knowledge of specific facts gained in a prior representation that are relevant to the matter in question ordinarily will preclude such a representation. A former client is not required to reveal the confidential information learned by the lawyer in order to establish a substantial risk that the lawyer has confidential information to use in the subsequent matter. A conclusion about the possession of such information may be based on the nature of the services the lawyer provided the former client and information that would in ordinary practice be learned by a lawyer providing such services.

Lawyers Moving Between Firms

[4] When lawyers have been associated within a firm but then end their association, the question of whether a lawyer should undertake representation is more complicated. There are several competing considerations. First, the client previously represented by the former firm must be reasonably assured that the principle of loyalty to the client is not compromised. Second, the rule should not be so broadly cast as to preclude other persons from having reasonable choice of legal counsel. Third, the rule should not unreasonably hamper lawyers from forming new associations and taking on new clients after having left a previous association. In this connection, it should be recognized that today many lawyers practice in firms, that many lawyers to some degree limit their practice to one field or another, and that many move from one association to another several times in their careers. If the concept of imputation were applied with unqualified rigor, the result would be radical curtailment of the opportunity of lawyers to move from one practice setting to another and of the opportunity of clients to change counsel.

[5] Paragraph (b) operates to disqualify the lawyer only when the lawyer involved has actual knowledge of information protected by Rules 1.6 and 1.9(c). Thus, if a lawyer while with one firm acquired no knowledge or information relating to a particular client of the firm, and that lawyer later joined another firm, neither the lawyer individually nor the second firm is disqualified from representing another client in the same

or a related matter even though the interests of the two clients conflict. See Rule 1.10(b) for the restrictions on a firm once a lawyer has terminated association with the firm.

[6] Application of paragraph (b) depends on a situation's particular facts, aided by inferences, deductions or working presumptions that reasonably may be made about the way in which lawyers work together. A lawyer may have general access to files of all clients of a law firm and may regularly participate in discussions of their affairs; it should be inferred that such a lawyer in fact is privy to all information about all the firm's clients. In contrast, another lawyer may have access to the files of only a limited number of clients and participate in discussions of the affairs of no other clients; in the absence of information to the contrary, it should be inferred that such a lawyer in fact is privy to information about the clients actually served but not those of other clients. In such an inquiry, the burden of proof should rest upon the firm whose disqualification is sought.

[7] Independent of the question of disqualification of a firm, a lawyer changing professional association has a continuing duty to preserve confidentiality of information about a client formerly represented. See Rules 1.6 and 1.9(c).

[8] Paragraph (c) provides that information acquired by the lawyer in the course of representing a client may not subsequently be used or revealed by the lawyer to the disadvantage of the client. However, the fact that a lawyer has once served a client does not preclude the lawyer from using generally known information about that client when later representing another client.

[9] The provisions of this Rule are for the protection of former clients and can be waived if the client gives informed consent, which consent must be confirmed in writing under paragraphs (a) and (b). See Rule 1.0(e). With regard to the effectiveness of an advance waiver, see Comment [22] to Rule 1.7. With regard to disqualification of a firm with which a lawyer is or was formerly associated, see Rule 1.10.

Definitional Cross-References

"Confirmed in writing" *See* Rule 1.0(b)

"Firm" *See* Rule 1.0(c)

"Informed consent" *See* Rule 1.0(e)

"Knowingly" and "Known" *See* Rule 1.0(f)

"Writing" *See* Rule 1.0(n)

RULE 1.10: IMPUTATION OF CONFLICTS OF INTEREST: GENERAL RULE

(a) While lawyers are associated in a firm, none of them shall knowingly represent a client when any one of them practicing alone would be prohibited from doing so by Rules 1.7 or 1.9, unless

(1) the prohibition is based on a personal interest of the disqualified lawyer and does not present a significant risk of materially limiting the representation of the client by the remaining lawyers in the firm; or

(2) the prohibition is based upon Rule 1.9(a) or (b), and arises out of the disqualified lawyer's association with a prior firm, and

(i) the disqualified lawyer is timely screened from any participation in the matter and is apportioned no part of the fee therefrom;

(ii) written notice is promptly given to any affected former client to enable the former client to ascertain compliance with the provisions of this Rule, which shall include a description of the screening procedures employed; a statement of the firm's and of the screened lawyer's compliance with these Rules; a statement that review may be available before a tribunal; and an agreement by the firm to respond promptly to any written inquiries or objections by the former client about the screening procedures; and

(iii) certifications of compliance with these Rules and with the screening procedures are provided to the former client by the screened lawyer and by a partner of the firm, at reasonable intervals upon the former client's written request and upon termination of the screening procedures.

(b) When a lawyer has terminated an association with a firm, the firm is not prohibited from thereafter representing a person with interests materially adverse to those of a client represented by the formerly associated lawyer and not currently represented by the firm, unless:

(1) the matter is the same or substantially related to that in which the formerly associated lawyer represented the client; and

(2) any lawyer remaining in the firm has information protected by Rules 1.6 and 1.9(c) that is material to the matter.

    (c) A disqualification prescribed by this Rule may be waived by the affected client under the conditions stated in Rule 1.7.

    (d) The disqualification of lawyers associated in a firm with former or current government lawyers is governed by Rule 1.11.

Comment

Definition of "Firm"

[1] For purposes of the Rules of Professional Conduct, the term "firm" denotes lawyers in a law partnership, professional corporation, sole proprietorship or other association authorized to practice law; or lawyers employed in a legal services organization or the legal department of a corporation or other organization. See Rule 1.0(c). Whether two or more lawyers constitute a firm within this definition can depend on the specific facts. See Rule 1.0, Comments [2]–[4].

Principles of Imputed Disqualification

[2] The rule of imputed disqualification stated in paragraph (a) gives effect to the principle of loyalty to the client as it applies to lawyers who practice in a law firm. Such situations can be considered from the premise that a firm of lawyers is essentially one lawyer for purposes of the rules governing loyalty to the client, or from the premise that each lawyer is vicariously bound by the obligation of loyalty owed by each lawyer with whom the lawyer is associated. Paragraph (a)(1) operates only among the lawyers currently associated in a firm. When a lawyer moves from one firm to another, the situation is governed by Rules 1.9(b) and 1.10(a)(2) and 1.10(b).

[3] The rule in paragraph (a) does not prohibit representation where neither questions of client loyalty nor protection of confidential information are presented. Where one lawyer in a firm could not effectively represent a given client because of strong political beliefs, for example, but that lawyer will do no work on the case and the personal beliefs of the lawyer will not materially limit the representation by others in the firm, the firm should not be disqualified. On the other hand, if an opposing party in a case were owned by a lawyer in the law firm, and others in the firm would be materially limited in pursuing the matter because of loyalty to that lawyer, the personal disqualification of the lawyer would be imputed to all others in the firm.

[4] The rule in paragraph (a) also does not prohibit representation by others in the law firm where the person prohibited from involvement in a matter is a nonlawyer, such as a paralegal or legal secretary. Nor does

paragraph (a) prohibit representation if the lawyer is prohibited from acting because of events before the person became a lawyer, for example, work that the person did while a law student. Such persons, however, ordinarily must be screened from any personal participation in the matter to avoid communication to others in the firm of confidential information that both the nonlawyers and the firm have a legal duty to protect. See Rules 1.0(k) and 5.3.

[5] Rule 1.10(b) operates to permit a law firm, under certain circumstances, to represent a person with interests directly adverse to those of a client represented by a lawyer who formerly was associated with the firm. The Rule applies regardless of when the formerly associated lawyer represented the client. However, the law firm may not represent a person with interests adverse to those of a present client of the firm, which would violate Rule 1.7. Moreover, the firm may not represent the person where the matter is the same or substantially related to that in which the formerly associated lawyer represented the client and any other lawyer currently in the firm has material information protected by Rules 1.6 and 1.9(c).

[6] Rule 1.10(c) removes imputation with the informed consent of the affected client or former client under the conditions stated in Rule 1.7. The conditions stated in Rule 1.7 require the lawyer to determine that the representation is not prohibited by Rule 1.7(b) and that each affected client or former client has given informed consent to the representation, confirmed in writing. In some cases, the risk may be so severe that the conflict may not be cured by client consent. For a discussion of the effectiveness of client waivers of conflicts that might arise in the future, see Rule 1.7, Comment [22]. For a definition of informed consent, see Rule 1.0(e).

[7] Rule 1.10(a)(2) similarly removes the imputation otherwise required by Rule 1.10(a), but unlike section (c), it does so without requiring that there be informed consent by the former client. Instead, it requires that the procedures laid out in sections (a)(2)(i)-(iii) be followed. A description of effective screening mechanisms appears in Rule 1.0(k). Lawyers should be aware, however, that, even where screening mechanisms have been adopted, tribunals may consider additional factors in ruling upon motions to disqualify a lawyer from pending litigation.

[8] Paragraph (a)(2)(i) does not prohibit the screened lawyer from receiving a salary or partnership share established by prior independent agreement, but that lawyer may not receive compensation directly related to the matter in which the lawyer is disqualified.

[9] The notice required by paragraph (a)(2)(ii) generally should include a description of the screened lawyer's prior representation and be

given as soon as practicable after the need for screening becomes apparent. It also should include a statement by the screened lawyer and the firm that the client's material confidential information has not been disclosed or used in violation of the Rules. The notice is intended to enable the former client to evaluate and comment upon the effectiveness of the screening procedures.

[10] The certifications required by paragraph (a)(2)(iii) give the former client assurance that the client's material confidential information has not been disclosed or used inappropriately, either prior to timely implementation of a screen or thereafter. If compliance cannot be certified, the certificate must describe the failure to comply.

[11] Where a lawyer has joined a private firm after having represented the government, imputation is governed by Rule 1.11(b) and (c), not this Rule. Under Rule 1.11(d), where a lawyer represents the government after having served clients in private practice, nongovernmental employment or in another government agency, former-client conflicts are not imputed to government lawyers associated with the individually disqualified lawyer.

[12] Where a lawyer is prohibited from engaging in certain transactions under Rule 1.8, paragraph (k) of that Rule, and not this Rule, determines whether that prohibition also applies to other lawyers associated in a firm with the personally prohibited lawyer.

Definitional Cross-References

"Firm" *See* Rule 1.0(c)
"Knowingly" *See* Rule 1.0(f)
"Partner" *See* Rule 1.0(g)
"Screened" *See* Rule 1.0(k)
"Tribunal" *See* Rule 1.0(m)
"Written" *See* Rule 1.0(n)

RULE 1.11: SPECIAL CONFLICTS OF INTEREST FOR FORMER AND CURRENT GOVERNMENT OFFICERS AND EMPLOYEES

(a) Except as law may otherwise expressly permit, a lawyer who has formerly served as a public officer or employee of the government:

(1) is subject to Rule 1.9(c); and

62

(2) shall not otherwise represent a client in connection with a matter in which the lawyer participated personally and substantially as a public officer or employee, unless the appropriate government agency gives its informed consent, confirmed in writing, to the representation.

(b) When a lawyer is disqualified from representation under paragraph (a), no lawyer in a firm with which that lawyer is associated may knowingly undertake or continue representation in such a matter unless:

(1) the disqualified lawyer is timely screened from any participation in the matter and is apportioned no part of the fee therefrom; and

(2) written notice is promptly given to the appropriate government agency to enable it to ascertain compliance with the provisions of this Rule.

(c) Except as law may otherwise expressly permit, a lawyer having information that the lawyer knows is confidential government information about a person acquired when the lawyer was a public officer or employee, may not represent a private client whose interests are adverse to that person in a matter in which the information could be used to the material disadvantage of that person. As used in this Rule, the term "confidential government information" means information that has been obtained under governmental authority and which, at the time this Rule is applied, the government is prohibited by law from disclosing to the public or has a legal privilege not to disclose and which is not otherwise available to the public. A firm with which that lawyer is associated may undertake or continue representation in the matter only if the disqualified lawyer is timely screened from any participation in the matter and is apportioned no part of the fee therefrom.

(d) Except as law may otherwise expressly permit, a lawyer currently serving as a public officer or employee:

(1) is subject to Rules 1.7 and 1.9; and

(2) shall not:

(i) participate in a matter in w_
participated personally and subst_
practice or nongovernmental empl_
appropriate government agency giv_
consent, confirmed in writing; or

(ii) negotiate for private employment with any person who is involved as a party or as lawyer for a party in a matter in which the lawyer is participating personally and substantially, except that a lawyer serving as a law clerk to a judge, other adjudicative officer or arbitrator may negotiate for private employment as permitted by Rule 1.12(b) and subject to the conditions stated in Rule 1.12(b).

(e) As used in this Rule, the term "matter" includes:

(1) any judicial or other proceeding, application, request for a ruling or other determination, contract, claim, controversy, investigation, charge, accusation, arrest or other particular matter involving a specific party or parties, and

(2) any other matter covered by the conflict of interest rules of the appropriate government agency.

Comment

[1] A lawyer who has served or is currently serving as a public officer or employee is personally subject to the Rules of Professional Conduct, including the prohibition against concurrent conflicts of interest stated in Rule 1.7. In addition, such a lawyer may be subject to statutes and government regulations regarding conflict of interest. Such statutes and regulations may circumscribe the extent to which the government agency may give consent under this Rule. See Rule 1.0(e) for the definition of informed consent.

[2] Paragraphs (a)(1), (a)(2) and (d)(1) restate the obligations of an individual lawyer who has served or is currently serving as an officer or employee of the government toward a former government or private client. Rule 1.10 is not applicable to the conflicts of interest addressed by this Rule. Rather, paragraph (b) sets forth a special imputation rule for former government lawyers that provides for screening and notice. Because of the special problems raised by imputation within a government agency, paragraph (d) does not impute the conflicts of a lawyer currently serving as an officer or employee of the government to other associated government officers or employees, although ordinarily it will be prudent to screen such lawyers.

[3] Paragraphs (a)(2) and (d)(2) apply regardless of whether a lawyer adverse to a former client and are thus designed not only to protect the er client, but also to prevent a lawyer from exploiting public office advantage of another client. For example, a lawyer who has pur-

sued a claim on behalf of the government may not pursue the same claim on behalf of a later private client after the lawyer has left government service, except when authorized to do so by the government agency under paragraph (a). Similarly, a lawyer who has pursued a claim on behalf of a private client may not pursue the claim on behalf of the government, except when authorized to do so by paragraph (d). As with paragraphs (a)(1) and (d)(1), Rule 1.10 is not applicable to the conflicts of interest addressed by these paragraphs.

(4) This Rule represents a balancing of interests. On the one hand, where the successive clients are a government agency and another client, public or private, the risk exists that power or discretion vested in that agency might be used for the special benefit of the other client. A lawyer should not be in a position where benefit to the other client might affect performance of the lawyer's professional functions on behalf of the government. Also, unfair advantage could accrue to the other client by reason of access to confidential government information about the client's adversary obtainable only through the lawyer's government service. On the other hand, the rules governing lawyers presently or formerly employed by a government agency should not be so restrictive as to inhibit transfer of employment to and from the government. The government has a legitimate need to attract qualified lawyers as well as to maintain high ethical standards. Thus a former government lawyer is disqualified only from particular matters in which the lawyer participated personally and substantially. The provisions for screening and waiver in paragraph (b) are necessary to prevent the disqualification rule from imposing too severe a deterrent against entering public service. The limitation of disqualification in paragraphs (a)(2) and (d)(2) to matters involving a specific party or parties, rather than extending disqualification to all substantive issues on which the lawyer worked, serves a similar function.

(5) When a lawyer has been employed by one government agency and then moves to a second government agency, it may be appropriate to treat that second agency as another client for purposes of this Rule, as when a lawyer is employed by a city and subsequently is employed by a federal agency. However, because the conflict of interest is governed by paragraph (d), the latter agency is not required to screen the lawyer as paragraph (b) requires a law firm to do. The question of whether two government agencies should be regarded as the same or different clients for conflict of interest purposes is beyond the scope of these Rules. See Rule 1.13 Comment [9].

[6] Paragraphs (b) and (c) contemplate a screening arrangement. See Rule 1.0(k) (requirements for screening procedures). These paragraphs do not prohibit a lawyer from receiving a salary or partnership share established by prior independent agreement, but that lawyer may not receive compensation directly relating the lawyer's compensation to the fee in the matter in which the lawyer is disqualified.

[7] Notice, including a description of the screened lawyer's prior representation and of the screening procedures employed, generally should be given as soon as practicable after the need for screening becomes apparent.

[8] Paragraph (c) operates only when the lawyer in question has knowledge of the information, which means actual knowledge; it does not operate with respect to information that merely could be imputed to the lawyer.

[9] Paragraphs (a) and (d) do not prohibit a lawyer from jointly representing a private party and a government agency when doing so is permitted by Rule 1.7 and is not otherwise prohibited by law.

[10] For purposes of paragraph (e) of this Rule, a "matter" may continue in another form. In determining whether two particular matters are the same, the lawyer should consider the extent to which the matters involve the same basic facts, the same or related parties, and the time elapsed.

Definitional Cross-References

"Confirmed in writing" *See* Rule 1.0(b)
"Firm" *See* Rule 1.0(c)
"Informed consent" *See* Rule 1.0(e)
"Knowingly" and "Knows" *See* Rule 1.0(f)
"Screened" *See* Rule 1.0(k)
"Written" *See* Rule 1.0(n)

RULE 1.12: FORMER JUDGE, ARBITRATOR, MEDIATOR OR OTHER THIRD-PARTY NEUTRAL

(a) Except as stated in paragraph (d), a lawyer shall not represent anyone in connection with a matter in which the lawyer participated personally and substantially as a judge or other adjudicative officer or law clerk to such a person or as an arbitrator, mediator or other third-party neutral, unless all parties to the proceeding give informed consent, confirmed in writing.

(b) A lawyer shall not negotiate for employment with any person who is involved as a party or as lawyer for a party in a matter in which the lawyer is participating personally and substantially as a judge or other adjudicative officer or as an arbitrator, mediator or other third-party neutral. A lawyer serving as a law clerk to a judge or other adjudicative officer may negotiate for employment with a party or lawyer involved in a matter in which the clerk is participating personally and substantially, but only after the lawyer has notified the judge or other adjudicative officer.

(c) If a lawyer is disqualified by paragraph (a), no lawyer in a firm with which that lawyer is associated may knowingly undertake or continue representation in the matter unless:

(1) the disqualified lawyer is timely screened from any participation in the matter and is apportioned no part of the fee therefrom; and

(2) written notice is promptly given to the parties and any appropriate tribunal to enable them to ascertain compliance with the provisions of this Rule.

(d) An arbitrator selected as a partisan of a party in a multimember arbitration panel is not prohibited from subsequently representing that party.

Comment

[1] This Rule generally parallels Rule 1.11. The term "personally and substantially" signifies that a judge who was a member of a multimember court, and thereafter left judicial office to practice law, is not prohibited from representing a client in a matter pending in the court, but in which the former judge did not participate. So also the fact that a former judge exercised administrative responsibility in a court does not prevent the former judge from acting as a lawyer in a matter where the judge had previously exercised remote or incidental administrative responsibility that did not affect the merits. Compare the Comment to Rule 1.11. The term "adjudicative officer" includes such officials as judges pro tempore, referees, special masters, hearing officers and other parajudicial officers, and also lawyers who serve as part-time judges. Paragraphs C(2), D(2) and E(2) of the Application Section of the Model Code of Judicial Con-

duct provide that a part-time judge, judge pro tempore or retired judge recalled to active service, shall not "act as a lawyer in a proceeding in which the judge has served as a judge or in any other proceeding related thereto." Although phrased differently from this Rule, those Rules correspond in meaning.

[2] Like former judges, lawyers who have served as arbitrators, mediators or other third-party neutrals may be asked to represent a client in a matter in which the lawyer participated personally and substantially. This Rule forbids such representation unless all of the parties to the proceedings give their informed consent, confirmed in writing. See Rule 1.0(e) and (b). Other law or codes of ethics governing third-party neutrals may impose more stringent standards of personal or imputed disqualification. See Rule 2.4.

[3] Although lawyers who serve as third-party neutrals do not have information concerning the parties that is protected under Rule 1.6, they typically owe the parties an obligation of confidentiality under law or codes of ethics governing third-party neutrals. Thus, paragraph (c) provides that conflicts of the personally disqualified lawyer will be imputed to other lawyers in a law firm unless the conditions of this paragraph are met.

[4] Requirements for screening procedures are stated in Rule 1.0(k). Paragraph (c)(1) does not prohibit the screened lawyer from receiving a salary or partnership share established by prior independent agreement, but that lawyer may not receive compensation directly related to the matter in which the lawyer is disqualified.

[5] Notice, including a description of the screened lawyer's prior representation and of the screening procedures employed, generally should be given as soon as practicable after the need for screening becomes apparent.

Definitional Cross-References

"Confirmed in writing" *See* Rule 1.0(b)
"Firm" *See* Rule 1.0(c)
"Informed consent" *See* Rule 1.0(e)
"Knowingly" *See* Rule 1.0(f)
"Screened" *See* Rule 1.0(k)
"Tribunal" *See* Rule 1.0(m)
"Writing" and "Written" *See* Rule 1.0(n)

RULE 1.13: ORGANIZATION AS CLIENT

(a) A lawyer employed or retained by an organization represents the organization acting through its duly authorized constituents.

(b) If a lawyer for an organization knows that an officer, employee or other person associated with the organization is engaged in action, intends to act or refuses to act in a matter related to the representation that is a violation of a legal obligation to the organization, or a violation of law that reasonably might be imputed to the organization, and that is likely to result in substantial injury to the organization, then the lawyer shall proceed as is reasonably necessary in the best interest of the organization. Unless the lawyer reasonably believes that it is not necessary in the best interest of the organization to do so, the lawyer shall refer the matter to higher authority in the organization, including, if warranted by the circumstances, to the highest authority that can act on behalf of the organization as determined by applicable law.

(c) Except as provided in paragraph (d), if

(1) despite the lawyer's efforts in accordance with paragraph (b) the highest authority that can act on behalf of the organization insists upon or fails to address in a timely and appropriate manner an action or a refusal to act, that is clearly a violation of law; and

(2) the lawyer reasonably believes that the violation is reasonably certain to result in substantial injury to the organization,

then the lawyer may reveal information relating to the representation whether or not Rule 1.6 permits such disclosure, but only if and to the extent the lawyer reasonably believes necessary to prevent substantial injury to the organization.

(d) Paragraph (c) shall not apply with respect to information relating to a lawyer's representation of an organization to investigate an alleged violation of law, or to defend the organization or an officer, employee or other constituent associated with the organization against a claim arising out of an alleged violation of law.

(e) A lawyer who reasonably believes that he or she has been discharged because of the lawyer's actions taken pursuant to paragraphs (b) or (c), or who withdraws under circumstances that require or permit the lawyer to take action under either of those paragraphs, shall proceed as the lawyer reasonably believes necessary to assure that the organization's highest authority is informed of the lawyer's discharge or withdrawal.

(f) In dealing with an organization's directors, officers, employees, members, shareholders or other constituents, a lawyer shall explain the identity of the client when the lawyer knows or reasonably should know that the organization's interests are adverse to those of the constituents with whom the lawyer is dealing.

(g) A lawyer representing an organization may also represent any of its directors, officers, employees, members, shareholders or other constituents, subject to the provisions of Rule 1.7. If the organization's consent to the dual representation is required by Rule 1.7, the consent shall be given by an appropriate official of the organization other than the individual who is to be represented, or by the shareholders.

Comment

The Entity as the Client

[1] An organizational client is a legal entity, but it cannot act except through its officers, directors, employees, shareholders and other constituents. Officers, directors, employees and shareholders are the constituents of the corporate organizational client. The duties defined in this Comment apply equally to unincorporated associations. "Other constituents" as used in this Comment means the positions equivalent to officers, directors, employees and shareholders held by persons acting for organizational clients that are not corporations.

[2] When one of the constituents of an organizational client communicates with the organization's lawyer in that person's organizational capacity, the communication is protected by Rule 1.6. Thus, by way of example, if an organizational client requests its lawyer to investigate allegations of wrongdoing, interviews made in the course of that investigation between the lawyer and the client's employees or other constituents are covered by Rule 1.6. This does not mean, however, that constituents of an organizational client are the clients of the lawyer. The lawyer may not disclose to such constituents information relating to the representation except for disclosures explicitly or impliedly authorized by the organizational client in order to carry out the representation or as otherwise permitted by Rule 1.6.

[3] When constituents of the organization make decisions for it, the decisions ordinarily must be accepted by the lawyer even if their utility or prudence is doubtful. Decisions concerning policy and operations, including ones entailing serious risk, are not as such in the lawyer's province. Paragraph (b) makes clear, however, that when the lawyer knows that the organization is likely to be substantially injured by action of an officer or other constituent that violates a legal obligation to the organization or is in violation of law that might be imputed to the organization, the lawyer must proceed as is reasonably necessary in the best interest of the organization. As defined in Rule 1.0(f), knowledge can be inferred from circumstances, and a lawyer cannot ignore the obvious.

[4] In determining how to proceed under paragraph (b), the lawyer should give due consideration to the seriousness of the violation and its consequences, the responsibility in the organization and the apparent motivation of the person involved, the policies of the organization concerning such matters, and any other relevant considerations. Ordinarily, referral to a higher authority would be necessary. In some circumstances, however, it may be appropriate for the lawyer to ask the constituent to reconsider the matter; for example, if the circumstances involve a constituent's innocent misunderstanding of law and subsequent acceptance of the lawyer's advice, the lawyer may reasonably conclude that the best interest of the organization does not require that the matter be referred to higher authority. If a constituent persists in conduct contrary to the lawyer's advice, it will be necessary for the lawyer to take steps to have the matter reviewed by a higher authority in the organization. If the matter is of sufficient seriousness and importance or urgency to the organization, referral to higher authority in the organization may be necessary even if the lawyer has not communicated with the constituent. Any measures taken should, to the extent practicable, minimize the risk of revealing information relating to the representation to persons outside the organization. Even in circumstances where a lawyer is not obligated by Rule 1.13 to proceed, a lawyer may bring to the attention of an organizational client, including its highest authority, matters that the lawyer reasonably believes to be of sufficient importance to warrant doing so in the best interest of the organization.

[5] Paragraph (b) also makes clear that when it is reasonably necessary to enable the organization to address the matter in a timely and appropriate manner, the lawyer must refer the matter to higher authority, including, if warranted by the circumstances, the highest authority that

can act on behalf of the organization under applicable law. The organization's highest authority to whom a matter may be referred ordinarily will be the board of directors or similar governing body. However, applicable law may prescribe that under certain conditions the highest authority reposes elsewhere, for example, in the independent directors of a corporation.

Relation to Other Rules

[6] The authority and responsibility provided in this Rule are concurrent with the authority and responsibility provided in other Rules. In particular, this Rule does not limit or expand the lawyer's responsibility under Rules 1.8, 1.16, 3.3 or 4.1. Paragraph (c) of this Rule supplements Rule 1.6(b) by providing an additional basis upon which the lawyer may reveal information relating to the representation, but does not modify, restrict, or limit the provisions of Rule 1.6(b)(1) – (6). Under paragraph (c) the lawyer may reveal such information only when the organization's highest authority insists upon or fails to address threatened or ongoing action that is clearly a violation of law, and then only to the extent the lawyer reasonably believes necessary to prevent reasonably certain substantial injury to the organization. It is not necessary that the lawyer's services be used in furtherance of the violation, but it is required that the matter be related to the lawyer's representation of the organization. If the lawyer's services are being used by an organization to further a crime or fraud by the organization, Rules 1.6(b)(2) and 1.6(b)(3) may permit the lawyer to disclose confidential information. In such circumstances Rule 1.2(d) may also be applicable, in which event, withdrawal from the representation under Rule 1.16(a)(1) may be required.

[7] Paragraph (d) makes clear that the authority of a lawyer to disclose information relating to a representation in circumstances described in paragraph (c) does not apply with respect to information relating to a lawyer's engagement by an organization to investigate an alleged violation of law or to defend the organization or an officer, employee or other person associated with the organization against a claim arising out of an alleged violation of law. This is necessary in order to enable organizational clients to enjoy the full benefits of legal counsel in conducting an investigation or defending against a claim.

[8] A lawyer who reasonably believes that he or she has been discharged because of the lawyer's actions taken pursuant to paragraph (b) or (c), or who withdraws in circumstances that require or permit the

lawyer to take action under either of these paragraphs, must proceed as the lawyer reasonably believes necessary to assure that the organization's highest authority is informed of the lawyer's discharge or withdrawal.

Government Agency

[9] The duty defined in this Rule applies to governmental organizations. Defining precisely the identity of the client and prescribing the resulting obligations of such lawyers may be more difficult in the government context and is a matter beyond the scope of these Rules. See Scope [18]. Although in some circumstances the client may be a specific agency, it may also be a branch of government, such as the executive branch, or the government as a whole. For example, if the action or failure to act involves the head of a bureau, either the department of which the bureau is a part or the relevant branch of government may be the client for purposes of this Rule. Moreover, in a matter involving the conduct of government officials, a government lawyer may have authority under applicable law to question such conduct more extensively than that of a lawyer for a private organization in similar circumstances. Thus, when the client is a governmental organization, a different balance may be appropriate between maintaining confidentiality and assuring that the wrongful act is prevented or rectified, for public business is involved. In addition, duties of lawyers employed by the government or lawyers in military service may be defined by statutes and regulation. This Rule does not limit that authority. See Scope.

Clarifying the Lawyer's Role

[10] There are times when the organization's interest may be or become adverse to those of one or more of its constituents. In such circumstances the lawyer should advise any constituent, whose interest the lawyer finds adverse to that of the organization of the conflict or potential conflict of interest, that the lawyer cannot represent such constituent, and that such person may wish to obtain independent representation. Care must be taken to assure that the individual understands that, when there is such adversity of interest, the lawyer for the organization cannot provide legal representation for that constituent individual, and that discussions between the lawyer for the organization and the individual may not be privileged.

[11] Whether such a warning should be given by the lawyer for the organization to any constituent individual may turn on the facts of each case.

Dual Representation

[12] Paragraph (g) recognizes that a lawyer for an organization may also represent a principal officer or major shareholder.

Derivative Actions

[13] Under generally prevailing law, the shareholders or members of a corporation may bring suit to compel the directors to perform their legal obligations in the supervision of the organization. Members of unincorporated associations have essentially the same right. Such an action may be brought nominally by the organization, but usually is, in fact, a legal controversy over management of the organization.

[14] The question can arise whether counsel for the organization may defend such an action. The proposition that the organization is the lawyer's client does not alone resolve the issue. Most derivative actions are a normal incident of an organization's affairs, to be defended by the organization's lawyer like any other suit. However, if the claim involves serious charges of wrongdoing by those in control of the organization, a conflict may arise between the lawyer's duty to the organization and the lawyer's relationship with the board. In those circumstances, Rule 1.7 governs who should represent the directors and the organization.

Definitional Cross-References

"Knows" *See* Rule 1.0(f)
"Reasonably" *See* Rule 1.0(h)
"Reasonably believes" *See* Rule 1.0(i)
"Reasonably should know" *See* Rule 1.0(j)
"Substantial" *See* Rule 1.0(l)

RULE 1.14: CLIENT WITH DIMINISHED CAPACITY

(a) When a client's capacity to make adequately considered decisions in connection with a representation is diminished, whether because of minority, mental impairment or for some other reason, the lawyer shall, as far as reasonably possible, maintain a normal client-lawyer relationship with the client.

(b) When the lawyer reasonably believes that the client has diminished capacity, is at risk of substantial physical, financial or other harm unless action is taken and cannot adequately act in the client's own interest, the lawyer may take reasonably necessary protective action, including consulting with individuals or entities that have the ability to take action to protect the client and, in appropriate cases, seeking the appointment of a guardian ad litem, conservator or guardian.

(c) Information relating to the representation of a client with diminished capacity is protected by Rule 1.6. When taking protective action pursuant to paragraph (b), the lawyer is impliedly authorized under Rule 1.6(a) to reveal information about the client, but only to the extent reasonably necessary to protect the client's interests.

Comment

[1] The normal client-lawyer relationship is based on the assumption that the client, when properly advised and assisted, is capable of making decisions about important matters. When the client is a minor or suffers from a diminished mental capacity, however, maintaining the ordinary client-lawyer relationship may not be possible in all respects. In particular, a severely incapacitated person may have no power to make legally binding decisions. Nevertheless, a client with diminished capacity often has the ability to understand, deliberate upon, and reach conclusions about matters affecting the client's own well-being. For example, children as young as five or six years of age, and certainly those of ten or twelve, are regarded as having opinions that are entitled to weight in legal proceedings concerning their custody. So also, it is recognized that some persons of advanced age can be quite capable of handling routine financial matters while needing special legal protection concerning major transactions.

[2] The fact that a client suffers a disability does not diminish the lawyer's obligation to treat the client with attention and respect. Even if the person has a legal representative, the lawyer should as far as possible accord the represented person the status of client, particularly in maintaining communication.

[3] The client may wish to have family members or other persons participate in discussions with the lawyer. When necessary to assist in the representation, the presence of such persons generally does not affect the applicability of the attorney-client evidentiary privilege. Nevertheless, the lawyer must keep the client's interests foremost and, except for protective action authorized under paragraph (b), must look to the client, and not family members, to make decisions on the client's behalf.

[4] If a legal representative has already been appointed for the client, the lawyer should ordinarily look to the representative for decisions

on behalf of the client. In matters involving a minor, whether the lawyer should look to the parents as natural guardians may depend on the type of proceeding or matter in which the lawyer is representing the minor. If the lawyer represents the guardian as distinct from the ward, and is aware that the guardian is acting adversely to the ward's interest, the lawyer may have an obligation to prevent or rectify the guardian's misconduct. See Rule 1.2(d).

Taking Protective Action

[5] If a lawyer reasonably believes that a client is at risk of substantial physical, financial or other harm unless action is taken, and that a normal client-lawyer relationship cannot be maintained as provided in paragraph (a) because the client lacks sufficient capacity to communicate or to make adequately considered decisions in connection with the representation, then paragraph (b) permits the lawyer to take protective measures deemed necessary. Such measures could include: consulting with family members, using a reconsideration period to permit clarification or improvement of circumstances, using voluntary surrogate decisionmaking tools such as durable powers of attorney or consulting with support groups, professional services, adult-protective agencies or other individuals or entities that have the ability to protect the client. In taking any protective action, the lawyer should be guided by such factors as the wishes and values of the client to the extent known, the client's best interests and the goals of intruding into the client's decisionmaking autonomy to the least extent feasible, maximizing client capacities and respecting the client's family and social connections.

[6] In determining the extent of the client's diminished capacity, the lawyer should consider and balance such factors as: the client's ability to articulate reasoning leading to a decision, variability of state of mind and ability to appreciate consequences of a decision; the substantive fairness of a decision; and the consistency of a decision with the known long-term commitments and values of the client. In appropriate circumstances, the lawyer may seek guidance from an appropriate diagnostician.

[7] If a legal representative has not been appointed, the lawyer should consider whether appointment of a guardian ad litem, conservator or guardian is necessary to protect the client's interests. Thus, if a client with diminished capacity has substantial property that should be sold for the client's benefit, effective completion of the transaction may require appointment of a legal representative. In addition, rules of pro-

cedure in litigation sometimes provide that minors or persons with di-minished capacity must be represented by a guardian or next friend if they do not have a general guardian. In many circumstances, however, appointment of a legal representative may be more expensive or trau-matic for the client than circumstances in fact require. Evaluation of such circumstances is a matter entrusted to the professional judgment of the lawyer. In considering alternatives, however, the lawyer should be aware of any law that requires the lawyer to advocate the least restrictive action on behalf of the client.

Disclosure of the Client's Condition

[8] Disclosure of the client's diminished capacity could adversely af-fect the client's interests. For example, raising the question of diminished capacity could, in some circumstances, lead to proceedings for involun-tary commitment. Information relating to the representation is protected by Rule 1.6. Therefore, unless authorized to do so, the lawyer may not disclose such information. When taking protective action pursuant to paragraph (b), the lawyer is impliedly authorized to make the neces-sary disclosures, even when the client directs the lawyer to the contrary. Nevertheless, given the risks of disclosure, paragraph (c) limits what the lawyer may disclose in consulting with other individuals or entities or seeking the appointment of a legal representative. At the very least, the lawyer should determine whether it is likely that the person or entity consulted with will act adversely to the client's interests before discuss-ing matters related to the client. The lawyer's position in such cases is an unavoidably difficult one.

Emergency Legal Assistance

[9] In an emergency where the health, safety or a financial interest of a person with seriously diminished capacity is threatened with imminent and irreparable harm, a lawyer may take legal action on behalf of such a person even though the person is unable to establish a client-lawyer relationship or to make or express considered judgments about the mat-ter, when the person or another acting in good faith on that person's be-half has consulted with the lawyer. Even in such an emergency, however, the lawyer should not act unless the lawyer reasonably believes that the person has no other lawyer, agent or other representative available. The lawyer should take legal action on behalf of the person only to the extent reasonably necessary to maintain the status quo or otherwise avoid im-

minent and irreparable harm. A lawyer who undertakes to represent a person in such an exigent situation has the same duties under these Rules as the lawyer would with respect to a client.

[10] A lawyer who acts on behalf of a person with seriously diminished capacity in an emergency should keep the confidences of the person as if dealing with a client, disclosing them only to the extent necessary to accomplish the intended protective action. The lawyer should disclose to any tribunal involved and to any other counsel involved the nature of his or her relationship with the person. The lawyer should take steps to regularize the relationship or implement other protective solutions as soon as possible. Normally, a lawyer would not seek compensation for such emergency actions taken.

Definitional Cross-References

"Reasonably" *See* Rule 1.0(h)
"Reasonably believes" *See* Rule 1.0(i)
"Substantial" *See* Rule 1.0(l)

RULE 1.15: SAFEKEEPING PROPERTY

(a) A lawyer shall hold property of clients or third persons that is in a lawyer's possession in connection with a representation separate from the lawyer's own property. Funds shall be kept in a separate account maintained in the state where the lawyer's office is situated, or elsewhere with the consent of the client or third person. Other property shall be identified as such and appropriately safeguarded. Complete records of such account funds and other property shall be kept by the lawyer and shall be preserved for a period of [five years] after termination of the representation.

(b) A lawyer may deposit the lawyer's own funds in a client trust account for the sole purpose of paying bank service charges on that account, but only in an amount necessary for that purpose.

(c) A lawyer shall deposit into a client trust account legal fees and expenses that have been paid in advance, to be withdrawn by the lawyer only as fees are earned or expenses incurred.

(d) Upon receiving funds or other property in which a client or third person has an interest, a lawyer shall promptly notify the client or third person. Except as stated in this Rule or otherwise permitted by law or by agreement with the client, a lawyer shall promptly deliver to the client or third person any funds or other property that the client or third person is entitled to receive and, upon request by the client or third person, shall promptly render a full accounting regarding such property.

(e) When in the course of representation a lawyer is in possession of property in which two or more persons (one of whom may be the lawyer) claim interests, the property shall be kept separate by the lawyer until the dispute is resolved. The lawyer shall promptly distribute all portions of the property as to which the interests are not in dispute.

Comment

[1] A lawyer should hold property of others with the care required of a professional fiduciary. Securities should be kept in a safe deposit box, except when some other form of safekeeping is warranted by special circumstances. All property that is the property of clients or third persons, including prospective clients, must be kept separate from the lawyer's business and personal property and, if monies, in one or more trust accounts. Separate trust accounts may be warranted when administering estate monies or acting in similar fiduciary capacities. A lawyer should maintain on a current basis books and records in accordance with generally accepted accounting practice and comply with any recordkeeping rules established by law or court order. See, e.g., ABA Model Rules for Client Trust Account Records.

[2] While normally it is impermissible to commingle the lawyer's own funds with client funds, paragraph (b) provides that it is permissible when necessary to pay bank service charges on that account. Accurate records must be kept regarding which part of the funds are the lawyer's.

[3] Lawyers often receive funds from which the lawyer's fee will be paid. The lawyer is not required to remit to the client funds that the lawyer reasonably believes represent fees owed. However, a lawyer may not hold funds to coerce a client into accepting the lawyer's contention. The disputed portion of the funds must be kept in a trust account and the lawyer should suggest means for prompt resolution of the dispute, such as arbitration. The undisputed portion of the funds shall be promptly distributed.

[4] Paragraph (e) also recognizes that third parties may have lawful claims against specific funds or other property in a lawyer's custody, such as a client's creditor who has a lien on funds recovered in a personal injury action. A lawyer may have a duty under applicable law to protect such third-party claims against wrongful interference by the client. In

such cases, when the third-party claim is not frivolous under applicable law, the lawyer must refuse to surrender the property to the client until the claims are resolved. A lawyer should not unilaterally assume to arbitrate a dispute between the client and the third party, but, when there are substantial grounds for dispute as to the person entitled to the funds, the lawyer may file an action to have a court resolve the dispute.

[5] The obligations of a lawyer under this Rule are independent of those arising from activity other than rendering legal services. For example, a lawyer who serves only as an escrow agent is governed by the applicable law relating to fiduciaries even though the lawyer does not render legal services in the transaction and is not governed by this Rule.

[6] A lawyers' fund for client protection provides a means through the collective efforts of the bar to reimburse persons who have lost money or property as a result of dishonest conduct of a lawyer. Where such a fund has been established, a lawyer must participate where it is mandatory, and, even when it is voluntary, the lawyer should participate.

RULE 1.16: DECLINING OR TERMINATING REPRESENTATION

(a) Except as stated in paragraph (c), a lawyer shall not represent a client or, where representation has commenced, shall withdraw from the representation of a client if:

    (1) the representation will result in violation of the Rules of Professional Conduct or other law;

    (2) the lawyer's physical or mental condition materially impairs the lawyer's ability to represent the client; or

    (3) the lawyer is discharged.

(b) Except as stated in paragraph (c), a lawyer may withdraw from representing a client if:

    (1) withdrawal can be accomplished without material adverse effect on the interests of the client;

    (2) the client persists in a course of action involving the lawyer's services that the lawyer reasonably believes is criminal or fraudulent;

    (3) the client has used the lawyer's services to perpetrate a crime or fraud;

    (4) the client insists upon taking action that the lawyer considers repugnant or with which the lawyer has a fundamental disagreement;

(5) the client fails substantially to fulfill an obligation to the lawyer regarding the lawyer's services and has been given reasonable warning that the lawyer will withdraw unless the obligation is fulfilled;   ~ fees, information, acceptin/ way

(6) the representation will result in an unreasonable financial burden on the lawyer or has been rendered unreasonably difficult by the client; or

(7) other good cause for withdrawal exists.

(c) A lawyer must comply with applicable law requiring notice to or permission of a tribunal when terminating a representation. When ordered to do so by a tribunal, a lawyer shall continue representation notwithstanding good cause for terminating the representation.   *must give notice of withdrawal*

(d) Upon termination of representation, a lawyer shall take steps to the extent reasonably practicable to protect a client's interests, such as giving reasonable notice to the client, allowing time for employment of other counsel, surrendering papers and property to which the client is entitled and refunding any advance payment of fee or expense that has not been earned or incurred. The lawyer may retain papers relating to the client to the extent permitted by other law.

Comment

[1] A lawyer should not accept representation in a matter unless it can be performed competently, promptly, without improper conflict of interest and to completion. Ordinarily, a representation in a matter is completed when the agreed-upon assistance has been concluded. See Rules 1.2(c) and 6.5. See also Rule 1.3, Comment [4].

Mandatory Withdrawal

[2] A lawyer ordinarily must decline or withdraw from representation if the client demands that the lawyer engage in conduct that is illegal or violates the Rules of Professional Conduct or other law. The lawyer is not obliged to decline or withdraw simply because the client suggests such a course of conduct; a client may make such a suggestion in the hope that a lawyer will not be constrained by a professional obligation.

[3] When a lawyer has been appointed to represent a client, withdrawal ordinarily requires approval of the appointing authority. See also Rule 6.2. Similarly, court approval or notice to the court is often required by applicable law before a lawyer withdraws from pending litigation.

Difficulty may be encountered if withdrawal is based on the client's demand that the lawyer engage in unprofessional conduct. The court may request an explanation for the withdrawal, while the lawyer may be bound to keep confidential the facts that would constitute such an explanation. The lawyer's statement that professional considerations require termination of the representation ordinarily should be accepted as sufficient. Lawyers should be mindful of their obligations to both clients and the court under Rules 1.6 and 3.3.

Discharge

[4] A client has a right to discharge a lawyer at any time, with or without cause, subject to liability for payment for the lawyer's services. Where future dispute about the withdrawal may be anticipated, it may be advisable to prepare a written statement reciting the circumstances.

[5] Whether a client can discharge appointed counsel may depend on applicable law. A client seeking to do so should be given a full explanation of the consequences. These consequences may include a decision by the appointing authority that appointment of successor counsel is unjustified, thus requiring self-representation by the client.

[6] If the client has severely diminished capacity, the client may lack the legal capacity to discharge the lawyer, and in any event the discharge may be seriously adverse to the client's interests. The lawyer should make special effort to help the client consider the consequences and may take reasonably necessary protective action as provided in Rule 1.14.

Optional Withdrawal

[7] A lawyer may withdraw from representation in some circumstances. The lawyer has the option to withdraw if it can be accomplished without material adverse effect on the client's interests. Withdrawal is also justified if the client persists in a course of action that the lawyer reasonably believes is criminal or fraudulent, for a lawyer is not required to be associated with such conduct even if the lawyer does not further it. Withdrawal is also permitted if the lawyer's services were misused in the past even if that would materially prejudice the client. The lawyer may also withdraw where the client insists on taking action that the lawyer considers repugnant or with which the lawyer has a fundamental disagreement.

[8] A lawyer may withdraw if the client refuses to abide by the terms of an agreement relating to the representation, such as an agreement con-

cerning fees or court costs or an agreement limiting the objectives of the representation.

Assisting the Client upon Withdrawal

[9] Even if the lawyer has been unfairly discharged by the client, a lawyer must take all reasonable steps to mitigate the consequences to the client. The lawyer may retain papers as security for a fee only to the extent permitted by law. See Rule 1.15.

Definitional Cross-References

"Fraud" and "Fraudulent" *See* Rule 1.0(d)
"Reasonable" *See* Rule 1.0(h)
"Reasonably believes" *See* Rule 1.0(i)
"Tribunal" *See* Rule 1.0(m)

RULE 1.17: SALE OF
LAW PRACTICE

A lawyer or a law firm may sell or purchase a law practice, or an area of law practice, including good will, if the following conditions are satisfied:

(a) The seller ceases to engage in the private practice of law, or in the area of practice that has been sold, [in the geographic area] [in the jurisdiction] (a jurisdiction may elect either version) in which the practice has been conducted;

(b) The entire practice, or the entire area of practice, is sold to one or more lawyers or law firms;

(c) The seller gives written notice to each of the seller's clients regarding:

(1) the proposed sale;

(2) the client's right to retain other counsel or to take possession of the file; and

(3) the fact that the client's consent to the transfer of the client's files will be presumed if the client does not take any action or does not otherwise object within ninety (90) days of receipt of the notice.

If a client cannot be given notice, the representation of that client may be transferred to the purchaser only upon entry of an order so authorizing by a court having jurisdiction. The seller may disclose to the court in camera information relating to the representation only to the extent necessary to obtain an order authorizing the transfer of a file.

(d) The fees charged clients shall not be increased by reason of the sale.

Comment

[1] The practice of law is a profession, not merely a business. Clients are not commodities that can be purchased and sold at will. Pursuant to this Rule, when a lawyer or an entire firm ceases to practice, or ceases to practice in an area of law, and other lawyers or firms take over the representation, the selling lawyer or firm may obtain compensation for the reasonable value of the practice as may withdrawing partners of law firms. See Rules 5.4 and 5.6.

Termination of Practice by the Seller

[2] The requirement that all of the private practice, or all of an area of practice, be sold is satisfied if the seller in good faith makes the entire practice, or the area of practice, available for sale to the purchasers. The fact that a number of the seller's clients decide not to be represented by the purchasers but take their matters elsewhere, therefore, does not result in a violation. Return to private practice as a result of an unanticipated change in circumstances does not necessarily result in a violation. For example, a lawyer who has sold the practice to accept an appointment to judicial office does not violate the requirement that the sale be attendant to cessation of practice if the lawyer later resumes private practice upon being defeated in a contested or a retention election for the office or resigns from a judiciary position.

[3] The requirement that the seller cease to engage in the private practice of law does not prohibit employment as a lawyer on the staff of a public agency or a legal services entity that provides legal services to the poor, or as in-house counsel to a business.

[4] The Rule permits a sale of an entire practice attendant upon retirement from the private practice of law within the jurisdiction. Its provisions, therefore, accommodate the lawyer who sells the practice on the occasion of moving to another state. Some states are so large that a move from one locale therein to another is tantamount to leaving the jurisdiction in which the lawyer has engaged in the practice of law. To also accommodate lawyers so situated, states may permit the sale of the practice when the lawyer leaves the geographical area rather than the jurisdiction.

The alternative desired should be indicated by selecting one of the two provided for in Rule 1.17(a).

[5] This Rule also permits a lawyer or law firm to sell an area of practice. If an area of practice is sold and the lawyer remains in the active practice of law, the lawyer must cease accepting any matters in the area of practice that has been sold, either as counsel or co-counsel or by assuming joint responsibility for a matter in connection with the division of a fee with another lawyer as would otherwise be permitted by Rule 1.5(e). For example, a lawyer with a substantial number of estate planning matters and a substantial number of probate administration cases may sell the estate planning portion of the practice but remain in the practice of law by concentrating on probate administration; however, that practitioner may not thereafter accept any estate planning matters. Although a lawyer who leaves a jurisdiction or geographical area typically would sell the entire practice, this Rule permits the lawyer to limit the sale to one or more areas of the practice, thereby preserving the lawyer's right to continue practice in the areas of the practice that were not sold.

Sale of Entire Practice or Entire Area of Practice

[6] The Rule requires that the seller's entire practice, or an entire area of practice, be sold. The prohibition against sale of less than an entire practice area protects those clients whose matters are less lucrative and who might find it difficult to secure other counsel if a sale could be limited to substantial fee-generating matters. The purchasers are required to undertake all client matters in the practice or practice area, subject to client consent. This requirement is satisfied, however, even if a purchaser is unable to undertake a particular client matter because of a conflict of interest.

Client Confidences, Consent and Notice

[7] Negotiations between seller and prospective purchaser prior to disclosure of information relating to a specific representation of an identifiable client no more violate the confidentiality provisions of Model Rule 1.6 than do preliminary discussions concerning the possible association of another lawyer or mergers between firms, with respect to which client consent is not required. See Rule 1.6(b)(7). Providing the purchaser access to detailed information relating to the representation, such as the client's file, however, requires client consent. The Rule provides that be-

fore such information can be disclosed by the seller to the purchaser the client must be given actual written notice of the contemplated sale, including the identity of the purchaser, and must be told that the decision to consent or make other arrangements must be made within 90 days. If nothing is heard from the client within that time, consent to the sale is presumed.

[8] A lawyer or law firm ceasing to practice cannot be required to remain in practice because some clients cannot be given actual notice of the proposed purchase. Since these clients cannot themselves consent to the purchase or direct any other disposition of their files, the Rule requires an order from a court having jurisdiction authorizing their transfer or other disposition. The court can be expected to determine whether reasonable efforts to locate the client have been exhausted, and whether the absent client's legitimate interests will be served by authorizing the transfer of the file so that the purchaser may continue the representation. Preservation of client confidences requires that the petition for a court order be considered in camera. (A procedure by which such an order can be obtained needs to be established in jurisdictions in which it presently does not exist).

[9] All elements of client autonomy, including the client's absolute right to discharge a lawyer and transfer the representation to another, survive the sale of the practice or area of practice.

Fee Arrangements Between Client and Purchaser

[10] The sale may not be financed by increases in fees charged the clients of the practice. Existing arrangements between the seller and the client as to fees and the scope of the work must be honored by the purchaser.

Other Applicable Ethical Standards

[11] Lawyers participating in the sale of a law practice or a practice area are subject to the ethical standards applicable to involving another lawyer in the representation of a client. These include, for example, the seller's obligation to exercise competence in identifying a purchaser qualified to assume the practice and the purchaser's obligation to undertake the representation competently (see Rule 1.1); the obligation to avoid disqualifying conflicts, and to secure the client's informed consent for those conflicts that can be agreed to (see Rule 1.7 regarding conflicts and Rule 1.0(e) for the definition of informed consent); and the obligation to protect information relating to the representation (see Rules 1.6 and 1.9).

[12] If approval of the substitution of the purchasing lawyer for the selling lawyer is required by the rules of any tribunal in which a matter is pending, such approval must be obtained before the matter can be included in the sale (see Rule 1.16).

Applicability of the Rule

[13] This Rule applies to the sale of a law practice of a deceased, disabled or disappeared lawyer. Thus, the seller may be represented by a non-lawyer representative not subject to these Rules. Since, however, no lawyer may participate in a sale of a law practice which does not conform to the requirements of this Rule, the representatives of the seller as well as the purchasing lawyer can be expected to see to it that they are met.

[14] Admission to or retirement from a law partnership or professional association, retirement plans and similar arrangements, and a sale of tangible assets of a law practice, do not constitute a sale or purchase governed by this Rule.

[15] This Rule does not apply to the transfers of legal representation between lawyers when such transfers are unrelated to the sale of a practice or an area of practice.

Definitional Cross-References

"Law firm" *See* Rule 1.0(c)
"Written" *See* Rule 1.0(n)

RULE 1.18: DUTIES TO PROSPECTIVE CLIENT

(a) A person who consults with a lawyer about the possibility of forming a client-lawyer relationship with respect to a matter is a prospective client.

(b) Even when no client-lawyer relationship ensues, a lawyer who has learned information from a prospective client shall not use or reveal that information, except as Rule 1.9 would permit with respect to information of a former client.

(c) A lawyer subject to paragraph (b) shall not represent a client with interests materially adverse to those of a prospective client in the same or a substantially related matter if the lawyer received information from the prospective client that could be significantly harmful to that person in the matter, except as provided in paragraph (d). If a lawyer is disqualified from representation under this paragraph, no lawyer in a firm with

— improbable theory/

which that lawyer is associated may knowingly undertake or continue representation in such a matter, except as provided in paragraph (d).

(d) When the lawyer has received disqualifying information as defined in paragraph (c), representation is permissible if:

(1) both the affected client and the prospective client have given informed consent, confirmed in writing; or:

(2) the lawyer who received the information took reasonable measures to avoid exposure to more disqualifying information than was reasonably necessary to determine whether to represent the prospective client; and

(i) the disqualified lawyer is timely screened from any participation in the matter and is apportioned no part of the fee therefrom; and

(ii) written notice is promptly given to the prospective client.

Comment

[1] Prospective clients, like clients, may disclose information to a lawyer, place documents or other property in the lawyer's custody, or rely on the lawyer's advice. A lawyer's consultations with a prospective client usually are limited in time and depth and leave both the prospective client and the lawyer free (and sometimes required) to proceed no further. Hence, prospective clients should receive some but not all of the protection afforded clients.

[2] A person becomes a prospective client by consulting with a lawyer about the possibility of forming a client-lawyer relationship with respect to a matter. Whether communications, including written, oral, or electronic communications, constitute a consultation depends on the circumstances. For example, a consultation is likely to have occurred if a lawyer, either in person or through the lawyer's advertising in any medium, specifically requests or invites the submission of information about a potential representation without clear and reasonably understandable warnings and cautionary statements that limit the lawyer's obligations, and a person provides information in response. See also Comment [4]. In contrast, a consultation does not occur if a person provides information to a lawyer in response to advertising that merely describes the lawyer's education, experience, areas of practice, and contact information, or provides legal information of general interest. Such a person communicates information unilaterally to a lawyer, without any reasonable expectation

that the lawyer is willing to discuss the possibility of forming a client-lawyer relationship, and is thus not a "prospective client." Moreover, a person who communicates with a lawyer for the purpose of disqualifying the lawyer is not a "prospective client."

[3] It is often necessary for a prospective client to reveal information to the lawyer during an initial consultation prior to the decision about formation of a client-lawyer relationship. The lawyer often must learn such information to determine whether there is a conflict of interest with an existing client and whether the matter is one that the lawyer is willing to undertake. Paragraph (b) prohibits the lawyer from using or revealing that information, except as permitted by Rule 1.9, even if the client or lawyer decides not to proceed with the representation. The duty exists regardless of how brief the initial conference may be.

[4] In order to avoid acquiring disqualifying information from a prospective client, a lawyer considering whether or not to undertake a new matter should limit the initial consultation to only such information as reasonably appears necessary for that purpose. Where the information indicates that a conflict of interest or other reason for non-representation exists, the lawyer should so inform the prospective client or decline the representation. If the prospective client wishes to retain the lawyer, and if consent is possible under Rule 1.7, then consent from all affected present or former clients must be obtained before accepting the representation.

[5] A lawyer may condition a consultation with a prospective client on the person's informed consent that no information disclosed during the consultation will prohibit the lawyer from representing a different client in the matter. See Rule 1.0(e) for the definition of informed consent. If the agreement expressly so provides, the prospective client may also consent to the lawyer's subsequent use of information received from the prospective client.

[6] Even in the absence of an agreement, under paragraph (c), the lawyer is not prohibited from representing a client with interests adverse to those of the prospective client in the same or a substantially related matter unless the lawyer has received from the prospective client information that could be significantly harmful if used in the matter.

[7] Under paragraph (c), the prohibition in this Rule is imputed to other lawyers as provided in Rule 1.10, but, under paragraph (d)(1), imputation may be avoided if the lawyer obtains the informed consent, confirmed in writing, of both the prospective and affected clients. In the alternative, imputation may be avoided if the conditions of paragraph

(d)(2) are met and all disqualified lawyers are timely screened and written notice is promptly given to the prospective client. See Rule 1.0(k) (requirements for screening procedures). Paragraph (d)(2)(i) does not prohibit the screened lawyer from receiving a salary or partnership share established by prior independent agreement, but that lawyer may not receive compensation directly related to the matter in which the lawyer is disqualified.

⟨8⟩ Notice, including a general description of the subject matter about which the lawyer was consulted, and of the screening procedures employed, generally should be given as soon as practicable after the need for screening becomes apparent.

⟨9⟩ For the duty of competence of a lawyer who gives assistance on the merits of a matter to a prospective client, see Rule 1.1. For a lawyer's duties when a prospective client entrusts valuables or papers to the lawyer's care, see Rule 1.15.

Definitional Cross-References

"Confirmed in writing" *See* Rule 1.0(b)
"Firm" *See* Rule 1.0(c)
"Informed consent" *See* Rule 1.0(e)
"Knowingly" *See* Rule 1.0(f)
"Reasonable" and "Reasonably" *See* Rule 1.0(h)
"Screened" *See* Rule 1.0(k)
"Written" *See* Rule 1.0(n)

COUNSELOR

RULE 2.1: ADVISOR

In representing a client, a lawyer shall exercise independent professional judgment and render candid advice. In rendering advice, a lawyer may refer not only to law but to other considerations such as moral, economic, social and political factors, that may be relevant to the client's situation.

Comment

Scope of Advice

[1] A client is entitled to straightforward advice expressing the lawyer's honest assessment. Legal advice often involves unpleasant facts and alternatives that a client may be disinclined to confront. In present-

ing advice, a lawyer endeavors to sustain the client's morale and may put advice in as acceptable a form as honesty permits. However, a lawyer should not be deterred from giving candid advice by the prospect that the advice will be unpalatable to the client.

[2] Advice couched in narrow legal terms may be of little value to a client, especially where practical considerations, such as cost or effects on other people, are predominant. Purely technical legal advice, therefore, can sometimes be inadequate. It is proper for a lawyer to refer to relevant moral and ethical considerations in giving advice. Although a lawyer is not a moral advisor as such, moral and ethical considerations impinge upon most legal questions and may decisively influence how the law will be applied.

[3] A client may expressly or impliedly ask the lawyer for purely technical advice. When such a request is made by a client experienced in legal matters, the lawyer may accept it at face value. When such a request is made by a client inexperienced in legal matters, however, the lawyer's responsibility as advisor may include indicating that more may be involved than strictly legal considerations.

[4] Matters that go beyond strictly legal questions may also be in the domain of another profession. Family matters can involve problems within the professional competence of psychiatry, clinical psychology or social work; business matters can involve problems within the competence of the accounting profession or of financial specialists. Where consultation with a professional in another field is itself something a competent lawyer would recommend, the lawyer should make such a recommendation. At the same time, a lawyer's advice at its best often consists of recommending a course of action in the face of conflicting recommendations of experts.

Offering Advice

[5] In general, a lawyer is not expected to give advice until asked by the client. However, when a lawyer knows that a client proposes a course of action that is likely to result in substantial adverse legal consequences to the client, the lawyer's duty to the client under Rule 1.4 may require that the lawyer offer advice if the client's course of action is related to the representation. Similarly, when a matter is likely to involve litigation, it may be necessary under Rule 1.4 to inform the client of forms of dispute resolution that might constitute reasonable alternatives to litigation. A lawyer ordinarily has no duty to initiate investigation of a client's affairs

or to give advice that the client has indicated is unwanted, but a lawyer may initiate advice to a client when doing so appears to be in the client's interest.

RULE 2.2 (DELETED 2002)

 ## RULE 2.3: EVALUATION FOR USE BY THIRD PERSONS

(a) A lawyer may provide an evaluation of a matter affecting a client for the use of someone other than the client if the lawyer reasonably believes that making the evaluation is compatible with other aspects of the lawyer's relationship with the client.

(b) When the lawyer knows or reasonably should know that the evaluation is likely to affect the client's interests materially and adversely, the lawyer shall not provide the evaluation unless the client gives informed consent.

(c) Except as disclosure is authorized in connection with a report of an evaluation, information relating to the evaluation is otherwise protected by Rule 1.6.

Comment
Definition

[1] An evaluation may be performed at the client's direction or when impliedly authorized in order to carry out the representation. See Rule 1.2. Such an evaluation may be for the primary purpose of establishing information for the benefit of third parties; for example, an opinion concerning the title of property rendered at the behest of a vendor for the information of a prospective purchaser, or at the behest of a borrower for the information of a prospective lender. In some situations, the evaluation may be required by a government agency; for example, an opinion concerning the legality of the securities registered for sale under the securities laws. In other instances, the evaluation may be required by a third person, such as a purchaser of a business.

[2] A legal evaluation should be distinguished from an investigation of a person with whom the lawyer does not have a client-lawyer relationship. For example, a lawyer retained by a purchaser to analyze a vendor's title to property does not have a client-lawyer relationship with

the vendor. So also, an investigation into a person's affairs by a government lawyer or by special counsel employed by the government, is not an evaluation as that term is used in this Rule. The question is whether the lawyer is retained by the person whose affairs are being examined. When the lawyer is retained by that person, the general rules concerning loyalty to client and preservation of confidences apply, which is not the case if the lawyer is retained by someone else. For this reason, it is essential to identify the person by whom the lawyer is retained. This should be made clear not only to the person under examination, but also to others to whom the results are to be made available.

Duties Owed to Third Person and Client

[3] When the evaluation is intended for the information or use of a third person, a legal duty to that person may or may not arise. That legal question is beyond the scope of this Rule. However, since such an evaluation involves a departure from the normal client-lawyer relationship, careful analysis of the situation is required. The lawyer must be satisfied as a matter of professional judgment that making the evaluation is compatible with other functions undertaken in behalf of the client. For example, if the lawyer is acting as advocate in defending the client against charges of fraud, it would normally be incompatible with that responsibility for the lawyer to perform an evaluation for others concerning the same or a related transaction. Assuming no such impediment is apparent, however, the lawyer should advise the client of the implications of the evaluation, particularly the lawyer's responsibilities to third persons and the duty to disseminate the findings.

Access to and Disclosure of Information

[4] The quality of an evaluation depends on the freedom and extent of the investigation upon which it is based. Ordinarily a lawyer should have whatever latitude of investigation seems necessary as a matter of professional judgment. Under some circumstances, however, the terms of the evaluation may be limited. For example, certain issues or sources may be categorically excluded, or the scope of search may be limited by time constraints or the noncooperation of persons having relevant information. Any such limitations that are material to the evaluation should be described in the report. If after a lawyer has commenced an evaluation, the client refuses to comply with the terms upon which it was understood the evaluation was to have been made, the lawyer's obligations

are determined by law, having reference to the terms of the client's agreement and the surrounding circumstances. In no circumstances is the lawyer permitted to knowingly make a false statement of material fact or law in providing an evaluation under this Rule. See Rule 4.1.

Obtaining Client's Informed Consent

[5] Information relating to an evaluation is protected by Rule 1.6. In many situations, providing an evaluation to a third party poses no significant risk to the client; thus, the lawyer may be impliedly authorized to disclose information to carry out the representation. See Rule 1.6(a). Where, however, it is reasonably likely that providing the evaluation will affect the client's interests materially and adversely, the lawyer must first obtain the client's consent after the client has been adequately informed concerning the important possible effects on the client's interests. See Rules 1.6(a) and 1.0(e).

Financial Auditors' Requests for Information

[6] When a question concerning the legal situation of a client arises at the instance of the client's financial auditor and the question is referred to the lawyer, the lawyer's response may be made in accordance with procedures recognized in the legal profession. Such a procedure is set forth in the American Bar Association Statement of Policy Regarding Lawyers' Responses to Auditors' Requests for Information, adopted in 1975.

Definitional Cross-References

"Informed consent" *See* Rule 1.0(e)
"Knows" *See* Rule 1.0(f)
"Reasonably believes" *See* Rule 1.0(i)
"Reasonably should know" *See* Rule 1.0(j)

RULE 2.4: LAWYER SERVING AS THIRD-PARTY NEUTRAL

(a) A lawyer serves as a third-party neutral when the lawyer assists two or more persons who are not clients of the lawyer to reach a resolution of a dispute or other matter that has arisen between them. Service as a third-party neutral may include service as an arbitrator, a mediator or in such other capacity as will enable the lawyer to assist the parties to resolve the matter.

(b) A lawyer serving as a third-party neutral shall inform unrepresented parties that the lawyer is not representing them. When the lawyer knows or reasonably should know that a party does not understand the lawyer's role in the matter, the lawyer shall explain the difference between the lawyer's role as a third-party neutral and a lawyer's role as one who represents a client.

Comment

[1] Alternative dispute resolution has become a substantial part of the civil justice system. Aside from representing clients in dispute-resolution processes, lawyers often serve as third-party neutrals. A third-party neutral is a person, such as a mediator, arbitrator, conciliator or evaluator, who assists the parties, represented or unrepresented, in the resolution of a dispute or in the arrangement of a transaction. Whether a third-party neutral serves primarily as a facilitator, evaluator or decisionmaker depends on the particular process that is either selected by the parties or mandated by a court.

[2] The role of a third-party neutral is not unique to lawyers, although, in some court-connected contexts, only lawyers are allowed to serve in this role or to handle certain types of cases. In performing this role, the lawyer may be subject to court rules or other law that apply either to third-party neutrals generally or to lawyers serving as third-party neutrals. Lawyer-neutrals may also be subject to various codes of ethics, such as the Code of Ethics for Arbitrators in Commercial Disputes prepared by a joint committee of the American Bar Association and the American Arbitration Association or the Model Standards of Conduct for Mediators jointly prepared by the American Bar Association, the American Arbitration Association and the Society of Professionals in Dispute Resolution.

[3] Unlike nonlawyers who serve as third-party neutrals, lawyers serving in this role may experience unique problems as a result of differences between the role of a third-party neutral and a lawyer's service as a client representative. The potential for confusion is significant when the parties are unrepresented in the process. Thus, paragraph (b) requires a lawyer-neutral to inform unrepresented parties that the lawyer is not representing them. For some parties, particularly parties who frequently use dispute-resolution processes, this information will be sufficient. For others, particularly those who are using the process for the first time, more information will be required. Where appropriate, the lawyer should

inform unrepresented parties of the important differences between the lawyer's role as third-party neutral and a lawyer's role as a client representative, including the inapplicability of the attorney-client evidentiary privilege. The extent of disclosure required under this paragraph will depend on the particular parties involved and the subject matter of the proceeding, as well as the particular features of the dispute-resolution process selected.

[4] A lawyer who serves as a third-party neutral subsequently may be asked to serve as a lawyer representing a client in the same matter. The conflicts of interest that arise for both the individual lawyer and the lawyer's law firm are addressed in Rule 1.12.

[5] Lawyers who represent clients in alternative dispute-resolution processes are governed by the Rules of Professional Conduct. When the dispute-resolution process takes place before a tribunal, as in binding arbitration (see Rule 1.0(m)), the lawyer's duty of candor is governed by Rule 3.3. Otherwise, the lawyer's duty of candor toward both the third-party neutral and other parties is governed by Rule 4.1.

Definitional Cross-References

"Knows" *See* Rule 1.0(f)

"Reasonably should know" *See* Rule 1.0(j)

ADVOCATE

RULE 3.1: MERITORIOUS
CLAIMS AND CONTENTIONS

A lawyer shall not bring or defend a proceeding, or assert or controvert an issue therein, unless there is a basis in law and fact for doing so that is not frivolous, which includes a good faith argument for an extension, modification or reversal of existing law. A lawyer for the defendant in a criminal proceeding, or the respondent in a proceeding that could result in incarceration, may nevertheless so defend the proceeding as to require that every element of the case be established.

Comment

[1] The advocate has a duty to use legal procedure for the fullest benefit of the client's cause, but also a duty not to abuse legal procedure.

The law, both procedural and substantive, establishes the limits within which an advocate may proceed. However, the law is not always clear and never is static. Accordingly, in determining the proper scope of advocacy, account must be taken of the law's ambiguities and potential for change.

[2] The filing of an action or defense or similar action taken for a client is not frivolous merely because the facts have not first been fully substantiated or because the lawyer expects to develop vital evidence only by discovery. What is required of lawyers, however, is that they inform themselves about the facts of their clients' cases and the applicable law and determine that they can make good faith arguments in support of their clients' positions. Such action is not frivolous even though the lawyer believes that the client's position ultimately will not prevail. The action is frivolous, however, if the lawyer is unable either to make a good faith argument on the merits of the action taken or to support the action taken by a good faith argument for an extension, modification or reversal of existing law.

[3] The lawyer's obligations under this Rule are subordinate to federal or state constitutional law that entitles a defendant in a criminal matter to the assistance of counsel in presenting a claim or contention that otherwise would be prohibited by this Rule.

RULE 3.2: EXPEDITING LITIGATION

A lawyer shall make reasonable efforts to expedite litigation consistent with the interests of the client.

Comment

[1] Dilatory practices bring the administration of justice into disrepute. Although there will be occasions when a lawyer may properly seek a postponement for personal reasons, it is not proper for a lawyer to routinely fail to expedite litigation solely for the convenience of the advocates. Nor will a failure to expedite be reasonable if done for the purpose of frustrating an opposing party's attempt to obtain rightful redress or repose. It is not a justification that similar conduct is often tolerated by the bench and bar. The question is whether a competent lawyer acting in good faith would regard the course of action as having some substantial purpose other than delay. Realizing financial or other benefit from otherwise improper delay in litigation is not a legitimate interest of the client.

Definitional Cross-References

"Reasonable" *See* Rule 1.0(h)

RULE 3.3: CANDOR TOWARD THE TRIBUNAL

(a) A lawyer shall not knowingly:

(1) make a false statement of fact or law to a tribunal or fail to correct a false statement of material fact or law previously made to the tribunal by the lawyer;

(2) fail to disclose to the tribunal legal authority in the controlling jurisdiction known to the lawyer to be directly adverse to the position of the client and not disclosed by opposing counsel; or

(3) offer evidence that the lawyer knows to be false. If a lawyer, the lawyer's client, or a witness called by the lawyer, has offered material evidence and the lawyer comes to know of its falsity, the lawyer shall take reasonable remedial measures, including, if necessary, disclosure to the tribunal. A lawyer may refuse to offer evidence, other than the testimony of a defendant in a criminal matter, that the lawyer reasonably believes is false.

(b) A lawyer who represents a client in an adjudicative proceeding and who knows that a person intends to engage, is engaging or has engaged in criminal or fraudulent conduct related to the proceeding shall take reasonable remedial measures, including, if necessary, disclosure to the tribunal.

(c) The duties stated in paragraphs (a) and (b) continue to the conclusion of the proceeding, and apply even if compliance requires disclosure of information otherwise protected by Rule 1.6.

(d) In an ex parte proceeding, a lawyer shall inform the tribunal of all material facts known to the lawyer that will enable the tribunal to make an informed decision, whether or not the facts are adverse.

Comment

[1] This Rule governs the conduct of a lawyer who is representing a client in the proceedings of a tribunal. See Rule 1.0(m) for the definition of "tribunal." It also applies when the lawyer is representing a client in an ancillary proceeding conducted pursuant to the tribunal's adjudi-

cative authority, such as a deposition. Thus, for example, paragraph (a) (3) requires a lawyer to take reasonable remedial measures if the lawyer comes to know that a client who is testifying in a deposition has offered evidence that is false.

[2] This Rule sets forth the special duties of lawyers as officers of the court to avoid conduct that undermines the integrity of the adjudicative process. A lawyer acting as an advocate in an adjudicative proceeding has an obligation to present the client's case with persuasive force. Performance of that duty while maintaining confidences of the client, however, is qualified by the advocate's duty of candor to the tribunal. Consequently, although a lawyer in an adversary proceeding is not required to present an impartial exposition of the law or to vouch for the evidence submitted in a cause, the lawyer must not allow the tribunal to be misled by false statements of law or fact or evidence that the lawyer knows to be false.

Representations by a Lawyer

[3] An advocate is responsible for pleadings and other documents prepared for litigation, but is usually not required to have personal knowledge of matters asserted therein, for litigation documents ordinarily present assertions by the client, or by someone on the client's behalf, and not assertions by the lawyer. Compare Rule 3.1. However, an assertion purporting to be on the lawyer's own knowledge, as in an affidavit by the lawyer or in a statement in open court, may properly be made only when the lawyer knows the assertion is true or believes it to be true on the basis of a reasonably diligent inquiry. There are circumstances where failure to make a disclosure is the equivalent of an affirmative misrepresentation. The obligation prescribed in Rule 1.2(d) not to counsel a client to commit or assist the client in committing a fraud applies in litigation. Regarding compliance with Rule 1.2(d), see the Comment to that Rule. See also the Comment to Rule 8.4(b).

Legal Argument

[4] Legal argument based on a knowingly false representation of law constitutes dishonesty toward the tribunal. A lawyer is not required to make a disinterested exposition of the law, but must recognize the existence of pertinent legal authorities. Furthermore, as stated in paragraph (a)(2), an advocate has a duty to disclose directly adverse authority in the controlling jurisdiction that has not been disclosed by the opposing party.

The underlying concept is that legal argument is a discussion seeking to determine the legal premises properly applicable to the case.

Offering Evidence

[5] Paragraph (a)(3) requires that the lawyer refuse to offer evidence that the lawyer knows to be false, regardless of the client's wishes. This duty is premised on the lawyer's obligation as an officer of the court to prevent the trier of fact from being misled by false evidence. A lawyer does not violate this Rule if the lawyer offers the evidence for the purpose of establishing its falsity.

[6] If a lawyer knows that the client intends to testify falsely or wants the lawyer to introduce false evidence, the lawyer should seek to persuade the client that the evidence should not be offered. If the persuasion is ineffective and the lawyer continues to represent the client, the lawyer must refuse to offer the false evidence. If only a portion of a witness's testimony will be false, the lawyer may call the witness to testify but may not elicit or otherwise permit the witness to present the testimony that the lawyer knows is false.

[7] The duties stated in paragraphs (a) and (b) apply to all lawyers, including defense counsel in criminal cases. In some jurisdictions, however, courts have required counsel to present the accused as a witness or to give a narrative statement if the accused so desires, even if counsel knows that the testimony or statement will be false. The obligation of the advocate under the Rules of Professional Conduct is subordinate to such requirements. See also Comment [9].

[8] The prohibition against offering false evidence only applies if the lawyer knows that the evidence is false. A lawyer's reasonable belief that evidence is false does not preclude its presentation to the trier of fact. A lawyer's knowledge that evidence is false, however, can be inferred from the circumstances. See Rule 1.0(f). Thus, although a lawyer should resolve doubts about the veracity of testimony or other evidence in favor of the client, the lawyer cannot ignore an obvious falsehood.

[9] Although paragraph (a)(3) only prohibits a lawyer from offering evidence the lawyer knows to be false, it permits the lawyer to refuse to offer testimony or other proof that the lawyer reasonably believes is false. Offering such proof may reflect adversely on the lawyer's ability to discriminate in the quality of evidence and thus impair the lawyer's effectiveness as an advocate. Because of the special protections historically provided criminal defendants, however, this Rule does not permit a law-

yer to refuse to offer the testimony of such a client where the lawyer reasonably believes but does not know that the testimony will be false. Unless the lawyer knows the testimony will be false, the lawyer must honor the client's decision to testify. See also Comment [7].

Remedial Measures

[10] Having offered material evidence in the belief that it was true, a lawyer may subsequently come to know that the evidence is false. Or, a lawyer may be surprised when the lawyer's client, or another witness called by the lawyer, offers testimony the lawyer knows to be false, either during the lawyer's direct examination or in response to cross-examination by the opposing lawyer. In such situations or if the lawyer knows of the falsity of testimony elicited from the client during a deposition, the lawyer must take reasonable remedial measures. In such situations, the advocate's proper course is to remonstrate with the client confidentially, advise the client of the lawyer's duty of candor to the tribunal and seek the client's cooperation with respect to the withdrawal or correction of the false statements or evidence. If that fails, the advocate must take further remedial action. If withdrawal from the representation is not permitted or will not undo the effect of the false evidence, the advocate must make such disclosure to the tribunal as is reasonably necessary to remedy the situation, even if doing so requires the lawyer to reveal information that otherwise would be protected by Rule 1.6. It is for the tribunal then to determine what should be done—making a statement about the matter to the trier of fact, ordering a mistrial or perhaps nothing.

[11] The disclosure of a client's false testimony can result in grave consequences to the client, including not only a sense of betrayal but also loss of the case and perhaps a prosecution for perjury. But the alternative is that the lawyer cooperate in deceiving the court, thereby subverting the truth-finding process which the adversary system is designed to implement. See Rule 1.2(d). Furthermore, unless it is clearly understood that the lawyer will act upon the duty to disclose the existence of false evidence, the client can simply reject the lawyer's advice to reveal the false evidence and insist that the lawyer keep silent. Thus the client could in effect coerce the lawyer into being a party to fraud on the court.

Preserving Integrity of Adjudicative Process

[12] Lawyers have a special obligation to protect a tribunal against criminal or fraudulent conduct that undermines the integrity of the ad-

judicative process, such as bribing, intimidating or otherwise unlawfully communicating with a witness, juror, court official or other participant in the proceeding, unlawfully destroying or concealing documents or other evidence or failing to disclose information to the tribunal when required by law to do so. Thus, paragraph (b) requires a lawyer to take reasonable remedial measures, including disclosure if necessary, whenever the lawyer knows that a person, including the lawyer's client, intends to engage, is engaging or has engaged in criminal or fraudulent conduct related to the proceeding.

Duration of Obligation

[13] A practical time limit on the obligation to rectify false evidence or false statements of law and fact has to be established. The conclusion of the proceeding is a reasonably definite point for the termination of the obligation. A proceeding has concluded within the meaning of this Rule when a final judgment in the proceeding has been affirmed on appeal or the time for review has passed.

Ex Parte Proceedings

[14] Ordinarily, an advocate has the limited responsibility of presenting one side of the matters that a tribunal should consider in reaching a decision; the conflicting position is expected to be presented by the opposing party. However, in any ex parte proceeding, such as an application for a temporary restraining order, there is no balance of presentation by opposing advocates. The object of an ex parte proceeding is nevertheless to yield a substantially just result. The judge has an affirmative responsibility to accord the absent party just consideration. The lawyer for the represented party has the correlative duty to make disclosures of material facts known to the lawyer and that the lawyer reasonably believes are necessary to an informed decision.

Withdrawal

[15] Normally, a lawyer's compliance with the duty of candor imposed by this Rule does not require that the lawyer withdraw from the representation of a client whose interests will be or have been adversely affected by the lawyer's disclosure. The lawyer may, however, be required by Rule 1.16(a) to seek permission of the tribunal to withdraw if the lawyer's compliance with this Rule's duty of candor results in such an extreme deterioration of the client-lawyer relationship that the lawyer

can no longer competently represent the client. Also see Rule 1.16(b) for the circumstances in which a lawyer will be permitted to seek a tribunal's permission to withdraw. In connection with a request for permission to withdraw that is premised on a client's misconduct, a lawyer may reveal information relating to the representation only to the extent reasonably necessary to comply with this Rule or as otherwise permitted by Rule 1.6.

Definitional Cross-References

"Fraudulent" *See* Rule 1.0(d)
"Knowingly" and "Known" and "Knows" *See* Rule 1.0(f)
"Reasonable" *See* Rule 1.0(h)
"Reasonably believes" *See* Rule 1.0(i)
"Tribunal" *See* Rule 1.0(m)

RULE 3.4: FAIRNESS TO OPPOSING PARTY AND COUNSEL

A lawyer shall not:

(a) unlawfully obstruct another party's access to evidence or unlawfully alter, destroy or conceal a document or other material having potential evidentiary value. A lawyer shall not counsel or assist another person to do any such act;

(b) falsify evidence, counsel or assist a witness to testify falsely, or offer an inducement to a witness that is prohibited by law;

(c) knowingly disobey an obligation under the rules of a tribunal, except for an open refusal based on an assertion that no valid obligation exists;

(d) in pretrial procedure, make a frivolous discovery request or fail to make reasonably diligent effort to comply with a legally proper discovery request by an opposing party;

(e) in trial, allude to any matter that the lawyer does not reasonably believe is relevant or that will not be supported by admissible evidence, assert personal knowledge of facts in issue except when testifying as a witness, or state a personal opinion as to the justness of a cause, the credibility of a witness, the culpability of a civil litigant or the guilt or innocence of an accused; or

(f) request a person other than a client to refrain from voluntarily giving relevant information to another party unless:

(1) the person is a relative or an employee or other agent of a client; and

(2) the lawyer reasonably believes that the person's interests will not be adversely affected by refraining from giving such information.

Comment

[1] The procedure of the adversary system contemplates that the evidence in a case is to be marshalled competitively by the contending parties. Fair competition in the adversary system is secured by prohibitions against destruction or concealment of evidence, improperly influencing witnesses, obstructive tactics in discovery procedure, and the like.

[2] Documents and other items of evidence are often essential to establish a claim or defense. Subject to evidentiary privileges, the right of an opposing party, including the government, to obtain evidence through discovery or subpoena is an important procedural right. The exercise of that right can be frustrated if relevant material is altered, concealed or destroyed. Applicable law in many jurisdictions makes it an offense to destroy material for purpose of impairing its availability in a pending proceeding or one whose commencement can be foreseen. Falsifying evidence is also generally a criminal offense. Paragraph (a) applies to evidentiary material generally, including computerized information. Applicable law may permit a lawyer to take temporary possession of physical evidence of client crimes for the purpose of conducting a limited examination that will not alter or destroy material characteristics of the evidence. In such a case, applicable law may require the lawyer to turn the evidence over to the police or other prosecuting authority, depending on the circumstances.

[3] With regard to paragraph (b), it is not improper to pay a witness's expenses or to compensate an expert witness on terms permitted by law. The common law rule in most jurisdictions is that it is improper to pay an occurrence witness any fee for testifying and that it is improper to pay an expert witness a contingent fee.

[4] Paragraph (f) permits a lawyer to advise employees of a client to refrain from giving information to another party, for the employees may identify their interests with those of the client. See also Rule 4.2.

Definitional Cross-References

"Knowingly" *See* Rule 1.0(f)
"Reasonably" *See* Rule 1.0(h)
"Reasonably believes" *See* Rule 1.0(i)
"Tribunal" *See* Rule 1.0(m)

RULE 3.5: IMPARTIALITY AND DECORUM OF THE TRIBUNAL

A lawyer shall not:

(a) seek to influence a judge, juror, prospective juror or other official by means prohibited by law;

(b) communicate ex parte with such a person during the proceeding unless authorized to do so by law or court order;

(c) communicate with a juror or prospective juror after discharge of the jury if:

(1) the communication is prohibited by law or court order;

(2) the juror has made known to the lawyer a desire not to communicate; or

(3) the communication involves misrepresentation, coercion, duress or harassment; or

(d) engage in conduct intended to disrupt a tribunal.

Comment

[1] Many forms of improper influence upon a tribunal are proscribed by criminal law. Others are specified in the ABA Model Code of Judicial Conduct, with which an advocate should be familiar. A lawyer is required to avoid contributing to a violation of such provisions.

[2] During a proceeding a lawyer may not communicate ex parte with persons serving in an official capacity in the proceeding, such as judges, masters or jurors, unless authorized to do so by law or court order.

[3] A lawyer may on occasion want to communicate with a juror or prospective juror after the jury has been discharged. The lawyer may do so unless the communication is prohibited by law or a court order but must respect the desire of the juror not to talk with the lawyer. The lawyer may not engage in improper conduct during the communication.

[4] The advocate's function is to present evidence and argument so that the cause may be decided according to law. Refraining from abusive or obstreperous conduct is a corollary of the advocate's right to speak on

behalf of litigants. A lawyer may stand firm against abuse by a judge but should avoid reciprocation; the judge's default is no justification for similar dereliction by an advocate. An advocate can present the cause, protect the record for subsequent review and preserve professional integrity by patient firmness no less effectively than by belligerence or theatrics.

[5] The duty to refrain from disruptive conduct applies to any proceeding of a tribunal, including a deposition. See Rule 1.0(m).

Definitional Cross-References
"Known" *See* Rule 1.0(f)
"Tribunal" *See* Rule 1.0(m)

RULE 3.6: TRIAL PUBLICITY

(a) A lawyer who is participating or has participated in the investigation or litigation of a matter shall not make an extrajudicial statement that the lawyer knows or reasonably should know will be disseminated by means of public communication and will have a substantial likelihood of materially prejudicing an adjudicative proceeding in the matter.

(b) Notwithstanding paragraph (a), a lawyer may state:

(1) the claim, offense or defense involved and, except when prohibited by law, the identity of the persons involved;

(2) information contained in a public record;

(3) that an investigation of a matter is in progress;

(4) the scheduling or result of any step in litigation;

(5) a request for assistance in obtaining evidence and information necessary thereto;

(6) a warning of danger concerning the behavior of a person involved, when there is reason to believe that there exists the likelihood of substantial harm to an individual or to the public interest; and

(7) in a criminal case, in addition to subparagraphs (1) through (6):

(i) the identity, residence, occupation and family status of the accused;

(ii) if the accused has not been apprehended, information necessary to aid in apprehension of that person;

(iii) the fact, time and place of arrest; and

(iv) the identity of investigating and arresting officers or agencies and the length of the investigation.

(c) Notwithstanding paragraph (a), a lawyer may make a statement that a reasonable lawyer would believe is required to protect a client from the substantial undue prejudicial effect of recent publicity not initiated by the lawyer or the lawyer's client. A statement made pursuant to this paragraph shall be limited to such information as is necessary to mitigate the recent adverse publicity.

(d) No lawyer associated in a firm or government agency with a lawyer subject to paragraph (a) shall make a statement prohibited by paragraph (a).

Comment

[1] It is difficult to strike a balance between protecting the right to a fair trial and safeguarding the right of free expression. Preserving the right to a fair trial necessarily entails some curtailment of the information that may be disseminated about a party prior to trial, particularly where trial by jury is involved. If there were no such limits, the result would be the practical nullification of the protective effect of the rules of forensic decorum and the exclusionary rules of evidence. On the other hand, there are vital social interests served by the free dissemination of information about events having legal consequences and about legal proceedings themselves. The public has a right to know about threats to its safety and measures aimed at assuring its security. It also has a legitimate interest in the conduct of judicial proceedings, particularly in matters of general public concern. Furthermore, the subject matter of legal proceedings is often of direct significance in debate and deliberation over questions of public policy.

[2] Special rules of confidentiality may validly govern proceedings in juvenile, domestic relations and mental disability proceedings, and perhaps other types of litigation. Rule 3.4(c) requires compliance with such rules.

[3] The Rule sets forth a basic general prohibition against a lawyer's making statements that the lawyer knows or should know will have a substantial likelihood of materially prejudicing an adjudicative proceeding. Recognizing that the public value of informed commentary is great and the likelihood of prejudice to a proceeding by the commentary of a lawyer who is not involved in the proceeding is small, the Rule applies only to lawyers who are, or who have been involved in the investigation or litigation of a case, and their associates.

[4] Paragraph (b) identifies specific matters about which a lawyer's statements would not ordinarily be considered to present a substantial likelihood of material prejudice, and should not in any event be considered prohibited by the general prohibition of paragraph (a). Paragraph (b) is not intended to be an exhaustive listing of the subjects upon which a lawyer may make a statement, but statements on other matters may be subject to paragraph (a).

[5] There are, on the other hand, certain subjects that are more likely than not to have a material prejudicial effect on a proceeding, particularly when they refer to a civil matter triable to a jury, a criminal matter, or any other proceeding that could result in incarceration. These subjects relate to:

(1) the character, credibility, reputation or criminal record of a party, suspect in a criminal investigation or witness, or the identity of a witness, or the expected testimony of a party or witness;

(2) in a criminal case or proceeding that could result in incarceration, the possibility of a plea of guilty to the offense or the existence or contents of any confession, admission, or statement given by a defendant or suspect or that person's refusal or failure to make a statement;

(3) the performance or results of any examination or test or the refusal or failure of a person to submit to an examination or test, or the identity or nature of physical evidence expected to be presented;

(4) any opinion as to the guilt or innocence of a defendant or suspect in a criminal case or proceeding that could result in incarceration;

(5) information that the lawyer knows or reasonably should know is likely to be inadmissible as evidence in a trial and that would, if disclosed, create a substantial risk of prejudicing an impartial trial; or

(6) the fact that a defendant has been charged with a crime, unless there is included therein a statement explaining that the charge is merely an accusation and that the defendant is presumed innocent until and unless proven guilty.

[6] Another relevant factor in determining prejudice is the nature of the proceeding involved. Criminal jury trials will be most sensitive to extrajudicial speech. Civil trials may be less sensitive. Non-jury hearings and arbitration proceedings may be even less affected. The Rule will still place limitations on prejudicial comments in these cases, but the likelihood of prejudice may be different depending on the type of proceeding.

[7] Finally, extrajudicial statements that might otherwise raise a question under this Rule may be permissible when they are made in response to statements made publicly by another party, another party's lawyer,

or third persons, where a reasonable lawyer would believe a public response is required in order to avoid prejudice to the lawyer's client. When prejudicial statements have been publicly made by others, responsive statements may have the salutary effect of lessening any resulting adverse impact on the adjudicative proceeding. Such responsive statements should be limited to contain only such information as is necessary to mitigate undue prejudice created by the statements made by others.

[8] See Rule 3.8(f) for additional duties of prosecutors in connection with extrajudicial statements about criminal proceedings.

Definitional Cross-References

"Firm" *See* Rule 1.0(c)
"Knows" *See* Rule 1.0(f)
"Reasonable" *See* Rule 1.0(h)
"Reasonably should know" *See* Rule 1.0(j)
"Substantial" *See* Rule 1.0(l)

RULE 3.7: LAWYER AS WITNESS

(a) A lawyer shall not act as advocate at a trial in which the lawyer is likely to be a necessary witness unless:

(1) the testimony relates to an uncontested issue;

(2) the testimony relates to the nature and value of legal services rendered in the case; or

(3) disqualification of the lawyer would work substantial hardship on the client.

(b) A lawyer may act as advocate in a trial in which another lawyer in the lawyer's firm is likely to be called as a witness unless precluded from doing so by Rule 1.7 or Rule 1.9.

Comment

[1] Combining the roles of advocate and witness can prejudice the tribunal and the opposing party and can also involve a conflict of interest between the lawyer and client.

Advocate-Witness Rule

[2] The tribunal has proper objection when the trier of fact may be confused or misled by a lawyer serving as both advocate and witness. The opposing party has proper objection where the combination of roles may prejudice that party's rights in the litigation. A witness is required to

testify on the basis of personal knowledge, while an advocate is expected to explain and comment on evidence given by others. It may not be clear whether a statement by an advocate-witness should be taken as proof or as an analysis of the proof.

[3] To protect the tribunal, paragraph (a) prohibits a lawyer from simultaneously serving as advocate and necessary witness except in those circumstances specified in paragraphs (a)(1) through (a)(3). Paragraph (a)(1) recognizes that if the testimony will be uncontested, the ambiguities in the dual role are purely theoretical. Paragraph (a)(2) recognizes that where the testimony concerns the extent and value of legal services rendered in the action in which the testimony is offered, permitting the lawyers to testify avoids the need for a second trial with new counsel to resolve that issue. Moreover, in such a situation the judge has firsthand knowledge of the matter in issue; hence, there is less dependence on the adversary process to test the credibility of the testimony.

[4] Apart from these two exceptions, paragraph (a)(3) recognizes that a balancing is required between the interests of the client and those of the tribunal and the opposing party. Whether the tribunal is likely to be misled or the opposing party is likely to suffer prejudice depends on the nature of the case, the importance and probable tenor of the lawyer's testimony, and the probability that the lawyer's testimony will conflict with that of other witnesses. Even if there is risk of such prejudice, in determining whether the lawyer should be disqualified, due regard must be given to the effect of disqualification on the lawyer's client. It is relevant that one or both parties could reasonably foresee that the lawyer would probably be a witness. The conflict of interest principles stated in Rules 1.7, 1.9 and 1.10 have no application to this aspect of the problem.

[5] Because the tribunal is not likely to be misled when a lawyer acts as advocate in a trial in which another lawyer in the lawyer's firm will testify as a necessary witness, paragraph (b) permits the lawyer to do so except in situations involving a conflict of interest.

Conflict of Interest

[6] In determining if it is permissible to act as advocate in a trial in which the lawyer will be a necessary witness, the lawyer must also consider that the dual role may give rise to a conflict of interest that will require compliance with Rules 1.7 or 1.9. For example, if there is likely to be substantial conflict between the testimony of the client and that of the lawyer the representation involves a conflict of interest that requires com-

pliance with Rule 1.7. This would be true even though the lawyer might not be prohibited by paragraph (a) from simultaneously serving as advocate and witness because the lawyer's disqualification would work a substantial hardship on the client. Similarly, a lawyer who might be permitted to simultaneously serve as an advocate and a witness by paragraph (a) (3) might be precluded from doing so by Rule 1.9. The problem can arise whether the lawyer is called as a witness on behalf of the client or is called by the opposing party. Determining whether or not such a conflict exists is primarily the responsibility of the lawyer involved. If there is a conflict of interest, the lawyer must secure the client's informed consent, confirmed in writing. In some cases, the lawyer will be precluded from seeking the client's consent. See Rule 1.7. See Rule 1.0(b) for the definition of "confirmed in writing" and Rule 1.0(e) for the definition of "informed consent."

[7] Paragraph (b) provides that a lawyer is not disqualified from serving as an advocate because a lawyer with whom the lawyer is associated in a firm is precluded from doing so by paragraph (a). If, however, the testifying lawyer would also be disqualified by Rule 1.7 or Rule 1.9 from representing the client in the matter, other lawyers in the firm will be precluded from representing the client by Rule 1.10 unless the client gives informed consent under the conditions stated in Rule 1.7.

Definitional Cross-References

"Firm" *See* Rule 1.0(c)
"Substantial" *See* Rule 1.0(l)

RULE 3.8: SPECIAL RESPONSIBILITIES OF A PROSECUTOR

The prosecutor in a criminal case shall:

(a) refrain from prosecuting a charge that the prosecutor knows is not supported by probable cause;

(b) make reasonable efforts to assure that the accused has been advised of the right to, and the procedure for obtaining, counsel and has been given reasonable opportunity to obtain counsel;

(c) not seek to obtain from an unrepresented accused a waiver of important pretrial rights, such as the right to a preliminary hearing;

(d) make timely disclosure to the defense of all evidence or information known to the prosecutor that tends to negate the

guilt of the accused or mitigates the offense, and, in connection
with sentencing, disclose to the defense and to the tribunal all
unprivileged mitigating information known to the prosecutor,
except when the prosecutor is relieved of this responsibility
by a protective order of the tribunal;

(e) not subpoena a lawyer in a grand jury or other criminal
proceeding to present evidence about a past or present client
unless the prosecutor reasonably believes:

(1) the information sought is not protected from disclosure
by any applicable privilege;

(2) the evidence sought is essential to the successful
completion of an ongoing investigation or prosecution; and

(3) there is no other feasible alternative to obtain the
information;

(f) except for statements that are necessary to inform
the public of the nature and extent of the prosecutor's action
and that serve a legitimate law enforcement purpose, refrain
from making extrajudicial comments that have a substantial
likelihood of heightening public condemnation of the accused
and exercise reasonable care to prevent investigators, law
enforcement personnel, employees or other persons assisting or
associated with the prosecutor in a criminal case from making an
extrajudicial statement that the prosecutor would be prohibited
from making under Rule 3.6 or this Rule.

(g) When a prosecutor knows of new, credible and material
evidence creating a reasonable likelihood that a convicted
defendant did not commit an offense of which the defendant
was convicted, the prosecutor shall:

(1) promptly disclose that evidence to an appropriate
court or authority, and

(2) if the conviction was obtained in the prosecutor's
jurisdiction,

(i) promptly disclose that evidence to the defendant
unless a court authorizes delay, and

(ii) undertake further investigation, or make reasonable
efforts to cause an investigation, to determine whether the
defendant was convicted of an offense that the defendant
did not commit.

(h) When a prosecutor knows of clear and convincing evidence
establishing that a defendant in the prosecutor's jurisdiction was

convicted of an offense that the defendant did not commit, the prosecutor shall seek to remedy the conviction.

Comment

[1] A prosecutor has the responsibility of a minister of justice and not simply that of an advocate. This responsibility carries with it specific obligations to see that the defendant is accorded procedural justice, that guilt is decided upon the basis of sufficient evidence, and that special precautions are taken to prevent and to rectify the conviction of innocent persons. The extent of mandated remedial action is a matter of debate and varies in different jurisdictions. Many jurisdictions have adopted the ABA Standards for Criminal Justice Relating to the Prosecution Function, which are the product of prolonged and careful deliberation by lawyers experienced in both criminal prosecution and defense. Competent representation of the sovereignty may require a prosecutor to undertake some procedural and remedial measures as a matter of obligation. Applicable law may require other measures by the prosecutor and knowing disregard of those obligations or a systematic abuse of prosecutorial discretion could constitute a violation of Rule 8.4.

[2] In some jurisdictions, a defendant may waive a preliminary hearing and thereby lose a valuable opportunity to challenge probable cause. Accordingly, prosecutors should not seek to obtain waivers of preliminary hearings or other important pretrial rights from unrepresented accused persons. Paragraph (c) does not apply, however, to an accused appearing *pro se* with the approval of the tribunal. Nor does it forbid the lawful questioning of an uncharged suspect who has knowingly waived the rights to counsel and silence.

[3] The exception in paragraph (d) recognizes that a prosecutor may seek an appropriate protective order from the tribunal if disclosure of information to the defense could result in substantial harm to an individual or to the public interest.

[4] Paragraph (e) is intended to limit the issuance of lawyer subpoenas in grand jury and other criminal proceedings to those situations in which there is a genuine need to intrude into the client-lawyer relationship.

[5] Paragraph (f) supplements Rule 3.6, which prohibits extrajudicial statements that have a substantial likelihood of prejudicing an adjudicatory proceeding. In the context of a criminal prosecution, a prosecutor's extrajudicial statement can create the additional problem of increasing

public condemnation of the accused. Although the announcement of an indictment, for example, will necessarily have severe consequences for the accused, a prosecutor can, and should, avoid comments which have no legitimate law enforcement purpose and have a substantial likelihood of increasing public opprobrium of the accused. Nothing in this Comment is intended to restrict the statements which a prosecutor may make which comply with Rule 3.6(b) or 3.6(c).

[6] Like other lawyers, prosecutors are subject to Rules 5.1 and 5.3, which relate to responsibilities regarding lawyers and nonlawyers who work for or are associated with the lawyer's office. Paragraph (f) reminds the prosecutor of the importance of these obligations in connection with the unique dangers of improper extrajudicial statements in a criminal case. In addition, paragraph (f) requires a prosecutor to exercise reasonable care to prevent persons assisting or associated with the prosecutor from making improper extrajudicial statements, even when such persons are not under the direct supervision of the prosecutor. Ordinarily, the reasonable care standard will be satisfied if the prosecutor issues the appropriate cautions to law enforcement personnel and other relevant individuals.

[7] When a prosecutor knows of new, credible and material evidence creating a reasonable likelihood that a person outside the prosecutor's jurisdiction was convicted of a crime that the person did not commit, paragraph (g) requires prompt disclosure to the court or other appropriate authority, such as the chief prosecutor of the jurisdiction where the conviction occurred. If the conviction was obtained in the prosecutor's jurisdiction, paragraph (g) requires the prosecutor to examine the evidence and undertake further investigation to determine whether the defendant is in fact innocent or make reasonable efforts to cause another appropriate authority to undertake the necessary investigation, and to promptly disclose the evidence to the court and, absent court-authorized delay, to the defendant. Consistent with the objectives of Rules 4.2 and 4.3, disclosure to a represented defendant must be made through the defendant's counsel, and, in the case of an unrepresented defendant, would ordinarily be accompanied by a request to a court for the appointment of counsel to assist the defendant in taking such legal measures as may be appropriate.

[8] Under paragraph (h), once the prosecutor knows of clear and convincing evidence that the defendant was convicted of an offense that the

defendant did not commit, the prosecutor must seek to remedy the conviction. Necessary steps may include disclosure of the evidence to the defendant, requesting that the court appoint counsel for an unrepresented indigent defendant and, where appropriate, notifying the court that the prosecutor has knowledge that the defendant did not commit the offense of which the defendant was convicted.

[9] A prosecutor's independent judgment, made in good faith, that the new evidence is not of such nature as to trigger the obligations of sections (g) and (h), though subsequently determined to have been erroneous, does not constitute a violation of this Rule.

Definitional Cross-References

"Known" and "Knows" *See* Rule 1.0(f)
"Reasonable" *See* Rule 1.0(h)
"Reasonably believes" *See* Rule 1.0(i)
"Substantial" *See* Rule 1.0(l)
"Tribunal" *See* Rule 1.0(m)

RULE 3.9: ADVOCATE IN NONADJUDICATIVE PROCEEDINGS

A lawyer representing a client before a legislative body or administrative agency in a nonadjudicative proceeding shall disclose that the appearance is in a representative capacity and shall conform to the provisions of Rules 3.3(a) through (c), 3.4(a) through (c), and 3.5.

Comment

[1] In representation before bodies such as legislatures, municipal councils, and executive and administrative agencies acting in a rule-making or policy-making capacity, lawyers present facts, formulate issues and advance argument in the matters under consideration. The decision-making body, like a court, should be able to rely on the integrity of the submissions made to it. A lawyer appearing before such a body must deal with it honestly and in conformity with applicable rules of procedure. See Rules 3.3(a) through (c), 3.4(a) through (c) and 3.5.

[2] Lawyers have no exclusive right to appear before nonadjudicative bodies, as they do before a court. The requirements of this Rule therefore may subject lawyers to regulations inapplicable to advocates who are not

lawyers. However, legislatures and administrative agencies have a right to expect lawyers to deal with them as they deal with courts.

[3] This Rule only applies when a lawyer represents a client in connection with an official hearing or meeting of a governmental agency or a legislative body to which the lawyer or the lawyer's client is presenting evidence or argument. It does not apply to representation of a client in a negotiation or other bilateral transaction with a governmental agency or in connection with an application for a license or other privilege or the client's compliance with generally applicable reporting requirements, such as the filing of income-tax returns. Nor does it apply to the representation of a client in connection with an investigation or examination of the client's affairs conducted by government investigators or examiners. Representation in such matters is governed by Rules 4.1 through 4.4.

TRANSACTIONS WITH PERSONS OTHER THAN CLIENTS

RULE 4.1: TRUTHFULNESS IN STATEMENTS TO OTHERS

In the course of representing a client a lawyer shall not knowingly:

(a) make a false statement of material fact or law to a third person; or

(b) fail to disclose a material fact when disclosure is necessary to avoid assisting a criminal or fraudulent act by a client, unless disclosure is prohibited by Rule 1.6.

Comment

Misrepresentation

[1] A lawyer is required to be truthful when dealing with others on a client's behalf, but generally has no affirmative duty to inform an opposing party of relevant facts. A misrepresentation can occur if the lawyer incorporates or affirms a statement of another person that the lawyer knows is false. Misrepresentations can also occur by partially true but misleading statements or omissions that are the equivalent of affirmative false statements. For dishonest conduct that does not amount to a false statement or for misrepresentations by a lawyer other than in the course of representing a client, see Rule 8.4.

Statements of Fact

[2] This Rule refers to statements of fact. Whether a particular statement should be regarded as one of fact can depend on the circumstances. Under generally accepted conventions in negotiation, certain types of statements ordinarily are not taken as statements of material fact. Estimates of price or value placed on the subject of a transaction and a party's intentions as to an acceptable settlement of a claim are ordinarily in this category, and so is the existence of an undisclosed principal except where nondisclosure of the principal would constitute fraud. Lawyers should be mindful of their obligations under applicable law to avoid criminal and tortious misrepresentation.

Crime or Fraud by Client   *dangerous*

[3] Under Rule 1.2(d), a lawyer is prohibited from counseling or assisting a client in conduct that the lawyer knows is criminal or fraudulent. Paragraph (b) states a specific application of the principle set forth in Rule 1.2(d) and addresses the situation where a client's crime or fraud takes the form of a lie or misrepresentation. Ordinarily, a lawyer can avoid assisting a client's crime or fraud by withdrawing from the representation. Sometimes it may be necessary for the lawyer to give notice of the fact of withdrawal and to disaffirm an opinion, document, affirmation or the like. In extreme cases, substantive law may require a lawyer to disclose information relating to the representation to avoid being deemed to have assisted the client's crime or fraud. If the lawyer can avoid assisting a client's crime or fraud only by disclosing this information, then under paragraph (b) the lawyer is required to do so, unless the disclosure is prohibited by Rule 1.6.

Definitional Cross-References

"Fraudulent" *See* Rule 1.0(d)
"Knowingly" *See* Rule 1.0(f)

RULE 4.2: COMMUNICATION WITH PERSON REPRESENTED BY COUNSEL

In representing a client, a lawyer shall not communicate about the subject of the representation with a person the lawyer knows to be represented by another lawyer in the matter, unless

the lawyer has the consent of the other lawyer or is authorized
to do so by law or a court order.

Comment

[1] This Rule contributes to the proper functioning of the legal system by protecting a person who has chosen to be represented by a lawyer
in a matter against possible overreaching by other lawyers who are participating in the matter, interference by those lawyers with the client-lawyer relationship and the uncounselled disclosure of information relating
to the representation.

[2] This Rule applies to communications with any person who is represented by counsel concerning the matter to which the communication
relates.

[3] The Rule applies even though the represented person initiates or
consents to the communication. A lawyer must immediately terminate
communication with a person if, after commencing communication, the
lawyer learns that the person is one with whom communication is not
permitted by this Rule.

[4] This Rule does not prohibit communication with a represented
person, or an employee or agent of such a person, concerning matters
outside the representation. For example, the existence of a controversy
between a government agency and a private party, or between two organizations, does not prohibit a lawyer for either from communicating with
nonlawyer representatives of the other regarding a separate matter. Nor
does this Rule preclude communication with a represented person who is
seeking advice from a lawyer who is not otherwise representing a client
in the matter. A lawyer may not make a communication prohibited by
this Rule through the acts of another. See Rule 8.4(a). Parties to a matter
may communicate directly with each other, and a lawyer is not prohibited from advising a client concerning a communication that the client is
legally entitled to make. Also, a lawyer having independent justification
or legal authorization for communicating with a represented person is
permitted to do so.

[5] Communications authorized by law may include communications by a lawyer on behalf of a client who is exercising a constitutional
or other legal right to communicate with the government. Communications authorized by law may also include investigative activities of lawyers representing governmental entities, directly or through investigative

agents, prior to the commencement of criminal or civil enforcement proceedings. When communicating with the accused in a criminal matter, a government lawyer must comply with this Rule in addition to honoring the constitutional rights of the accused. The fact that a communication does not violate a state or federal constitutional right is insufficient to establish that the communication is permissible under this Rule.

[6] A lawyer who is uncertain whether a communication with a represented person is permissible may seek a court order. A lawyer may also seek a court order in exceptional circumstances to authorize a communication that would otherwise be prohibited by this Rule, for example, where communication with a person represented by counsel is necessary to avoid reasonably certain injury.

[7] In the case of a represented organization, this Rule prohibits communications with a constituent of the organization who supervises, directs or regularly consults with the organization's lawyer concerning the matter or has authority to obligate the organization with respect to the matter or whose act or omission in connection with the matter may be imputed to the organization for purposes of civil or criminal liability. Consent of the organization's lawyer is not required for communication with a former constituent. If a constituent of the organization is represented in the matter by his or her own counsel, the consent by that counsel to a communication will be sufficient for purposes of this Rule. Compare Rule 3.4(f). In communicating with a current or former constituent of an organization, a lawyer must not use methods of obtaining evidence that violate the legal rights of the organization. See Rule 4.4.

[8] The prohibition on communications with a represented person only applies in circumstances where the lawyer knows that the person is in fact represented in the matter to be discussed. This means that the lawyer has actual knowledge of the fact of the representation; but such actual knowledge may be inferred from the circumstances. See Rule 1.0(f). Thus, the lawyer cannot evade the requirement of obtaining the consent of counsel by closing eyes to the obvious.

[9] In the event the person with whom the lawyer communicates is not known to be represented by counsel in the matter, the lawyer's communications are subject to Rule 4.3.

Definitional Cross-References

"Knows" *See* Rule 1.0(f)

RULE 4.3: DEALING WITH UNREPRESENTED PERSON

In dealing on behalf of a client with a person who is not represented by counsel, a lawyer shall not state or imply that the lawyer is disinterested. When the lawyer knows or reasonably should know that the unrepresented person misunderstands the lawyer's role in the matter, the lawyer shall make reasonable efforts to correct the misunderstanding. The lawyer shall not give legal advice to an unrepresented person, other than the advice to secure counsel, if the lawyer knows or reasonably should know that the interests of such a person are or have a reasonable possibility of being in conflict with the interests of the client.

Comment

[1] An unrepresented person, particularly one not experienced in dealing with legal matters, might assume that a lawyer is disinterested in loyalties or is a disinterested authority on the law even when the lawyer represents a client. In order to avoid a misunderstanding, a lawyer will typically need to identify the lawyer's client and, where necessary, explain that the client has interests opposed to those of the unrepresented person. For misunderstandings that sometimes arise when a lawyer for an organization deals with an unrepresented constituent, see Rule 1.13(f).

[2] The Rule distinguishes between situations involving unrepresented persons whose interests may be adverse to those of the lawyer's client and those in which the person's interests are not in conflict with the client's. In the former situation, the possibility that the lawyer will compromise the unrepresented person's interests is so great that the Rule prohibits the giving of any advice, apart from the advice to obtain counsel. Whether a lawyer is giving impermissible advice may depend on the experience and sophistication of the unrepresented person, as well as the setting in which the behavior and comments occur. This Rule does not prohibit a lawyer from negotiating the terms of a transaction or settling a dispute with an unrepresented person. So long as the lawyer has explained that the lawyer represents an adverse party and is not representing the person, the lawyer may inform the person of the terms on which the lawyer's client will enter into an agreement or settle a matter, prepare documents that require the person's signature and explain the lawyer's own view of the meaning of the document or the lawyer's view of the underlying legal obligations.

Definitional Cross-References

"Knows" *See* Rule 1.0(f)
"Reasonable" *See* Rule 1.0(h)
"Reasonably should know" *See* Rule 1.0(j)

RULE 4.4: RESPECT FOR RIGHTS OF THIRD PERSONS

(a) In representing a client, a lawyer shall not use means that have no substantial purpose other than to embarrass, delay, or burden a third person, or use methods of obtaining evidence that violate the legal rights of such a person.

(b) A lawyer who receives a document or electronically stored information relating to the representation of the lawyer's client and knows or reasonably should know that the document or electronically stored information was inadvertently sent shall promptly notify the sender.

Comment

[1] Responsibility to a client requires a lawyer to subordinate the interests of others to those of the client, but that responsibility does not imply that a lawyer may disregard the rights of third persons. It is impractical to catalogue all such rights, but they include legal restrictions on methods of obtaining evidence from third persons and unwarranted intrusions into privileged relationships, such as the client-lawyer relationship.

[2] Paragraph (b) recognizes that lawyers sometimes receive a document or electronically stored information that was mistakenly sent or produced by opposing parties or their lawyers. A document or electronically stored information is inadvertently sent when it is accidentally transmitted, such as when an email or letter is misaddressed or a document or electronically stored information is accidentally included with information that was intentionally transmitted. If a lawyer knows or reasonably should know that such a document or electronically stored information was sent inadvertently, then this Rule requires the lawyer to promptly notify the sender in order to permit that person to take protective measures. Whether the lawyer is required to take additional steps, such as returning the document or deleting electronically stored information, is a matter of law beyond the scope of these Rules, as is the question of whether the privileged status of a document or electronically stored

— Anything beyond
notification is beyond the
scope of the rules

information has been waived. Similarly, this Rule does not address the legal duties of a lawyer who receives a document or electronically stored information that the lawyer knows or reasonably should know may have been inappropriately obtained by the sending person. For purposes of this Rule, "document or electronically stored information" includes, in addition to paper documents, email and other forms of electronically stored information, including embedded data (commonly referred to as "metadata"), that is subject to being read or put into readable form. Metadata in electronic documents creates an obligation under this Rule only if the receiving lawyer knows or reasonably should know that the metadata was inadvertently sent to the receiving lawyer.

[3] Some lawyers may choose to return a document or delete electronically stored information unread, for example, when the lawyer learns before receiving it that it was inadvertently sent. Where a lawyer is not required by applicable law to do so, the decision to voluntarily return such a document or delete electronically stored information is a matter of professional judgment ordinarily reserved to the lawyer. See Rules 1.2 and 1.4.

Definitional Cross-References

"Knows" *See* Rule 1.0(f)
"Reasonably should know" *See* Rule 1.0(j)
"Substantial" *See* Rule 1.0(l)

LAW FIRMS AND ASSOCIATIONS

RULE 5.1: RESPONSIBILITIES OF PARTNERS, MANAGERS, AND SUPERVISORY LAWYERS

(a) A partner in a law firm, and a lawyer who individually or together with other lawyers possesses comparable managerial authority in a law firm, shall make reasonable efforts to ensure that the firm has in effect measures giving reasonable assurance that all lawyers in the firm conform to the Rules of Professional Conduct.

(b) A lawyer having direct supervisory authority over another lawyer shall make reasonable efforts to ensure that the other lawyer conforms to the Rules of Professional Conduct.

(c) A lawyer shall be responsible for another lawyer's violation of the Rules of Professional Conduct if:

(1) the lawyer orders or, with knowledge of the specific conduct, ratifies the conduct involved; or

(2) the lawyer is a partner or has comparable managerial authority in the law firm in which the other lawyer practices, or has direct supervisory authority over the other lawyer, and knows of the conduct at a time when its consequences can be avoided or mitigated but fails to take reasonable remedial action.

Comment

[1] Paragraph (a) applies to lawyers who have managerial authority over the professional work of a firm. See Rule 1.0(c). This includes members of a partnership, the shareholders in a law firm organized as a professional corporation, and members of other associations authorized to practice law; lawyers having comparable managerial authority in a legal services organization or a law department of an enterprise or government agency; and lawyers who have intermediate managerial responsibilities in a firm. Paragraph (b) applies to lawyers who have supervisory authority over the work of other lawyers in a firm.

[2] Paragraph (a) requires lawyers with managerial authority within a firm to make reasonable efforts to establish internal policies and procedures designed to provide reasonable assurance that all lawyers in the firm will conform to the Rules of Professional Conduct. Such policies and procedures include those designed to detect and resolve conflicts of interest, identify dates by which actions must be taken in pending matters, account for client funds and property and ensure that inexperienced lawyers are properly supervised.

[3] Other measures that may be required to fulfill the responsibility prescribed in paragraph (a) can depend on the firm's structure and the nature of its practice. In a small firm of experienced lawyers, informal supervision and periodic review of compliance with the required systems ordinarily will suffice. In a large firm, or in practice situations in which difficult ethical problems frequently arise, more elaborate measures may be necessary. Some firms, for example, have a procedure whereby junior lawyers can make confidential referral of ethical problems directly to a designated senior partner or special committee. See Rule 5.2. Firms, whether large or small, may also rely on continuing legal education in professional ethics. In any event, the ethical atmosphere of a firm can influence the

conduct of all its members, and the partners may not assume that all lawyers associated with the firm will inevitably conform to the Rules.

[4] Paragraph (c) expresses a general principle of personal responsibility for acts of another. See also Rule 8.4(a).

[5] Paragraph (c)(2) defines the duty of a partner or other lawyer having comparable managerial authority in a law firm, as well as a lawyer who has direct supervisory authority over performance of specific legal work by another lawyer. Whether a lawyer has supervisory authority in particular circumstances is a question of fact. Partners and lawyers with comparable authority have at least indirect responsibility for all work being done by the firm, while a partner or manager in charge of a particular matter ordinarily also has supervisory responsibility for the work of other firm lawyers engaged in the matter. Appropriate remedial action by a partner or managing lawyer would depend on the immediacy of that lawyer's involvement and the seriousness of the misconduct. A supervisor is required to intervene to prevent avoidable consequences of misconduct if the supervisor knows that the misconduct occurred. Thus, if a supervising lawyer knows that a subordinate misrepresented a matter to an opposing party in negotiation, the supervisor as well as the subordinate has a duty to correct the resulting misapprehension.

[6] Professional misconduct by a lawyer under supervision could reveal a violation of paragraph (b) on the part of the supervisory lawyer even though it does not entail a violation of paragraph (c) because there was no direction, ratification or knowledge of the violation.

[7] Apart from this Rule and Rule 8.4(a), a lawyer does not have disciplinary liability for the conduct of a partner, associate or subordinate. Whether a lawyer may be liable civilly or criminally for another lawyer's conduct is a question of law beyond the scope of these Rules.

[8] The duties imposed by this Rule on managing and supervising lawyers do not alter the personal duty of each lawyer in a firm to abide by the Rules of Professional Conduct. See Rule 5.2(a).

Definitional Cross-References

"Firm" and "Law firm" *See* Rule 1.0(c)
"Knows" *See* Rule 1.0(f)
"Partner" *See* Rule 1.0(g)
"Reasonable" *See* Rule 1.0(h)

RULE 5.2: RESPONSIBILITIES
OF A SUBORDINATE LAWYER

(a) A lawyer is bound by the Rules of Professional Conduct notwithstanding that the lawyer acted at the direction of another person.

(b) A subordinate lawyer does not violate the Rules of Professional Conduct if that lawyer acts in accordance with a supervisory lawyer's reasonable resolution of an arguable question of professional duty.

Comment

[1] Although a lawyer is not relieved of responsibility for a violation by the fact that the lawyer acted at the direction of a supervisor, that fact may be relevant in determining whether a lawyer had the knowledge required to render conduct a violation of the Rules. For example, if a subordinate filed a frivolous pleading at the direction of a supervisor, the subordinate would not be guilty of a professional violation unless the subordinate knew of the document's frivolous character.

[2] When lawyers in a supervisor-subordinate relationship encounter a matter involving professional judgment as to ethical duty, the supervisor may assume responsibility for making the judgment. Otherwise a consistent course of action or position could not be taken. If the question can reasonably be answered only one way, the duty of both lawyers is clear and they are equally responsible for fulfilling it. However, if the question is reasonably arguable, someone has to decide upon the course of action. That authority ordinarily reposes in the supervisor, and a subordinate may be guided accordingly. For example, if a question arises whether the interests of two clients conflict under Rule 1.7, the supervisor's reasonable resolution of the question should protect the subordinate professionally if the resolution is subsequently challenged.

Definitional Cross-References

"Reasonable" *See* Rule 1.0(h)

Rule 5.3: Responsibilities Regarding Nonlawyer Assistance

With respect to a nonlawyer employed or retained by or associated with a lawyer:

(a) a partner, and a lawyer who individually or together with other lawyers possesses comparable managerial authority in a law firm shall make reasonable efforts to ensure that the firm has in effect measures giving reasonable assurance that the person's conduct is compatible with the professional obligations of the lawyer;

(b) a lawyer having direct supervisory authority over the nonlawyer shall make reasonable efforts to ensure that the person's conduct is compatible with the professional obligations of the lawyer; and

(c) a lawyer shall be responsible for conduct of such a person that would be a violation of the Rules of Professional Conduct if engaged in by a lawyer if:

(1) the lawyer orders or, with the knowledge of the specific conduct, ratifies the conduct involved; or

(2) the lawyer is a partner or has comparable managerial authority in the law firm in which the person is employed, or has direct supervisory authority over the person, and knows of the conduct at a time when its consequences can be avoided or mitigated but fails to take reasonable remedial action.

Comment

[1] Paragraph (a) requires lawyers with managerial authority within a law firm to make reasonable efforts to ensure that the firm has in effect measures giving reasonable assurance that nonlawyers in the firm and nonlawyers outside the firm who work on firm matters act in a way compatible with the professional obligations of the lawyer. See Comment [6] to Rule 1.1 (retaining lawyers outside the firm) and Comment [1] to Rule 5.1 (responsibilities with respect to lawyers within a firm). Paragraph (b) applies to lawyers who have supervisory authority over such nonlawyers within or outside the firm. Paragraph (c) specifies the circumstances in which a lawyer is responsible for the conduct of such nonlawyers within or outside the firm that would be a violation of the Rules of Professional Conduct if engaged in by a lawyer.

Nonlawyers Within the Firm

[2] Lawyers generally employ assistants in their practice, including secretaries, investigators, law student interns, and paraprofessionals. Such assistants, whether employees or independent contractors, act for the lawyer in rendition of the lawyer's professional services. A lawyer must give such assistants appropriate instruction and supervision concerning the ethical aspects of their employment, particularly regarding the obligation not to disclose information relating to representation of the client, and should be responsible for their work product. The measures employed in supervising nonlawyers should take account of the fact that they do not have legal training and are not subject to professional discipline.

Nonlawyers Outside the Firm

[3] A lawyer may use nonlawyers outside the firm to assist the lawyer in rendering legal services to the client. Examples include the retention of an investigative or paraprofessional service, hiring a document management company to create and maintain a database for complex litigation, sending client documents to a third party for printing or scanning, and using an Internet-based service to store client information. When using such services outside the firm, a lawyer must make reasonable efforts to ensure that the services are provided in a manner that is compatible with the lawyer's professional obligations. The extent of this obligation will depend upon the circumstances, including the education, experience and reputation of the nonlawyer; the nature of the services involved; the terms of any arrangements concerning the protection of client information; and the legal and ethical environments of the jurisdictions in which the services will be performed, particularly with regard to confidentiality. See also Rules 1.1 (competence), 1.2 (allocation of authority), 1.4 (communication with client), 1.6 (confidentiality), 5.4(a) (professional independence of the lawyer), and 5.5(a) (unauthorized practice of law). When retaining or directing a nonlawyer outside the firm, a lawyer should communicate directions appropriate under the circumstances to give reasonable assurance that the nonlawyer's conduct is compatible with the professional obligations of the lawyer.

[4] Where the client directs the selection of a particular nonlawyer service provider outside the firm, the lawyer ordinarily should agree with the client concerning the allocation of responsibility for monitoring

as between the client and the lawyer. See Rule 1.2. When making such an allocation in a matter pending before a tribunal, lawyers and parties may have additional obligations that are a matter of law beyond the scope of these Rules.

Definitional Cross-References

"Firm" and "Law firm" *See* Rule 1.0(c)
"Knows" *See* Rule 1.0(f)
"Partner" *See* Rule 1.0(g)
"Reasonable" *See* Rule 1.0(h)

RULE 5.4: PROFESSIONAL INDEPENDENCE OF A LAWYER

(a) A lawyer or law firm shall not share legal fees with a nonlawyer, except that:

(1) an agreement by a lawyer with the lawyer's firm, partner, or associate may provide for the payment of money, over a reasonable period of time after the lawyer's death, to the lawyer's estate or to one or more specified persons;

(2) a lawyer who purchases the practice of a deceased, disabled, or disappeared lawyer may, pursuant to the provisions of Rule 1.17, pay to the estate or other representative of that lawyer the agreed-upon purchase price;

(3) a lawyer or law firm may include nonlawyer employees in a compensation or retirement plan, even though the plan is based in whole or in part on a profit-sharing arrangement; and

(4) a lawyer may share court-awarded legal fees with a nonprofit organization that employed, retained or recommended employment of the lawyer in the matter.

(b) A lawyer shall not form a partnership with a nonlawyer if any of the activities of the partnership consist of the practice of law.

(c) A lawyer shall not permit a person who recommends, employs, or pays the lawyer to render legal services for another to direct or regulate the lawyer's professional judgment in rendering such legal services.

(d) A lawyer shall not practice with or in the form of a professional corporation or association authorized to practice law for a profit, if:

(1) a nonlawyer owns any interest therein, except that a fiduciary representative of the estate of a lawyer may hold the stock or interest of the lawyer for a reasonable time during administration;

(2) a nonlawyer is a corporate director or officer thereof or occupies the position of similar responsibility in any form of association other than a corporation; or

(3) a nonlawyer has the right to direct or control the professional judgment of a lawyer.

Comment

[1] The provisions of this Rule express traditional limitations on sharing fees. These limitations are to protect the lawyer's professional independence of judgment. Where someone other than the client pays the lawyer's fee or salary, or recommends employment of the lawyer, that arrangement does not modify the lawyer's obligation to the client. As stated in paragraph (c), such arrangements should not interfere with the lawyer's professional judgment.

[2] This Rule also expresses traditional limitations on permitting a third party to direct or regulate the lawyer's professional judgment in rendering legal services to another. See also Rule 1.8(f) (lawyer may accept compensation from a third party as long as there is no interference with the lawyer's independent professional judgment and the client gives informed consent).

Definitional Cross-References

"Firm" and "Law firm" *See* Rule 1.0(c)
"Partner" *See* Rule 1.0(g)

RULE 5.5: UNAUTHORIZED PRACTICE OF LAW; MULTIJURISDICTIONAL PRACTICE OF LAW

(a) A lawyer shall not practice law in a jurisdiction in violation of the regulation of the legal profession in that jurisdiction, or assist another in doing so.

(b) A lawyer who is not admitted to practice in this jurisdiction shall not:

(1) except as authorized by these Rules or other law, establish an office or other systematic and continuous presence in this jurisdiction for the practice of law; or

(2) hold out to the public or otherwise represent that the lawyer is admitted to practice law in this jurisdiction.

(c) A lawyer admitted in another United States jurisdiction, and not disbarred or suspended from practice in any jurisdiction, may provide legal services on a temporary basis in this jurisdiction that:

(1) are undertaken in association with a lawyer who is admitted to practice in this jurisdiction and who actively participates in the matter;

(2) are in or reasonably related to a pending or potential proceeding before a tribunal in this or another jurisdiction, if the lawyer, or a person the lawyer is assisting, is authorized by law or order to appear in such proceeding or reasonably expects to be so authorized;

(3) are in or reasonably related to a pending or potential arbitration, mediation, or other alternative dispute resolution proceeding in this or another jurisdiction, if the services arise out of or are reasonably related to the lawyer's practice in a jurisdiction in which the lawyer is admitted to practice and are not services for which the forum requires pro hac vice admission; or

(4) are not within paragraphs (c)(2) or (c)(3) and arise out of or are reasonably related to the lawyer's practice in a jurisdiction in which the lawyer is admitted to practice.

(d) A lawyer admitted in another United States jurisdiction or in a foreign jurisdiction, and not disbarred or suspended from practice in any jurisdiction or the equivalent thereof, or a person otherwise lawfully practicing as an in-house counsel under the laws of a foreign jurisdiction, may provide legal services through an office or other systematic and continuous presence in this jurisdiction that:

(1) are provided to the lawyer's employer or its organizational affiliates; are not services for which the forum requires pro hac vice admission; and, when performed by a foreign lawyer and requires advice on the law of this or another jurisdiction or of the United States, such advice shall be based upon the advice of a lawyer who is duly licensed and authorized by the jurisdiction to provide such advice; or

(2) are services that the lawyer is authorized by federal law or other law or rule to provide in this jurisdiction.

(e) For purposes of paragraph (d):

(1) the foreign lawyer must be a member in good standing of a recognized legal profession in a foreign jurisdiction, the members of which are admitted to practice as lawyers or counselors at law or the equivalent, and subject to effective regulation and discipline by a duly constituted professional body or a public authority; or

(2) the person otherwise lawfully practicing as an in-house counsel under the laws of a foreign jurisdiction must be authorized to practice under this Rule by, in the exercise of its discretion, [the highest court of this jurisdiction].

Comment

[1] A lawyer may practice law only in a jurisdiction in which the lawyer is authorized to practice. A lawyer may be admitted to practice law in a jurisdiction on a regular basis or may be authorized by court rule or order or by law to practice for a limited purpose or on a restricted basis. Paragraph (a) applies to unauthorized practice of law by a lawyer, whether through the lawyer's direct action or by the lawyer assisting another person. For example, a lawyer may not assist a person in practicing law in violation of the rules governing professional conduct in that person's jurisdiction.

[2] The definition of the practice of law is established by law and varies from one jurisdiction to another. Whatever the definition, limiting the practice of law to members of the bar protects the public against rendition of legal services by unqualified persons. This Rule does not prohibit a lawyer from employing the services of paraprofessionals and delegating functions to them, so long as the lawyer supervises the delegated work and retains responsibility for their work. See Rule 5.3.

[3] A lawyer may provide professional advice and instruction to nonlawyers whose employment requires knowledge of the law; for example, claims adjusters, employees of financial or commercial institutions, social workers, accountants and persons employed in government agencies. Lawyers also may assist independent nonlawyers, such as paraprofessionals, who are authorized by the law of a jurisdiction to provide particular law-related services. In addition, a lawyer may counsel nonlawyers who wish to proceed pro se.

[4] Other than as authorized by law or this Rule, a lawyer who is not admitted to practice generally in this jurisdiction violates paragraph

(b)(1) if the lawyer establishes an office or other systematic and continuous presence in this jurisdiction for the practice of law. Presence may be systematic and continuous even if the lawyer is not physically present here. Such a lawyer must not hold out to the public or otherwise represent that the lawyer is admitted to practice law in this jurisdiction. See also Rule 7.1.

[5] There are occasions in which a lawyer admitted to practice in another United States jurisdiction, and not disbarred or suspended from practice in any jurisdiction, may provide legal services on a temporary basis in this jurisdiction under circumstances that do not create an unreasonable risk to the interests of their clients, the public or the courts. Paragraph (c) identifies four such circumstances. The fact that conduct is not so identified does not imply that the conduct is or is not authorized. With the exception of paragraphs (d)(1) and (d)(2), this Rule does not authorize a U.S. or foreign lawyer to establish an office or other systematic and continuous presence in this jurisdiction without being admitted to practice generally here.

[6] There is no single test to determine whether a lawyer's services are provided on a "temporary basis" in this jurisdiction, and may therefore be permissible under paragraph (c). Services may be "temporary" even though the lawyer provides services in this jurisdiction on a recurring basis, or for an extended period of time, as when the lawyer is representing a client in a single lengthy negotiation or litigation.

[7] Paragraphs (c) and (d) apply to lawyers who are admitted to practice law in any United States jurisdiction, which includes the District of Columbia and any state, territory or commonwealth of the United States. Paragraph (d) also applies to lawyers admitted in a foreign jurisdiction. The word "admitted" in paragraphs (c), (d) and (e) contemplates that the lawyer is authorized to practice in the jurisdiction in which the lawyer is admitted and excludes a lawyer who while technically admitted is not authorized to practice, because, for example, the lawyer is on inactive status.

[8] Paragraph (c)(1) recognizes that the interests of clients and the public are protected if a lawyer admitted only in another jurisdiction associates with a lawyer licensed to practice in this jurisdiction. For this paragraph to apply, however, the lawyer admitted to practice in this jurisdiction must actively participate in and share responsibility for the representation of the client.

[9] Lawyers not admitted to practice generally in a jurisdiction may be authorized by law or order of a tribunal or an administrative agency

to appear before the tribunal or agency. This authority may be granted pursuant to formal rules governing admission pro hac vice or pursuant to informal practice of the tribunal or agency. Under paragraph (c)(2), a lawyer does not violate this Rule when the lawyer appears before a tribunal or agency pursuant to such authority. To the extent that a court rule or other law of this jurisdiction requires a lawyer who is not admitted to practice in this jurisdiction to obtain admission pro hac vice before appearing before a tribunal or administrative agency, this Rule requires the lawyer to obtain that authority.

[10] Paragraph (c)(2) also provides that a lawyer rendering services in this jurisdiction on a temporary basis does not violate this Rule when the lawyer engages in conduct in anticipation of a proceeding or hearing in a jurisdiction in which the lawyer is authorized to practice law or in which the lawyer reasonably expects to be admitted pro hac vice. Examples of such conduct include meetings with the client, interviews of potential witnesses, and the review of documents. Similarly, a lawyer admitted only in another jurisdiction may engage in conduct temporarily in this jurisdiction in connection with pending litigation in another jurisdiction in which the lawyer is or reasonably expects to be authorized to appear, including taking depositions in this jurisdiction.

[11] When a lawyer has been or reasonably expects to be admitted to appear before a court or administrative agency, paragraph (c)(2) also permits conduct by lawyers who are associated with that lawyer in the matter, but who do not expect to appear before the court or administrative agency. For example, subordinate lawyers may conduct research, review documents, and attend meetings with witnesses in support of the lawyer responsible for the litigation.

[12] Paragraph (c)(3) permits a lawyer admitted to practice law in another jurisdiction to perform services on a temporary basis in this jurisdiction if those services are in or reasonably related to a pending or potential arbitration, mediation, or other alternative dispute resolution proceeding in this or another jurisdiction, if the services arise out of or are reasonably related to the lawyer's practice in a jurisdiction in which the lawyer is admitted to practice. The lawyer, however, must obtain admission pro hac vice in the case of a court-annexed arbitration or mediation or otherwise if court rules or law so require.

[13] Paragraph (c)(4) permits a lawyer admitted in another jurisdiction to provide certain legal services on a temporary basis in this jurisdiction that arise out of or are reasonably related to the lawyer's practice in

a jurisdiction in which the lawyer is admitted but are not within paragraphs (c)(2) or (c)(3). These services include both legal services and services that nonlawyers may perform but that are considered the practice of law when performed by lawyers.

[14] Paragraphs (c)(3) and (c)(4) require that the services arise out of or be reasonably related to the lawyer's practice in a jurisdiction in which the lawyer is admitted. A variety of factors evidence such a relationship. The lawyer's client may have been previously represented by the lawyer, or may be resident in or have substantial contacts with the jurisdiction in which the lawyer is admitted. The matter, although involving other jurisdictions, may have a significant connection with that jurisdiction. In other cases, significant aspects of the lawyer's work might be conducted in that jurisdiction or a significant aspect of the matter may involve the law of that jurisdiction. The necessary relationship might arise when the client's activities or the legal issues involve multiple jurisdictions, such as when the officers of a multinational corporation survey potential business sites and seek the services of their lawyer in assessing the relative merits of each. In addition, the services may draw on the lawyer's recognized expertise developed through the regular practice of law on behalf of clients in matters involving a particular body of federal, nationally-uniform, foreign, or international law. Lawyers desiring to provide pro bono legal services on a temporary basis in a jurisdiction that has been affected by a major disaster, but in which they are not otherwise authorized to practice law, as well as lawyers from the affected jurisdiction who seek to practice law temporarily in another jurisdiction, but in which they are not otherwise authorized to practice law, should consult the [*Model Court Rule on Provision of Legal Services Following Determination of Major Disaster*].

[15] Paragraph (d) identifies two circumstances in which a lawyer who is admitted to practice in another United States or a foreign jurisdiction, and is not disbarred or suspended from practice in any jurisdiction, or the equivalent thereof, may establish an office or other systematic and continuous presence in this jurisdiction for the practice of law. Pursuant to paragraph (c) of this Rule, a lawyer admitted in any U.S. jurisdiction may also provide legal services in this jurisdiction on a temporary basis. See also *Model Rule on Temporary Practice by Foreign Lawyers*. Except as provided in paragraphs (d)(1) and (d)(2), a lawyer who is admitted to practice law in another United States or foreign jurisdiction and who establishes an office or other systematic or continuous presence in this jurisdiction must become admitted to practice law generally in this jurisdiction.

[16] Paragraph (d)(1) applies to a U.S. or foreign lawyer who is employed by a client to provide legal services to the client or its organizational affiliates, i.e., entities that control, are controlled by, or are under common control with the employer. This paragraph does not authorize the provision of personal legal services to the employer's officers or employees. The paragraph applies to in-house corporate lawyers, government lawyers and others who are employed to render legal services to the employer. The lawyer's ability to represent the employer outside the jurisdiction in which the lawyer is licensed generally serves the interests of the employer and does not create an unreasonable risk to the client and others because the employer is well situated to assess the lawyer's qualifications and the quality of the lawyer's work. To further decrease any risk to the client, when advising on the domestic law of a United States jurisdiction or on the law of the United States, the foreign lawyer authorized to practice under paragraph (d)(1) of this Rule needs to base that advice on the advice of a lawyer licensed and authorized by the jurisdiction to provide it.

[17] If an employed lawyer establishes an office or other systematic presence in this jurisdiction for the purpose of rendering legal services to the employer, the lawyer may be subject to registration or other requirements, including assessments for client protection funds and mandatory continuing legal education. See *Model Rule for Registration of In-House Counsel*.

[18] Paragraph (d)(2) recognizes that a U.S. or foreign lawyer may provide legal services in a jurisdiction in which the lawyer is not licensed when authorized to do so by federal or other law, which includes statute, court rule, executive regulation or judicial precedent. See, e.g., *Model Rule on Practice Pending Admission*.

[19] A lawyer who practices law in this jurisdiction pursuant to paragraphs (c) or (d) or otherwise is subject to the disciplinary authority of this jurisdiction. See Rule 8.5(a).

[20] In some circumstances, a lawyer who practices law in this jurisdiction pursuant to paragraphs (c) or (d) may have to inform the client that the lawyer is not licensed to practice law in this jurisdiction. For example, that may be required when the representation occurs primarily in this jurisdiction and requires knowledge of the law of this jurisdiction. See Rule 1.4(b).

[21] Paragraphs (c) and (d) do not authorize communications advertising legal services in this jurisdiction by lawyers who are admitted to

practice in other jurisdictions. Whether and how lawyers may communicate the availability of their services in this jurisdiction is governed by Rules 7.1 to 7.3.

Definitional Cross-References
"Reasonably" *See* Rule 1.0(h)
"Tribunal" *See* Rule 1.0(m)

RULE 5.6: RESTRICTIONS ON RIGHT TO PRACTICE

A lawyer shall not participate in offering or making:
(a) a partnership, shareholders, operating, employment, or other similar type of agreement that restricts the right of a lawyer to practice after termination of the relationship, except an agreement concerning benefits upon retirement; or
(b) an agreement in which a restriction on the lawyer's right to practice is part of the settlement of a client controversy.

Comment

[1] An agreement restricting the right of lawyers to practice after leaving a firm not only limits their professional autonomy but also limits the freedom of clients to choose a lawyer. Paragraph (a) prohibits such agreements except for restrictions incident to provisions concerning retirement benefits for service with the firm.

[2] Paragraph (b) prohibits a lawyer from agreeing not to represent other persons in connection with settling a claim on behalf of a client.

[3] This Rule does not apply to prohibit restrictions that may be included in the terms of the sale of a law practice pursuant to Rule 1.17.

RULE 5.7: RESPONSIBILITIES REGARDING LAW-RELATED SERVICES

(a) A lawyer shall be subject to the Rules of Professional Conduct with respect to the provision of law-related services, as defined in paragraph (b), if the law-related services are provided:
(1) by the lawyer in circumstances that are not distinct from the lawyer's provision of legal services to clients; or

> (2) in other circumstances by an entity controlled by the lawyer individually or with others if the lawyer fails to take reasonable measures to assure that a person obtaining the law-related services knows that the services are not legal services and that the protections of the client-lawyer relationship do not exist.
>
> (b) The term "law-related services" denotes services that might reasonably be performed in conjunction with and in substance are related to the provision of legal services, and that are not prohibited as unauthorized practice of law when provided by a nonlawyer.

Comment

[1] When a lawyer performs law-related services or controls an organization that does so, there exists the potential for ethical problems. Principal among these is the possibility that the person for whom the law-related services are performed fails to understand that the services may not carry with them the protections normally afforded as part of the client-lawyer relationship. The recipient of the law-related services may expect, for example, that the protection of client confidences, prohibitions against representation of persons with conflicting interests, and obligations of a lawyer to maintain professional independence apply to the provision of law-related services when that may not be the case.

[2] Rule 5.7 applies to the provision of law-related services by a lawyer even when the lawyer does not provide any legal services to the person for whom the law-related services are performed and whether the law-related services are performed through a law firm or a separate entity. The Rule identifies the circumstances in which all of the Rules of Professional Conduct apply to the provision of law-related services. Even when those circumstances do not exist, however, the conduct of a lawyer involved in the provision of law-related services is subject to those Rules that apply generally to lawyer conduct, regardless of whether the conduct involves the provision of legal services. See, e.g., Rule 8.4.

[3] When law-related services are provided by a lawyer under circumstances that are not distinct from the lawyer's provision of legal services to clients, the lawyer in providing the law-related services must adhere to the requirements of the Rules of Professional Conduct as provided in paragraph (a)(1). Even when the law-related and legal services are provided in circumstances that are distinct from each other, for example through sepa-

rate entities or different support staff within the law firm, the Rules of Professional Conduct apply to the lawyer as provided in paragraph (a)(2) unless the lawyer takes reasonable measures to assure that the recipient of the law-related services knows that the services are not legal services and that the protections of the client-lawyer relationship do not apply.

[4] Law-related services also may be provided through an entity that is distinct from that through which the lawyer provides legal services. If the lawyer individually or with others has control of such an entity's operations, the Rule requires the lawyer to take reasonable measures to assure that each person using the services of the entity knows that the services provided by the entity are not legal services and that the Rules of Professional Conduct that relate to the client-lawyer relationship do not apply. A lawyer's control of an entity extends to the ability to direct its operation. Whether a lawyer has such control will depend upon the circumstances of the particular case.

[5] When a client-lawyer relationship exists with a person who is referred by a lawyer to a separate law-related service entity controlled by the lawyer, individually or with others, the lawyer must comply with Rule 1.8(a).

[6] In taking the reasonable measures referred to in paragraph (a)(2) to assure that a person using law-related services understands the practical effect or significance of the inapplicability of the Rules of Professional Conduct, the lawyer should communicate to the person receiving the law-related services, in a manner sufficient to assure that the person understands the significance of the fact, that the relationship of the person to the business entity will not be a client-lawyer relationship. The communication should be made before entering into an agreement for provision of or providing law-related services, and preferably should be in writing.

[7] The burden is upon the lawyer to show that the lawyer has taken reasonable measures under the circumstances to communicate the desired understanding. For instance, a sophisticated user of law-related services, such as a publicly held corporation, may require a lesser explanation than someone unaccustomed to making distinctions between legal services and law-related services, such as an individual seeking tax advice from a lawyer-accountant or investigative services in connection with a lawsuit.

[8] Regardless of the sophistication of potential recipients of law-related services, a lawyer should take special care to keep separate the provision of law-related and legal services in order to minimize the

risk that the recipient will assume that the law-related services are legal services. The risk of such confusion is especially acute when the lawyer renders both types of services with respect to the same matter. Under some circumstances the legal and law-related services may be so closely entwined that they cannot be distinguished from each other, and the requirement of disclosure and consultation imposed by paragraph (a)(2) of the Rule cannot be met. In such a case a lawyer will be responsible for assuring that both the lawyer's conduct and, to the extent required by Rule 5.3, that of nonlawyer employees in the distinct entity that the lawyer controls complies in all respects with the Rules of Professional Conduct.

[9] A broad range of economic and other interests of clients may be served by lawyers' engaging in the delivery of law-related services. Examples of law-related services include providing title insurance, financial planning, accounting, trust services, real estate counseling, legislative lobbying, economic analysis, social work, psychological counseling, tax preparation, and patent, medical or environmental consulting.

[10] When a lawyer is obliged to accord the recipients of such services the protections of those Rules that apply to the client-lawyer relationship, the lawyer must take special care to heed the proscriptions of the Rules addressing conflict of interest (Rules 1.7 through 1.11, especially Rules 1.7(a)(2) and 1.8(a), (b) and (f)), and to scrupulously adhere to the requirements of Rule 1.6 relating to disclosure of confidential information. The promotion of the law-related services must also in all respects comply with Rules 7.1 through 7.3, dealing with advertising and solicitation. In that regard, lawyers should take special care to identify the obligations that may be imposed as a result of a jurisdiction's decisional law.

[11] When the full protections of all of the Rules of Professional Conduct do not apply to the provision of law-related services, principles of law external to the Rules, for example, the law of principal and agent, govern the legal duties owed to those receiving the services. Those other legal principles may establish a different degree of protection for the recipient with respect to confidentiality of information, conflicts of interest and permissible business relationships with clients. See also Rule 8.4 (Misconduct).

Definitional Cross-References

"Knows" *See* Rule 1.0(f)
"Reasonable" *See* Rule 1.0(h)

PUBLIC SERVICE

RULE 6.1: VOLUNTARY PRO BONO PUBLICO SERVICE

Every lawyer has a professional responsibility to provide legal services to those unable to pay. A lawyer should aspire to render at least (50) hours of pro bono publico legal services per year. In fulfilling this responsibility, the lawyer should:

(a) provide a substantial majority of the (50) hours of legal services without fee or expectation of fee to:

(1) persons of limited means; or

(2) charitable, religious, civic, community, governmental and educational organizations in matters that are designed primarily to address the needs of persons of limited means; and

(b) provide any additional services through:

(1) delivery of legal services at no fee or substantially reduced fee to individuals, groups or organizations seeking to secure or protect civil rights, civil liberties or public rights, or charitable, religious, civic, community, governmental and educational organizations in matters in furtherance of their organizational purposes, where the payment of standard legal fees would significantly deplete the organization's economic resources or would be otherwise inappropriate;

(2) delivery of legal services at a substantially reduced fee to persons of limited means; or

(3) participation in activities for improving the law, the legal system or the legal profession.

In addition, a lawyer should voluntarily contribute financial support to organizations that provide legal services to persons of limited means.

Comment

[1] Every lawyer, regardless of professional prominence or professional work load, has a responsibility to provide legal services to those unable to pay, and personal involvement in the problems of the disadvantaged can be one of the most rewarding experiences in the life of a lawyer. The American Bar Association urges all lawyers to provide a minimum of 50 hours of pro bono services annually. States, however, may

decide to choose a higher or lower number of hours of annual service (which may be expressed as a percentage of a lawyer's professional time) depending upon local needs and local conditions. It is recognized that in some years a lawyer may render greater or fewer hours than the annual standard specified, but during the course of his or her legal career, each lawyer should render on average per year, the number of hours set forth in this Rule. Services can be performed in civil matters or in criminal or quasi-criminal matters for which there is no government obligation to provide funds for legal representation, such as post-conviction death penalty appeal cases.

[2] Paragraphs (a)(1) and (2) recognize the critical need for legal services that exists among persons of limited means by providing that a substantial majority of the legal services rendered annually to the disadvantaged be furnished without fee or expectation of fee. Legal services under these paragraphs consist of a full range of activities, including individual and class representation, the provision of legal advice, legislative lobbying, administrative rule making and the provision of free training or mentoring to those who represent persons of limited means. The variety of these activities should facilitate participation by government lawyers, even when restrictions exist on their engaging in the outside practice of law.

[3] Persons eligible for legal services under paragraphs (a)(1) and (2) are those who qualify for participation in programs funded by the Legal Services Corporation and those whose incomes and financial resources are slightly above the guidelines utilized by such programs but nevertheless, cannot afford counsel. Legal services can be rendered to individuals or to organizations such as homeless shelters, battered women's centers and food pantries that serve those of limited means. The term "governmental organizations" includes, but is not limited to, public protection programs and sections of governmental or public sector agencies.

[4] Because service must be provided without fee or expectation of fee, the intent of the lawyer to render free legal services is essential for the work performed to fall within the meaning of paragraphs (a)(1) and (2). Accordingly, services rendered cannot be considered pro bono if an anticipated fee is uncollected, but the award of statutory attorneys' fees in a case originally accepted as pro bono would not disqualify such services from inclusion under this section. Lawyers who do receive fees in such cases are encouraged to contribute an appropriate portion of such fees to organizations or projects that benefit persons of limited means.

[5] While it is possible for a lawyer to fulfill the annual responsibility to perform pro bono services exclusively through activities described in paragraphs (a)(1) and (2), to the extent that any hours of service remained unfulfilled, the remaining commitment can be met in a variety of ways as set forth in paragraph (b). Constitutional, statutory or regulatory restrictions may prohibit or impede government and public sector lawyers and judges from performing the pro bono services outlined in paragraphs (a)(1) and (2). Accordingly, where those restrictions apply, government and public sector lawyers and judges may fulfill their pro bono responsibility by performing services outlined in paragraph (b).

[6] Paragraph (b)(1) includes the provision of certain types of legal services to those whose incomes and financial resources place them above limited means. It also permits the pro bono lawyer to accept a substantially reduced fee for services. Examples of the types of issues that may be addressed under this paragraph include First Amendment claims, Title VII claims and environmental protection claims. Additionally, a wide range of organizations may be represented, including social service, medical research, cultural and religious groups.

[7] Paragraph (b)(2) covers instances in which lawyers agree to and receive a modest fee for furnishing legal services to persons of limited means. Participation in judicare programs and acceptance of court appointments in which the fee is substantially below a lawyer's usual rate are encouraged under this section.

[8] Paragraph (b)(3) recognizes the value of lawyers engaging in activities that improve the law, the legal system or the legal profession. Serving on bar association committees, serving on boards of pro bono or legal services programs, taking part in Law Day activities, acting as a continuing legal education instructor, a mediator or an arbitrator and engaging in legislative lobbying to improve the law, the legal system or the profession are a few examples of the many activities that fall within this paragraph.

[9] Because the provision of pro bono services is a professional responsibility, it is the individual ethical commitment of each lawyer. Nevertheless, there may be times when it is not feasible for a lawyer to engage in pro bono services. At such times a lawyer may discharge the pro bono responsibility by providing financial support to organizations providing free legal services to persons of limited means. Such financial support should be reasonably equivalent to the value of the hours of service that would have otherwise been provided. In addition, at times it may be

more feasible to satisfy the pro bono responsibility collectively, as by a firm's aggregate pro bono activities.

[10] Because the efforts of individual lawyers are not enough to meet the need for free legal services that exists among persons of limited means, the government and the profession have instituted additional programs to provide those services. Every lawyer should financially support such programs, in addition to either providing direct pro bono services or making financial contributions when pro bono service is not feasible.

[11] Law firms should act reasonably to enable and encourage all lawyers in the firm to provide the pro bono legal services called for by this Rule.

[12] The responsibility set forth in this Rule is not intended to be enforced through disciplinary process.

Definitional Cross-References
"Substantial" *See* Rule 1.0(l)

RULE 6.2: ACCEPTING APPOINTMENTS

A lawyer shall not seek to avoid appointment by a tribunal to represent a person except for good cause, such as:

(a) representing the client is likely to result in violation of the Rules of Professional Conduct or other law;

(b) representing the client is likely to result in an unreasonable financial burden on the lawyer; or

(c) the client or the cause is so repugnant to the lawyer as to be likely to impair the client-lawyer relationship or the lawyer's ability to represent the client.

Comment

[1] A lawyer ordinarily is not obliged to accept a client whose character or cause the lawyer regards as repugnant. The lawyer's freedom to select clients is, however, qualified. All lawyers have a responsibility to assist in providing pro bono publico service. See Rule 6.1. An individual lawyer fulfills this responsibility by accepting a fair share of unpopular matters or indigent or unpopular clients. A lawyer may also be subject to appointment by a court to serve unpopular clients or persons unable to afford legal services.

Appointed Counsel

[2] For good cause a lawyer may seek to decline an appointment to represent a person who cannot afford to retain counsel or whose cause is unpopular. Good cause exists if the lawyer could not handle the matter competently, see Rule 1.1, or if undertaking the representation would result in an improper conflict of interest, for example, when the client or the cause is so repugnant to the lawyer as to be likely to impair the client-lawyer relationship or the lawyer's ability to represent the client. A lawyer may also seek to decline an appointment if acceptance would be unreasonably burdensome, for example, when it would impose a financial sacrifice so great as to be unjust.

[3] An appointed lawyer has the same obligations to the client as retained counsel, including the obligations of loyalty and confidentiality, and is subject to the same limitations on the client-lawyer relationship, such as the obligation to refrain from assisting the client in violation of the Rules.

Definitional Cross-References

"Tribunal" *See* Rule 1.0(m)

RULE 6.3: MEMBERSHIP IN LEGAL SERVICES ORGANIZATION

A lawyer may serve as a director, officer or member of a legal services organization, apart from the law firm in which the lawyer practices, notwithstanding that the organization serves persons having interests adverse to a client of the lawyer. The lawyer shall not knowingly participate in a decision or action of the organization:

(a) if participating in the decision or action would be incompatible with the lawyer's obligations to a client under Rule 1.7; or

(b) where the decision or action could have a material adverse effect on the representation of a client of the organization whose interests are adverse to a client of the lawyer.

Comment

[1] Lawyers should be encouraged to support and participate in legal service organizations. A lawyer who is an officer or a member of such an organization does not thereby have a client-lawyer relationship with

persons served by the organization. However, there is potential conflict between the interests of such persons and the interests of the lawyer's clients. If the possibility of such conflict disqualified a lawyer from serving on the board of a legal services organization, the profession's involvement in such organizations would be severely curtailed.

[2] It may be necessary in appropriate cases to reassure a client of the organization that the representation will not be affected by conflicting loyalties of a member of the board. Established, written policies in this respect can enhance the credibility of such assurances.

Definitional Cross-References

"Law firm" *See* Rule 1.0(c)
"Knowingly" *See* Rule 1.0(f)

RULE 6.4: LAW REFORM ACTIVITIES AFFECTING CLIENT INTERESTS

A lawyer may serve as a director, officer or member of an organization involved in reform of the law or its administration notwithstanding that the reform may affect the interests of a client of the lawyer. When the lawyer knows that the interests of a client may be materially benefitted by a decision in which the lawyer participates, the lawyer shall disclose that fact but need not identify the client.

Comment

[1] Lawyers involved in organizations seeking law reform generally do not have a client-lawyer relationship with the organization. Otherwise, it might follow that a lawyer could not be involved in a bar association law reform program that might indirectly affect a client. See also Rule 1.2(b). For example, a lawyer specializing in antitrust litigation might be regarded as disqualified from participating in drafting revisions of rules governing that subject. In determining the nature and scope of participation in such activities, a lawyer should be mindful of obligations to clients under other Rules, particularly Rule 1.7. A lawyer is professionally obligated to protect the integrity of the program by making an appropriate disclosure within the organization when the lawyer knows a private client might be materially benefitted.

Definitional Cross-References

"Knows" *See* Rule 1.0(f)

RULE 6.5: NONPROFIT AND COURT-ANNEXED LIMITED LEGAL SERVICES PROGRAMS

(a) A lawyer who, under the auspices of a program sponsored by a nonprofit organization or court, provides short-term limited legal services to a client without expectation by either the lawyer or the client that the lawyer will provide continuing representation in the matter:

(1) is subject to Rules 1.7 and 1.9(a) only if the lawyer knows that the representation of the client involves a conflict of interest; and

(2) is subject to Rule 1.10 only if the lawyer knows that another lawyer associated with the lawyer in a law firm is disqualified by Rule 1.7 or 1.9(a) with respect to the matter.

(b) Except as provided in paragraph (a)(2), Rule 1.10 is inapplicable to a representation governed by this Rule.

Comment

[1] Legal services organizations, courts and various nonprofit organizations have established programs through which lawyers provide short-term limited legal services—such as advice or the completion of legal forms—that will assist persons to address their legal problems without further representation by a lawyer. In these programs, such as legal-advice hotlines, advice-only clinics or pro se counseling programs, a client-lawyer relationship is established, but there is no expectation that the lawyer's representation of the client will continue beyond the limited consultation. Such programs are normally operated under circumstances in which it is not feasible for a lawyer to systematically screen for conflicts of interest as is generally required before undertaking a representation. See, e.g., Rules 1.7, 1.9 and 1.10.

[2] A lawyer who provides short-term limited legal services pursuant to this Rule must secure the client's informed consent to the limited scope of the representation. See Rule 1.2(c). If a short-term limited representation would not be reasonable under the circumstances, the lawyer may offer advice to the client but must also advise the client of the need for further assistance of counsel. Except as provided in this Rule, the Rules of

Professional Conduct, including Rules 1.6 and 1.9(c), are applicable to the limited representation.

[3] Because a lawyer who is representing a client in the circumstances addressed by this Rule ordinarily is not able to check systematically for conflicts of interest, paragraph (a) requires compliance with Rules 1.7 or 1.9(a) only if the lawyer knows that the representation presents a conflict of interest for the lawyer, and with Rule 1.10 only if the lawyer knows that another lawyer in the lawyer's firm is disqualified by Rules 1.7 or 1.9(a) in the matter.

[4] Because the limited nature of the services significantly reduces the risk of conflicts of interest with other matters being handled by the lawyer's firm, paragraph (b) provides that Rule 1.10 is inapplicable to a representation governed by this Rule except as provided by paragraph (a)(2). Paragraph (a)(2) requires the participating lawyer to comply with Rule 1.10 when the lawyer knows that the lawyer's firm is disqualified by Rules 1.7 or 1.9(a). By virtue of paragraph (b), however, a lawyer's participation in a short-term limited legal services program will not preclude the lawyer's firm from undertaking or continuing the representation of a client with interests adverse to a client being represented under the program's auspices. Nor will the personal disqualification of a lawyer participating in the program be imputed to other lawyers participating in the program.

[5] If, after commencing a short-term limited representation in accordance with this Rule, a lawyer undertakes to represent the client in the matter on an ongoing basis, Rules 1.7, 1.9(a) and 1.10 become applicable.

Definitional Cross-References
"Law firm" *See* Rule 1.0(c)
"Knows" *See* Rule 1.0(f)

INFORMATION ABOUT LEGAL SERVICES

Rule 7.1: Communications Concerning a Lawyer's Services

A lawyer shall not make a false or misleading communication about the lawyer or the lawyer's services. A communication is false or misleading if it contains a material misrepresentation of fact or law, or omits a fact necessary to make the statement considered as a whole not materially misleading.

Comment

[1] This Rule governs all communications about a lawyer's services, including advertising. Whatever means are used to make known a lawyer's services, statements about them must be truthful.

[2] Misleading truthful statements are prohibited by this Rule. A truthful statement is misleading if it omits a fact necessary to make the lawyer's communication considered as a whole not materially misleading. A truthful statement is misleading if a substantial likelihood exists that it will lead a reasonable person to formulate a specific conclusion about the lawyer or the lawyer's services for which there is no reasonable factual foundation. A truthful statement is also misleading if presented in a way that creates a substantial likelihood that a reasonable person would believe the lawyer's communication requires that person to take further action when, in fact, no action is required.

[3] A communication that truthfully reports a lawyer's achievements on behalf of clients or former clients may be misleading if presented so as to lead a reasonable person to form an unjustified expectation that the same results could be obtained for other clients in similar matters without reference to the specific factual and legal circumstances of each client's case. Similarly, an unsubstantiated claim about a lawyer's or law firm's services or fees, or an unsubstantiated comparison of the lawyer's or law firm's services or fees with those of other lawyers or law firms, may be misleading if presented with such specificity as would lead a reasonable person to conclude that the comparison or claim can be substantiated. The inclusion of an appropriate disclaimer or qualifying language may preclude a finding that a statement is likely to create unjustified expectations or otherwise mislead the public.

[4] It is professional misconduct for a lawyer to engage in conduct involving dishonesty, fraud, deceit or misrepresentation. Rule 8.4(c). See also Rule 8.4(e) for the prohibition against stating or implying an ability to improperly influence a government agency or official or to achieve results by means that violate the Rules of Professional Conduct or other law.

[5] Firm names, letterhead and professional designations are communications concerning a lawyer's services. A firm may be designated by the names of all or some of its current members, by the names of deceased members where there has been a succession in the firm's identity or by a trade name if it is not false or misleading. A lawyer or law firm also may be designated by a distinctive website address, social media

username or comparable professional designation that is not misleading. A law firm name or designation is misleading if it implies a connection with a government agency, with a deceased lawyer who was not a former member of the firm, with a lawyer not associated with the firm or a predecessor firm, with a nonlawyer or with a public or charitable legal services organization. If a firm uses a trade name that includes a geographical name such as "Springfield Legal Clinic," an express statement explaining that it is not a public legal aid organization may be required to avoid a misleading implication.

[6] A law firm with offices in more than one jurisdiction may use the same name or other professional designation in each jurisdiction.

[7] Lawyers may not imply or hold themselves out as practicing together in one firm when they are not a firm, as defined in Rule 1.0(c), because to do so would be false and misleading.

[8] It is misleading to use the name of a lawyer holding a public office in the name of a law firm, or in communications on the law firm's behalf, during any substantial period in which the lawyer is not actively and regularly practicing with the firm.

RULE 7.2: COMMUNICATIONS CONCERNING A LAWYER'S SERVICES: SPECIFIC RULES

(a) A lawyer may communicate information regarding the lawyer's services through any media.

(b) A lawyer shall not compensate, give or promise anything of value to a person for recommending the lawyer's services except that a lawyer may:

(1) pay the reasonable costs of advertisements or communications permitted by this Rule;

(2) pay the usual charges of a legal service plan or a not-for-profit or qualified lawyer referral service;

(3) pay for a law practice in accordance with Rule 1.17;

(4) refer clients to another lawyer or a nonlawyer professional pursuant to an agreement not otherwise prohibited under these Rules that provides for the other person to refer clients or customers to the lawyer, if:

(i) the reciprocal referral agreement is not exclusive; and

(ii) the client is informed of the existence and nature of the agreement; and

(5) give nominal gifts as an expression of appreciation that are neither intended nor reasonably expected to be a form of compensation for recommending a lawyer's services.

(c) A lawyer shall not state or imply that a lawyer is certified as a specialist in a particular field of law, unless:

(1) the lawyer has been certified as a specialist by an organization that has been approved by an appropriate authority of the state or the District of Columbia or a U.S. Territory or that has been accredited by the American Bar Association; and

(2) the name of the certifying organization is clearly identified in the communication.

(d) Any communication made under this Rule must include the name and contact information of at least one lawyer or law firm responsible for its content.

Comment

[1] This Rule permits public dissemination of information concerning a lawyer's or law firm's name, address, email address, website, and telephone number; the kinds of services the lawyer will undertake; the basis on which the lawyer's fees are determined, including prices for specific services and payment and credit arrangements; a lawyer's foreign language ability; names of references and, with their consent, names of clients regularly represented; and other information that might invite the attention of those seeking legal assistance.

Paying Others to Recommend a Lawyer

[2] Except as permitted under paragraphs (b)(1)-(b)(5), lawyers are not permitted to pay others for recommending the lawyer's services. A communication contains a recommendation if it endorses or vouches for a lawyer's credentials, abilities, competence, character, or other professional qualities. Directory listings and group advertisements that list lawyers by practice area, without more, do not constitute impermissible "recommendations."

[3] Paragraph (b)(1) allows a lawyer to pay for advertising and communications permitted by this Rule, including the costs of print directory listings, on-line directory listings, newspaper ads, television and radio airtime, domain-name registrations, sponsorship fees, Internet-based advertisements, and group advertising. A lawyer may compensate em-

ployees, agents and vendors who are engaged to provide marketing or client development services, such as publicists, public-relations personnel, business-development staff, television and radio station employees or spokespersons and website designers.

[4] Paragraph (b)(5) permits lawyers to give nominal gifts as an expression of appreciation to a person for recommending the lawyer's services or referring a prospective client. The gift may not be more than a token item as might be given for holidays, or other ordinary social hospitality. A gift is prohibited if offered or given in consideration of any promise, agreement or understanding that such a gift would be forthcoming or that referrals would be made or encouraged in the future.

[5] A lawyer may pay others for generating client leads, such as Internet-based client leads, as long as the lead generator does not recommend the lawyer, any payment to the lead generator is consistent with Rules 1.5(e) (division of fees) and 5.4 (professional independence of the lawyer), and the lead generator's communications are consistent with Rule 7.1 (communications concerning a lawyer's services). To comply with Rule 7.1, a lawyer must not pay a lead generator that states, implies, or creates a reasonable impression that it is recommending the lawyer, is making the referral without payment from the lawyer, or has analyzed a person's legal problems when determining which lawyer should receive the referral. See Comment [2] (definition of "recommendation"). See also Rule 5.3 (duties of lawyers and law firms with respect to the conduct of nonlawyers); Rule 8.4(a) (duty to avoid violating the Rules through the acts of another).

[6] A lawyer may pay the usual charges of a legal service plan or a not-for-profit or qualified lawyer referral service. A legal service plan is a prepaid or group legal service plan or a similar delivery system that assists people who seek to secure legal representation. A lawyer referral service, on the other hand, is any organization that holds itself out to the public as a lawyer referral service. Qualified referral services are consumer-oriented organizations that provide unbiased referrals to lawyers with appropriate experience in the subject matter of the representation and afford other client protections, such as complaint procedures or malpractice insurance requirements. Consequently, this Rule only permits a lawyer to pay the usual charges of a not-for-profit or qualified lawyer referral service. A qualified lawyer referral service is one that is approved by an appropriate regulatory authority as affording adequate protections for the public. See, e.g., the American Bar Association's Model Supreme

Court Rules Governing Lawyer Referral Services and Model Lawyer Referral and Information Service Quality Assurance Act.

[7] A lawyer who accepts assignments or referrals from a legal service plan or referrals from a lawyer referral service must act reasonably to assure that the activities of the plan or service are compatible with the lawyer's professional obligations. Legal service plans and lawyer referral services may communicate with the public, but such communication must be in conformity with these Rules. Thus, advertising must not be false or misleading, as would be the case if the communications of a group advertising program or a group legal services plan would mislead the public to think that it was a lawyer referral service sponsored by a state agency or bar association.

[8] A lawyer also may agree to refer clients to another lawyer or a nonlawyer professional, in return for the undertaking of that person to refer clients or customers to the lawyer. Such reciprocal referral arrangements must not interfere with the lawyer's professional judgment as to making referrals or as to providing substantive legal services. See Rules 2.1 and 5.4(c). Except as provided in Rule 1.5(e), a lawyer who receives referrals from a lawyer or nonlawyer professional must not pay anything solely for the referral, but the lawyer does not violate paragraph (b) of this Rule by agreeing to refer clients to the other lawyer or nonlawyer professional, so long as the reciprocal referral agreement is not exclusive and the client is informed of the referral agreement. Conflicts of interest created by such arrangements are governed by Rule 1.7. Reciprocal referral agreements should not be of indefinite duration and should be reviewed periodically to determine whether they comply with these Rules. This Rule does not restrict referrals or divisions of revenues or net income among lawyers within firms comprised of multiple entities.

Communications about Fields of Practice

[9] Paragraph (c) of this Rule permits a lawyer to communicate that the lawyer does or does not practice in particular areas of law. A lawyer is generally permitted to state that the lawyer "concentrates in" or is a "specialist," practices a "specialty," or "specializes in" particular fields based on the lawyer's experience, specialized training or education, but such communications are subject to the "false and misleading" standard applied in Rule 7.1 to communications concerning a lawyer's services.

[10] The Patent and Trademark Office has a long-established policy of designating lawyers practicing before the Office. The designation of

Admiralty practice also has a long historical tradition associated with maritime commerce and the federal courts. A lawyer's communications about these practice areas are not prohibited by this Rule.

[11] This Rule permits a lawyer to state that the lawyer is certified as a specialist in a field of law if such certification is granted by an organization approved by an appropriate authority of a state, the District of Columbia or a U.S. Territory or accredited by the American Bar Association or another organization, such as a state supreme court or a state bar association, that has been approved by the authority of the state, the District of Columbia or a U.S. Territory to accredit organizations that certify lawyers as specialists. Certification signifies that an objective entity has recognized an advanced degree of knowledge and experience in the specialty area greater than is suggested by general licensure to practice law. Certifying organizations may be expected to apply standards of experience, knowledge and proficiency to ensure that a lawyer's recognition as a specialist is meaningful and reliable. To ensure that consumers can obtain access to useful information about an organization granting certification, the name of the certifying organization must be included in any communication regarding the certification.

Required Contact Information

[12] This Rule requires that any communication about a lawyer or law firm's services include the name of, and contact information for, the lawyer or law firm. Contact information includes a website address, a telephone number, an email address or a physical office location.

RULE 7.3: SOLICITATION OF CLIENTS

(a) "Solicitation" or "solicit" denotes a communication initiated by or on behalf of a lawyer or law firm that is directed to a specific person the lawyer knows or reasonably should know needs legal services in a particular matter and that offers to provide, or reasonably can be understood as offering to provide, legal services for that matter.

(b) A lawyer shall not solicit professional employment by live person-to-person contact when a significant motive for the lawyer's doing so is the lawyer's or law firm's pecuniary gain, unless the contact is with a:

(1) lawyer;

(2) person who has a family, close personal, or prior business or professional relationship with the lawyer or law firm; or

(3) person who routinely uses for business purposes the type of legal services offered by the lawyer.

(c) A lawyer shall not solicit professional employment even when not otherwise prohibited by paragraph (b), if:

(1) the target of the solicitation has made known to the lawyer a desire not to be solicited by the lawyer; or

(2) the solicitation involves coercion, duress or harassment.

(d) This Rule does not prohibit communications authorized by law or ordered by a court or other tribunal.

(e) Notwithstanding the prohibitions in this Rule, a lawyer may participate with a prepaid or group legal service plan operated by an organization not owned or directed by the lawyer that uses live person-to-person contact to enroll members or sell subscriptions for the plan from persons who are not known to need legal services in a particular matter covered by the plan.

Comment

[1] Paragraph (b) prohibits a lawyer from soliciting professional employment by live person-to-person contact when a significant motive for the lawyer's doing so is the lawyer's or the law firm's pecuniary gain. A lawyer's communication is not a solicitation if it is directed to the general public, such as through a billboard, an Internet banner advertisement, a website or a television commercial, or if it is in response to a request for information or is automatically generated in response to electronic searches.

[2] "Live person-to-person contact" means in-person, face-to-face, live telephone and other real-time visual or auditory person-to-person communications where the person is subject to a direct personal encounter without time for reflection. Such person-to-person contact does not include chat rooms, text messages or other written communications that recipients may easily disregard. A potential for overreaching exists when a lawyer, seeking pecuniary gain, solicits a person known to be in need of legal services. This form of contact subjects a person to the private importuning of the trained advocate in a direct interpersonal encounter. The person, who may already feel overwhelmed by the circumstances giving rise to the need for legal services, may find it difficult to fully evaluate all available alternatives with reasoned judgment and appropriate selfinter-

est in the face of the lawyer's presence and insistence upon an immediate response. The situation is fraught with the possibility of undue influence, intimidation, and overreaching.

[3] The potential for overreaching inherent in live person-to-person contact justifies its prohibition, since lawyers have alternative means of conveying necessary information. In particular, communications can be mailed or transmitted by email or other electronic means that do not violate other laws. These forms of communications make it possible for the public to be informed about the need for legal services, and about the qualifications of available lawyers and law firms, without subjecting the public to live person-to-person persuasion that may overwhelm a person's judgment.

[4] The contents of live person-to-person contact can be disputed and may not be subject to thirdparty scrutiny. Consequently, they are much more likely to approach (and occasionally cross) the dividing line between accurate representations and those that are false and misleading.

[5] There is far less likelihood that a lawyer would engage in overreaching against a former client, or a person with whom the lawyer has a close personal, family, business or professional relationship, or in situations in which the lawyer is motivated by considerations other than the lawyer's pecuniary gain. Nor is there a serious potential for overreaching when the person contacted is a lawyer or is known to routinely use the type of legal services involved for business purposes. Examples include persons who routinely hire outside counsel to represent the entity; entrepreneurs who regularly engage business, employment law or intellectual property lawyers; small business proprietors who routinely hire lawyers for lease or contract issues; and other people who routinely retain lawyers for business transactions or formations. Paragraph (b) is not intended to prohibit a lawyer from participating in constitutionally protected activities of public or charitable legal-service organizations or bona fide political, social, civic, fraternal, employee or trade organizations whose purposes include providing or recommending legal services to their members or beneficiaries.

[6] A solicitation that contains false or misleading information within the meaning of Rule 7.1, that involves coercion, duress or harassment within the meaning of Rule 7.3(c)(2), or that involves contact with someone who has made known to the lawyer a desire not to be solicited by the lawyer within the meaning of Rule 7.3(c)(1) is prohibited. Live, person-to-person contact of individuals who may be especially vulnerable to co-

ercion or duress is ordinarily not appropriate, for example, the elderly, those whose first language is not English, or the disabled.

[7] This Rule does not prohibit a lawyer from contacting representatives of organizations or groups that may be interested in establishing a group or prepaid legal plan for their members, insureds, beneficiaries or other third parties for the purpose of informing such entities of the availability of and details concerning the plan or arrangement which the lawyer or lawyer's firm is willing to offer. This form of communication is not directed to people who are seeking legal services for themselves. Rather, it is usually addressed to an individual acting in a fiduciary capacity seeking a supplier of legal services for others who may, if they choose, become prospective clients of the lawyer. Under these circumstances, the activity which the lawyer undertakes in communicating with such representatives and the type of information transmitted to the individual are functionally similar to and serve the same purpose as advertising permitted under Rule 7.2.

[8] Communications authorized by law or ordered by a court or tribunal include a notice to potential members of a class in class action litigation.

[9] Paragraph (e) of this Rule permits a lawyer to participate with an organization which uses personal contact to enroll members for its group or prepaid legal service plan, provided that the personal contact is not undertaken by any lawyer who would be a provider of legal services through the plan. The organization must not be owned by or directed (whether as manager or otherwise) by any lawyer or law firm that participates in the plan. For example, paragraph (e) would not permit a lawyer to create an organization controlled directly or indirectly by the lawyer and use the organization for the person-to-person solicitation of legal employment of the lawyer through memberships in the plan or otherwise. The communication permitted by these organizations must not be directed to a person known to need legal services in a particular matter, but must be designed to inform potential plan members generally of another means of affordable legal services. Lawyers who participate in a legal service plan must reasonably assure that the plan sponsors are in compliance with Rules 7.1, 7.2 and 7.3(c).

RULE 7.4 (DELETED 2018)

RULE 7.5 (DELETED 2018)

RULE 7.6: POLITICAL CONTRIBUTIONS TO OBTAIN GOVERNMENT LEGAL ENGAGEMENTS OR APPOINTMENTS BY JUDGES

A lawyer or law firm shall not accept a government legal engagement or an appointment by a judge if the lawyer or law firm makes a political contribution or solicits political contributions for the purpose of obtaining or being considered for that type of legal engagement or appointment.

Comment

[1] Lawyers have a right to participate fully in the political process, which includes making and soliciting political contributions to candidates for judicial and other public office. Nevertheless, when lawyers make or solicit political contributions in order to obtain an engagement for legal work awarded by a government agency, or to obtain appointment by a judge, the public may legitimately question whether the lawyers engaged to perform the work are selected on the basis of competence and merit. In such a circumstance, the integrity of the profession is undermined.

[2] The term "political contribution" denotes any gift, subscription, loan, advance or deposit of anything of value made directly or indirectly to a candidate, incumbent, political party or campaign committee to influence or provide financial support for election to or retention in judicial or other government office. Political contributions in initiative and referendum elections are not included. For purposes of this Rule, the term "political contribution" does not include uncompensated services.

[3] Subject to the exceptions below, (i) the term "government legal engagement" denotes any engagement to provide legal services that a public official has the direct or indirect power to award; and (ii) the term "appointment by a judge" denotes an appointment to a position such as referee, commissioner, special master, receiver, guardian or other similar position that is made by a judge. Those terms do not, however, include (a) substantially uncompensated services; (b) engagements or appointments made on the basis of experience, expertise, professional qualifications and cost following a request for proposal or other process that is

free from influence based upon political contributions; and (c) engagements or appointments made on a rotational basis from a list compiled without regard to political contributions.

[4] The term "lawyer or law firm" includes a political action committee or other entity owned or controlled by a lawyer or law firm.

[5] Political contributions are for the purpose of obtaining or being considered for a government legal engagement or appointment by a judge if, but for the desire to be considered for the legal engagement or appointment, the lawyer or law firm would not have made or solicited the contributions. The purpose may be determined by an examination of the circumstances in which the contributions occur. For example, one or more contributions that in the aggregate are substantial in relation to other contributions by lawyers or law firms, made for the benefit of an official in a position to influence award of a government legal engagement, and followed by an award of the legal engagement to the contributing or soliciting lawyer or the lawyer's firm would support an inference that the purpose of the contributions was to obtain the engagement, absent other factors that weigh against existence of the proscribed purpose. Those factors may include among others that the contribution or solicitation was made to further a political, social, or economic interest or because of an existing personal, family, or professional relationship with a candidate.

[6] If a lawyer makes or solicits a political contribution under circumstances that constitute bribery or another crime, Rule 8.4(b) is implicated.

Definitional Cross-References

"Law firm" *See* Rule 1.0(c)

MAINTAINING THE INTEGRITY OF THE PROFESSION

RULE 8.1: BAR ADMISSION AND DISCIPLINARY MATTERS

An applicant for admission to the bar, or a lawyer in connection with a bar admission application or in connection with a disciplinary matter, shall not:

(a) knowingly make a false statement of material fact; or

(b) fail to disclose a fact necessary to correct a misapprehension known by the person to have arisen in the matter, or knowingly fail

to respond to a lawful demand for information from an admissions or disciplinary authority, except that this Rule does not require disclosure of information otherwise protected by Rule 1.6.

Comment

[1] The duty imposed by this Rule extends to persons seeking admission to the bar as well as to lawyers. Hence, if a person makes a material false statement in connection with an application for admission, it may be the basis for subsequent disciplinary action if the person is admitted, and in any event may be relevant in a subsequent admission application. The duty imposed by this Rule applies to a lawyer's own admission or discipline as well as that of others. Thus, it is a separate professional offense for a lawyer to knowingly make a misrepresentation or omission in connection with a disciplinary investigation of the lawyer's own conduct. Paragraph (b) of this Rule also requires correction of any prior misstatement in the matter that the applicant or lawyer may have made and affirmative clarification of any misunderstanding on the part of the admissions or disciplinary authority of which the person involved becomes aware.

[2] This Rule is subject to the provisions of the Fifth Amendment of the United States Constitution and corresponding provisions of state constitutions. A person relying on such a provision in response to a question, however, should do so openly and not use the right of nondisclosure as a justification for failure to comply with this Rule.

[3] A lawyer representing an applicant for admission to the bar, or representing a lawyer who is the subject of a disciplinary inquiry or proceeding, is governed by the Rules applicable to the client-lawyer relationship, including Rule 1.6 and, in some cases, Rule 3.3.

Definitional Cross-References

"Knowingly" and "Known" *See* Rule 1.0(f)

RULE 8.2: JUDICIAL AND LEGAL OFFICIALS

(a) A lawyer shall not make a statement that the lawyer knows to be false or with reckless disregard as to its truth or falsity concerning the qualifications or integrity of a judge, adjudicatory officer or public legal officer, or of a candidate for election or appointment to judicial or legal office.

(b) A lawyer who is a candidate for judicial office shall comply with the applicable provisions of the Code of Judicial Conduct.

Comment

[1] Assessments by lawyers are relied on in evaluating the professional or personal fitness of persons being considered for election or appointment to judicial office and to public legal offices, such as attorney general, prosecuting attorney and public defender. Expressing honest and candid opinions on such matters contributes to improving the administration of justice. Conversely, false statements by a lawyer can unfairly undermine public confidence in the administration of justice.

[2] When a lawyer seeks judicial office, the lawyer should be bound by applicable limitations on political activity.

[3] To maintain the fair and independent administration of justice, lawyers are encouraged to continue traditional efforts to defend judges and courts unjustly criticized.

Definitional Cross-References

"Knows" *See* Rule 1.0(f)

RULE 8.3: REPORTING PROFESSIONAL MISCONDUCT

(a) A lawyer who knows that another lawyer has committed a violation of the Rules of Professional Conduct that raises a substantial question as to that lawyer's honesty, trustworthiness or fitness as a lawyer in other respects, shall inform the appropriate professional authority.

(b) A lawyer who knows that a judge has committed a violation of applicable rules of judicial conduct that raises a substantial question as to the judge's fitness for office shall inform the appropriate authority.

(c) This Rule does not require disclosure of information otherwise protected by Rule 1.6 or information gained by a lawyer or judge while participating in an approved lawyers assistance program.

Comment

[1] Self-regulation of the legal profession requires that members of the profession initiate disciplinary investigation when they know of a violation of the Rules of Professional Conduct. Lawyers have a similar obligation with respect to judicial misconduct. An apparently isolated violation may indicate a pattern of misconduct that only a disciplinary investigation can uncover. Reporting a violation is especially important where the victim is unlikely to discover the offense.

[2] A report about misconduct is not required where it would involve violation of Rule 1.6. However, a lawyer should encourage a client to consent to disclosure where prosecution would not substantially prejudice the client's interests.

[3] If a lawyer were obliged to report every violation of the Rules, the failure to report any violation would itself be a professional offense. Such a requirement existed in many jurisdictions but proved to be unenforceable. This Rule limits the reporting obligation to those offenses that a self-regulating profession must vigorously endeavor to prevent. A measure of judgment is, therefore, required in complying with the provisions of this Rule. The term "substantial" refers to the seriousness of the possible offense and not the quantum of evidence of which the lawyer is aware. A report should be made to the bar disciplinary agency unless some other agency, such as a peer review agency, is more appropriate in the circumstances. Similar considerations apply to the reporting of judicial misconduct.

[4] The duty to report professional misconduct does not apply to a lawyer retained to represent a lawyer whose professional conduct is in question. Such a situation is governed by the Rules applicable to the client-lawyer relationship.

[5] Information about a lawyer's or judge's misconduct or fitness may be received by a lawyer in the course of that lawyer's participation in an approved lawyers or judges assistance program. In that circumstance, providing for an exception to the reporting requirements of paragraphs (a) and (b) of this Rule encourages lawyers and judges to seek treatment through such a program. Conversely, without such an exception, lawyers and judges may hesitate to seek assistance from these programs, which may then result in additional harm to their professional careers and additional injury to the welfare of clients and the public. These Rules do not otherwise address the confidentiality of information received by a lawyer or judge participating in an approved lawyers assistance program; such an obligation, however, may be imposed by the rules of the program or other law.

Definitional Cross-References

"Knows" *See* Rule 1.0(f)

"Substantial" *See* Rule 1.0(l)

RULE 8.4: MISCONDUCT

It is professional misconduct for a lawyer to:

(a) violate or attempt to violate the Rules of Professional Conduct, knowingly assist or induce another to do so, or do so through the acts of another;

(b) commit a criminal act that reflects adversely on the lawyer's honesty, trustworthiness or fitness as a lawyer in other respects;

(c) engage in conduct involving dishonesty, fraud, deceit or misrepresentation;

(d) engage in conduct that is prejudicial to the administration of justice;

(e) state or imply an ability to influence improperly a government agency or official or to achieve results by means that violate the Rules of Professional Conduct or other law;

(f) knowingly assist a judge or judicial officer in conduct that is a violation of applicable rules of judicial conduct or other law; or

(g) engage in conduct that the lawyer knows or reasonably should know is harassment or discrimination on the basis of race, sex, religion, national origin, ethnicity, disability, age, sexual orientation, gender identity, marital status or socioeconomic status in conduct related to the practice of law. This paragraph does not limit the ability of a lawyer to accept, decline or withdraw from a representation in accordance with Rule 1.16. This paragraph does not preclude legitimate advice or advocacy consistent with these Rules.

Comment

[1] Lawyers are subject to discipline when they violate or attempt to violate the Rules of Professional Conduct, knowingly assist or induce another to do so or do so through the acts of another, as when they request or instruct an agent to do so on the lawyer's behalf. Paragraph (a), however, does not prohibit a lawyer from advising a client concerning action the client is legally entitled to take.

[2] Many kinds of illegal conduct reflect adversely on fitness to practice law, such as offenses involving fraud and the offense of willful fail-

ure to file an income tax return. However, some kinds of offenses carry no such implication. Traditionally, the distinction was drawn in terms of offenses involving "moral turpitude." That concept can be construed to include offenses concerning some matters of personal morality, such as adultery and comparable offenses, that have no specific connection to fitness for the practice of law. Although a lawyer is personally answerable to the entire criminal law, a lawyer should be professionally answerable only for offenses that indicate lack of those characteristics relevant to law practice. Offenses involving violence, dishonesty, breach of trust, or serious interference with the administration of justice are in that category. A pattern of repeated offenses, even ones of minor significance when considered separately, can indicate indifference to legal obligation.

[3] Discrimination and harassment by lawyers in violation of paragraph (g) undermine confidence in the legal profession and the legal system. Such discrimination includes harmful verbal or physical conduct that manifests bias or prejudice towards others. Harassment includes sexual harassment and derogatory or demeaning verbal or physical conduct. Sexual harassment includes unwelcome sexual advances, requests for sexual favors, and other unwelcome verbal or physical conduct of a sexual nature. The substantive law of antidiscrimination and antiharassment statutes and case law may guide application of paragraph (g).

[4] Conduct related to the practice of law includes representing clients; interacting with witnesses, coworkers, court personnel, lawyers and others while engaged in the practice of law; operating or managing a law firm or law practice; and participating in bar association, business or social activities in connection with the practice of law. Lawyers may engage in conduct undertaken to promote diversity and inclusion without violating this Rule by, for example, implementing initiatives aimed at recruiting, hiring, retaining and advancing diverse employees or sponsoring diverse law student organizations.

[5] A trial judge's finding that peremptory challenges were exercised on a discriminatory basis does not alone establish a violation of paragraph (g). A lawyer does not violate paragraph (g) by limiting the scope or subject matter of the lawyer's practice or by limiting the lawyer's practice to members of underserved populations in accordance with these Rules and other law. A lawyer may charge and collect reasonable fees and expenses for a representation. Rule 1.5(a). Lawyers also should be mindful of their professional obligations under Rule 6.1 to provide legal services to those who are unable to pay, and their obligation under Rule

6.2 not to avoid appointments from a tribunal except for good cause. See Rule 6.2(a), (b) and (c). A lawyer's representation of a client does not constitute an endorsement by the lawyer of the client's views or activities. See Rule 1.2(b).

[6] A lawyer may refuse to comply with an obligation imposed by law upon a good faith belief that no valid obligation exists. The provisions of Rule 1.2(d) concerning a good faith challenge to the validity, scope, meaning or application of the law apply to challenges of legal regulation of the practice of law.

[7] Lawyers holding public office assume legal responsibilities going beyond those of other citizens. A lawyer's abuse of public office can suggest an inability to fulfill the professional role of lawyers. The same is true of abuse of positions of private trust such as trustee, executor, administrator, guardian, agent and officer, director or manager of a corporation or other organization.

Definitional Cross-References

"Fraud" *See* Rule 1.0(d)
"Knowingly and knows" *See* Rule 1.0(f)
"Reasonably should know" *See* Rule 1.0(j)

RULE 8.5: DISCIPLINARY AUTHORITY; CHOICE OF LAW

(a) Disciplinary Authority. A lawyer admitted to practice in this jurisdiction is subject to the disciplinary authority of this jurisdiction, regardless of where the lawyer's conduct occurs. A lawyer not admitted in this jurisdiction is also subject to the disciplinary authority of this jurisdiction if the lawyer provides or offers to provide any legal services in this jurisdiction. A lawyer may be subject to the disciplinary authority of both this jurisdiction and another jurisdiction for the same conduct.

(b) Choice of Law. In any exercise of the disciplinary authority of this jurisdiction, the rules of professional conduct to be applied shall be as follows:

(1) for conduct in connection with a matter pending before a tribunal, the rules of the jurisdiction in which the tribunal sits, unless the rules of the tribunal provide otherwise; and

(2) for any other conduct, the rules of the jurisdiction in which the lawyer's conduct occurred, or, if the predominant

effect of the conduct is in a different jurisdiction, the rules of that jurisdiction shall be applied to the conduct. <u>A lawyer shall not be subject to discipline if the lawyer's conduct conforms to the rules of a jurisdiction in which the lawyer reasonably believes the predominant effect of the lawyer's conduct will occur.</u>

Comment

Disciplinary Authority

[1] It is longstanding law that the conduct of a lawyer admitted to practice in this jurisdiction is subject to the disciplinary authority of this jurisdiction. Extension of the disciplinary authority of this jurisdiction to other lawyers who provide or offer to provide legal services in this jurisdiction is for the protection of the citizens of this jurisdiction. Reciprocal enforcement of a jurisdiction's disciplinary findings and sanctions will further advance the purposes of this Rule. See, Rules 6 and 22, ABA *Model Rules for Lawyer Disciplinary Enforcement*. A lawyer who is subject to the disciplinary authority of this jurisdiction under Rule 8.5(a) appoints an official to be designated by this court to receive service of process in this jurisdiction. The fact that the lawyer is subject to the disciplinary authority of this jurisdiction may be a factor in determining whether personal jurisdiction may be asserted over the lawyer for civil matters.

Choice of Law

[2] A lawyer may be potentially subject to more than one set of rules of professional conduct which impose different obligations. The lawyer may be licensed to practice in more than one jurisdiction with differing rules, or may be admitted to practice before a particular court with rules that differ from those of the jurisdiction or jurisdictions in which the lawyer is licensed to practice. Additionally, the lawyer's conduct may involve significant contacts with more than one jurisdiction.

[3] Paragraph (b) seeks to resolve such potential conflicts. Its premise is that minimizing conflicts between rules, as well as uncertainty about which rules are applicable, is in the best interest of both clients and the profession (as well as the bodies having authority to regulate the profession). Accordingly, it takes the approach of (i) providing that any particular conduct of a lawyer shall be subject to only one set of rules of professional conduct, (ii) making the determination of which set of rules applies to particular conduct as straightforward as possible, consistent with recognition of appropriate regulatory interests of relevant jurisdictions, and

(iii) providing protection from discipline for lawyers who act reasonably in the face of uncertainty.

[4] Paragraph (b)(1) provides that as to a lawyer's conduct relating to a proceeding pending before a tribunal, the lawyer shall be subject only to the rules of professional conduct of that tribunal. As to all other conduct, including conduct in anticipation of a proceeding not yet pending before a tribunal, paragraph (b)(2) provides that a lawyer shall be subject to the rules of the jurisdiction in which the lawyer's conduct occurred, or, if the predominant effect of the conduct is in another jurisdiction, the rules of that jurisdiction shall be applied to the conduct. In the case of conduct in anticipation of a proceeding that is likely to be before a tribunal, the predominant effect of such conduct could be where the conduct occurred, where the tribunal sits or in another jurisdiction.

[5] When a lawyer's conduct involves significant contacts with more than one jurisdiction, it may not be clear whether the predominant effect of the lawyer's conduct will occur in a jurisdiction other than the one in which the conduct occurred. So long as the lawyer's conduct conforms to the rules of a jurisdiction in which the lawyer reasonably believes the predominant effect will occur, the lawyer shall not be subject to discipline under this Rule. With respect to conflicts of interest, in determining a lawyer's reasonable belief under paragraph (b)(2), a written agreement between the lawyer and client that reasonably specifies a particular jurisdiction as within the scope of that paragraph may be considered if the agreement was obtained with the client's informed consent confirmed in the agreement.

[6] If two admitting jurisdictions were to proceed against a lawyer for the same conduct, they should, applying this rule, identify the same governing ethics rules. They should take all appropriate steps to see that they do apply the same rule to the same conduct, and in all events should avoid proceeding against a lawyer on the basis of two inconsistent rules.

[7] The choice of law provision applies to lawyers engaged in transnational practice, unless international law, treaties or other agreements between competent regulatory authorities in the affected jurisdictions provide otherwise.

Definitional Cross-References

"Reasonably believes" *See* Rule 1.0(i)

"Tribunal" *See* Rule 1.0(m)

SUBJECT GUIDE

N

S

CORRELATION TABLES

TABLES A AND B: RELATED SECTIONS IN THE ABA MODEL CODE OF PROFESSIONAL RESPONSIBILITY

TABLE A*

ABA MODEL RULES	ABA MODEL CODE
Competence	
Rule 1.1	EC 1-1, EC 1-2, EC 6-1, EC 6-2, EC 6-3, EC 6-4, EC 6-5, DR 6-101(A)

Scope of Representation and Allocation of Authority between Client and Lawyer

Rule 1.2(a)	EC 5-12, EC 7-7, EC 7-8, DR 7-101(A)(1)
Rule 1.2(b)	EC 7-17
Rule 1.2(c)	EC 7-8, EC 7-9, DR 7-101(B)(1)
Rule 1.2(d)	EC 7-1, EC 7-2, EC 7-5, EC 7-22, DR 7-102(A)(6), (7), & (8), DR 7-106

Diligence	
Rule 1.3	EC 2-31, EC 6-4, EC 7-1, EC 7-38, DR 6-101(A)(3), DR 7-101(A)(1) & (3)

Communication	
Rule 1.4(a)	EC 7-8, EC 9-2, DR 2-110(C)(1)(c), DR 6-101(A)(3), DR 9-102(B)(1)
Rule 1.4(b)	EC 7-8

Fees	
Rule 1.5(a)	EC 2-16, EC 2-17, EC 2-18, DR 2-106(A) & (B)
Rule 1.5(b)	EC 2-19
Rule 1.5(c)	EC 2-20, EC 5-7
Rule 1.5(d)	EC 2-20, DR 2-106(C)
Rule 1.5(e)	EC 2-22, DR 2-107(A)

---

* Table A provides cross-references to related provisions, but only in the sense that the provisions consider substantially similar subject matter or reflect similar concerns. A cross-reference does not indicate that a provision of the ABA Model Code of Professional Responsibility has been incorporated by the provision of a Model Rule. The Canons of the Code are not cross-referenced.

ABA **MODEL RULES**	ABA **MODEL CODE**

Confidentiality of Information

Rule 1.6(a)	EC 4-1, EC 4-2, EC 4-3, EC 4-4, DR 4-101(A), (B), & (C)
Rule 1.6(b)(1)	EC 4-2, DR 4-101(C)(3), DR 7-102(B)
Rule 1.6(b)(2)	DR 4-101(C)(3)
Rule 1.6(b)(3)	None
Rule 1.6(b)(4)	None
Rule 1.6(b)(5)	DR 4-101(C)(4)
Rule 1.6(b)(6)	DR 4-101(C)(2)
Rule 1.6(b)(7)	None
Rule 1.6(c)	None

Conflict of Interest: Current Clients

Rule 1.7(a)	EC 2-21, EC 5-1, EC 5-2, EC 5-3, EC 5-9, EC 5-11, EC 5-13, EC 5-14, EC 5-15, EC 5-17, EC 5-21, EC 5-22, EC 5-23, DR 5-101(A) & (B), DR 5-102, DR 5-104(A), DR 5-105(A) & (B), DR 5-107(A) & (B)
Rule 1.7(b)	EC 2-21, EC 5-15, EC 5-16, EC 5-17, EC 5-19, EC 5-23, DR 5-101(A) & (B), DR 5-102, DR 5-104(A), DR 5-105(C), DR 5-107(A)

Conflict of Interest: Current Clients: Specific Rules

Rule 1.8(a)	EC 5-3, EC 5-5, DR 5-104(A)
Rule 1.8(b)	EC 4-5, DR 4-101(B)
Rule 1.8(c)	EC 5-1, EC 5-2, EC 5-5, EC 5-6
Rule 1.8(d)	EC 5-1, EC 5-3, EC 5-4, DR 5-104(B)
Rule 1.8(e)	EC 5-1, EC 5-3, EC 5-7, EC 5-8, DR 5-103(B)
Rule 1.8(f)	EC 2-21, EC 5-1, EC 5-22, EC 5-23, DR 5-107(A) & (B)
Rule 1.8(g)	EC 5-1, DR 5-106(A)
Rule 1.8(h)	EC 6-6, DR 6-102(A)
Rule 1.8(i)	EC 5-1, EC 5-7, DR 5-101(A), DR 5-103(A)
Rule 1.8(j)	None
Rule 1.8(k)	None

Duties to Former Clients

Rule 1.9(a)	DR 5-105(C)
Rule 1.9(b)	EC 4-5, EC 4-6
Rule 1.9(c)	None

Imputation of Conflicts of Interest: General Rule

Rule 1.10(a)	EC 4-5, DR 5-105(D)
Rule 1.10(b)	EC 4-5, DR 5-105(D)

ABA MODEL RULES	ABA MODEL CODE
Rule 1.10(c)	DR 5-105(A)
Rule 1.10(d)	None

Special Conflicts of Interest for Former and
Current Government Officers and Employees

Rule 1.11(a)	EC 9-3, DR 9-101(B)
Rule 1.11(b)	None
Rule 1.11(c)	None
Rule 1.11(d)	EC 8-8
Rule 1.11(e)	None

Former Judge, Arbitrator, Mediator or Other Third-Party Neutral

Rule 1.12(a)&(b)	EC 5-20, EC 9-3, DR 9-101(A) & (B)
Rule 1.12(c)	DR 5-105(D)
Rule 1.12(d)	None

Organization as Client

Rule 1.13(a)	EC 5-18, EC 5-24
Rule 1.13(b)	EC 5-18, EC 5-24, DR 5-107(B)
Rule 1.13(c)	EC 5-18, EC 5-24, DR 5-105(D), DR 5-107(B)
Rule 1.13(d)	None
Rule 1.13(e)	None
Rule 1.13(f)	EC 5-16
Rule 1.13(g)	EC 4-4, EC 5-16, DR 5-105(B) & (C)

Client with Diminished Capacity

Rule 1.14(a)	EC 7-11, EC 7-12
Rule 1.14(b)	EC 7-12
Rule 1.14(c)	None

Safekeeping Property

Rule 1.15	EC 5-7, EC 9-5, EC 9-7, DR 5-103(A)(1), DR 9-102

Declining or Terminating Representation

Rule 1.16(a)(1)	EC 2-30, EC 2-31, EC 2-32, DR 2-103(E), DR 2-104(A), DR 2-109(A), DR 2-110(B)(1) & (2)
Rule 1.16(a)(2)	EC 1-6, EC 2-30, EC 2-31, EC 2-32, DR 2-110(B)(3), DR 2-110(C)(4)
Rule 1.16(a)(3)	EC 2-31, EC 2-32, DR 2-110(B)(4)
Rule 1.16(b)(1)	EC 2-32, DR 2-110(A)(2), DR 2-110(C)(5)
Rule 1.16(b)(2)	EC 2-31, EC 2-32, DR 2-110(C)(1)(b) & (c), DR 2-110(C)(2)

ABA MODEL RULES	ABA MODEL CODE
Rule 1.16(b)(3)	EC 2-31, EC 2-32, DR 2-110(C)(2)
Rule 1.16(b)(4)	EC 2-30, EC 2-31, EC 2-32, DR 2-110(C)(1)(d)
Rule 1.16(b)(5)	EC 2-31, EC 2-32, DR 2-110(C)(1)(f)(i)(j)
Rule 1.16(b)(6)	EC 2-32, DR 2-110(C)(1)(d) & (e)
Rule 1.16(b)(7)	EC 2-32, DR 2-110(C)(6)
Rule 1.16(c)	EC 2-32, DR 2-110(A)(1)
Rule 1.16(d)	EC 2-32, DR 2-110(A)(2) & (3)

Sale of Law Practice

Rule 1.17	None

Duties to Prospective Client

Rule 1.18	EC 4-1

Advisor

Rule 2.1	EC 5-11, EC 7-3, EC 7-8, DR 5-107(B)

Evaluation for Use by Third Persons

Rule 2.3	None

Lawyer Serving as Third-Party Neutral

Rule 2.4	EC 5-20

Meritorious Claims and Contentions

Rule 3.1	EC 7-1, EC 7-4, EC 7-5, EC 7-14, EC 7-25, DR 5-102(A)(5), DR 2-109(A)(B)(1), DR 7-102(A)(1) & (2)

Expediting Litigation

Rule 3.2	EC 7-20, DR 1-102(A)(5), DR 7-101(A)(1) & (2)

Candor toward the Tribunal

Rule 3.3(a)(1)	EC 7-4, EC 7-26, EC 7-32, EC 8-5, DR 1-102(A)(4) & (5), DR 7-102(A)(4) & (5)
Rule 3.3(a)(2)	EC 7-23, DR 1-102(A)(5), DR 7-106(B)(1)
Rule 3.3(a)(3)	EC 7-5, EC 7-6, EC 7-26, EC 8-5, DR 1-102(A)(4) & (5), DR 7-102(A)(4), (6), & (7), DR 7-102(B)(1) & (2)
Rule 3.3(b)	EC 7-5, EC 7-26, EC 7-27, EC 7-32, EC 8-5, DR 1-102(A)(4) & (5), DR 7-102(A)(4), (6), & (7), DR 7-102(B)(1) & (2), DR 7-108(G), DR 7-109(A) & (B)
Rule 3.3(c)	EC 8-5, DR 7-102(B)
Rule 3.3(d)	EC 7-24, EC 7-27

ABA MODEL RULES	ABA MODEL CODE

Fairness to Opposing Party and Counsel

Rule 3.4(a)	EC 7-6, EC 7-27, DR 1-102(A)(4) & (5), DR 7-106(C)(7), DR 7-109(A) & (B)
Rule 3.4(b)	EC 7-6, EC 7-28, DR 1-102(A)(4), (5), & (6), DR 7-102(A)(6), DR 7-109(C)
Rule 3.4(c)	EC 7-22, EC 7-25, EC 7-38, DR 1-102(A)(5), DR 7-106(A), DR 7-106(C)(5) & (7)
Rule 3.4(d)	DR 1-102(A)(5), DR 7-106(A), DR 7-106(C)(7)
Rule 3.4(e)	EC 7-24, EC 7-25, DR 1-102(A)(5), DR 7-106(C)(1), (2), (3), & (4)
Rule 3.4(f)	EC 7-27, DR 1-102(A)(5), DR 7-104(A)(2), DR 7-109(B)

Impartiality and Decorum of the Tribunal

Rule 3.5(a)	EC 7-20, EC 7-29, EC 7-31, EC 7-32, EC 7-34, DR 7-106, DR 7-108, DR 7-109, DR 7-110, DR 8-101(A)
Rule 3.5(b)	EC 7-35, DR 7-108, DR 7-110(A) & (B)
Rule 3.5(c)	EC 7-29, EC 7-30, EC 7-31, EC 7-32, DR 7-108
Rule 3.5(d)	EC 7-20, EC 7-25, EC 7-36, EC 7-37, DR 7-101(A)(1), DR 7-106(C)(6)

Trial Publicity

Rule 3.6	EC 7-25, EC 7-33, DR 7-107

Lawyer as Witness

Rule 3.7(a)	EC 5-9, EC 5-10, DR 5-101(B)(1) & (2), DR 5-102
Rule 3.7(b)	EC 5-9, DR 5-101(B), DR 5-102

Special Responsibilities of a Prosecutor

Rule 3.8(a)	EC 7-11, EC 7-13, EC 7-14, DR 7-103(A)
Rule 3.8(b)	EC 7-11, EC 7-13
Rule 3.8(c)	EC 7-11, EC 7-13, EC 7-18
Rule 3.8(d)	EC 7-11, EC 7-13, DR 7-103(B)
Rule 3.8(e)	None
Rule 3.8(f)	EC 7-14
Rule 3.8(g)	None
Rule 3.8(h)	None

Advocate in Nonadjudicative Proceedings

Rule 3.9	EC 7-11, EC 7-15, EC 7-16, EC 8-4, EC 8-5, DR 7-106(B)(2), DR 9-101(C)

ABA MODEL RULES	ABA MODEL CODE

Truthfulness in Statements to Others

Rule 4.1	EC 7-5, DR 7-102(A)(3), (4), (5), & (7), DR 7-102(B)

Communication with Person Represented by Counsel

Rule 4.2	EC 2-30, EC 7-18, DR 7-104(A)(1)

Dealing with Unrepresented Person

Rule 4.3	EC 2-3, EC 7-18, DR 7-104(A)(2)

Respect for Rights of Third Persons

Rule 4.4(a)	EC 7-10, EC 7-14, EC 7-21, EC 7-25, EC 7-29, EC 7-30, EC 7-37, DR 2-110(B)(1), DR 7-101(A)(1), DR 7-102(A)(1), DR 7-106(C)(2), DR 7-107(D), (E), & (F), DR 7-108(D), (E), & (F)
Rule 4.4(b)	None

Responsibilities of Partners, Managers, and Supervisory Lawyers

Rule 5.1(a) & (b)	EC 4-5, DR 4-101(D), DR 7-107(J)
Rule 5.1(c)	DR 1-102(A)(2), DR 1-103(A), DR 7-108(E)

Responsibilities of a Subordinate Lawyer

Rule 5.2	None

Responsibilities regarding Nonlawyer Assistance

Rule 5.3(a)	EC 3-6, EC 4-2, EC 4-5, EC 7-28, DR 4-101(D), DR 7-107(J)
Rule 5.3(b)	DR 1-102(A)(2), DR 7-107(J), DR 7-108(B), DR 7-108(E)
Rule 5.3(c)	None

Professional Independence of a Lawyer

Rule 5.4(a)	EC 2-33, EC 3-8, EC 5-24, DR 2-103(D)(1), DR 2-103(D)(2), DR 2-103(D)(4)(a), (d), (e), & (f), DR 3-102(A), DR 5-107(C)(3)
Rule 5.4(b)	EC 2-33, EC 3-8, DR 3-103(A)
Rule 5.4(c)	EC 2-33, EC 5-22, EC 5-23, DR 2-103(C), DR 5-107(B)
Rule 5.4(d)	EC 2-33, EC 3-8, DR 5-107(C)

Unauthorized Practice of Law; Multijurisdictional Practice of Law

Rule 5.5(a)	DR 3-101(A) & (B)
Rule 5.5(b)	None

ABA MODEL RULES	ABA MODEL CODE
Rule 5.5(c)	None
Rule 5.5(d)	None
Rule 5.5(e)	None

Restrictions on Right to Practice

Rule 5.6	DR 2-108

Responsibilities regarding Law-Related Services

Rule 5.7	None

Voluntary Pro Bono Publico Service

Rule 6.1	EC 1-2, EC 1-4, EC 2-1, EC 2-2, EC 2-16, EC 2-24, EC 2-25, EC 6-2, EC 8-1, EC 8-2, EC 8-3, EC 8-7, EC 8-9

Accepting Appointments

Rule 6.2 (a)	EC 2-1, EC 2-25, EC 2-27, EC 2-28, EC 2-29, EC 8-3
Rule 6.2(b)	EC 2-16, EC 2-25, EC 2-29, EC 2-30
Rule 6.2(c)	EC 2-25, EC 2-27, EC 2-29, EC 2-30

Membership in Legal Services Organization

Rule 6.3	EC 2-33, DR 5-101(A)

Law Reform Activities Affecting Client Interests

Rule 6.4	EC 2-33, DR 5-101(A), DR 8-101

Nonprofit and Court-Annexed Limited Legal Services Programs

Rule 6.5	None

Communications Concerning a Lawyer's Services

Rule 7.1	EC 2-8, EC 2-9, EC 2-10, DR 2-101(A), (B), (C), (E), (F), & (G), DR 2-102(E)

Advertising

Rule 7.2(a)	EC 2-1, EC 2-2, EC 2-6, EC 2-7, EC 2-8, EC 2-15, DR 2-101(B) & (H), DR 2-102(A) & (B), DR 2-103(B), DR 2-104(A)(4) & (5)
Rule 7.2(b)	EC 2-8, EC 2-15, DR 2-101(I), DR 2-103(B), (C), & (D)
Rule 7.2(c)	EC 2-8, EC 2-14, DR 2-105(A)(2) & (3)
Rule 7.2(d)	None

ABA MODEL RULES	ABA MODEL CODE

Solicitation of Clients

Rule 7.3	EC 2-3, EC 2-4, EC 5-6, DR 2-103(A), DR 2-103(C)(1), DR 2-103(D)(4)(b) & (c), DR 2-104(A)(1), (2), (3), & (5)

Communication of Fields of Practice and Specialization

Rule 7.2(c)	EC 2-1, EC 2-7, EC 2-8, EC 2-14, DR 2-101(B)(2), DR 2-102(A)(3), DR 2-102(E), DR 2-105(A)

Firm Names and Letterheads

Rule 7.1 (Comment)	EC 2-11, EC 2-12, EC 2-13, DR 2-102(A)(4), DR 2-102(B), (C), (D), & (E), DR 2-105

Political Contributions to Obtain Government
Legal Engagements or Appointments by Judges

Rule 7.6	None

Bar Admission and Disciplinary Matters

Rule 8.1(a)	EC 1-1, EC 1-2, EC 1-3, DR 1-101(A) & (B)
Rule 8.1(b)	DR 1-102(A)(5), DR 1-103(B)

Judicial and Legal Officials

Rule 8.2(a)	EC 8-6, DR 8-102
Rule 8.2(b)	DR 8-103

Reporting Professional Misconduct

Rule 8.3	EC 1-3, DR 1-103(A)

Misconduct

Rule 8.4(a)	EC 1-5, EC 1-6, EC 9-6, DR 1-102(A)(1) & (2), DR 2-103(E), DR 7-102(A) & (B)
Rule 8.4(b)	EC 1-5, DR 1-102(A)(3) & (6), DR 7-102(A)(8), DR 8-101(A)(3)
Rule 8.4(c)	EC 1-5, EC 9-4, DR 1-102(A)(4), DR 8-101(A)(3)
Rule 8.4(d)	EC 3-9, EC 8-3, DR 1-102(A)(5), DR 3-101(B)
Rule 8.4(e)	EC 1-5, EC 9-2, EC 9-4, EC 9-6, DR 9-101(C)
Rule 8.4(f)	EC 1-5, EC 7-34, EC 9-1, DR 1-102(A)(3), (4), (5), & (6), DR 7-110(A), DR 8-101(A)(2)
Rule 8.4(g)	None

Disciplinary Authority; Choice of Law

Rule 8.5	None

TABLE B*

ABA MODEL CODE	ABA MODEL RULES

Canon 1: Integrity of Profession

EC 1-1	Rules 1.1, 8.1(a)
EC 1-2	Rules 1.1, 6.1, 8.1(a)
EC 1-3	Rules 8.1(a), 8.3
EC 1-4	Rule 6.1
EC 1-5	Rule 8.4(a), (b), (c), (e), & (f)
EC 1-6	Rules 1.16(a)(2), 8.4(a)
DR 1-101	Rule 8.1(a)
DR 1-102(A)(1)	Rule 8.4(a)
DR 1-102(A)(2)	Rules 5.1(c), 5.3(b), 8.4(a)
DR 1-102(A)(3)	Rule 8.4(b) & (f)
DR 1-102(A)(4)	Rules 3.3(a)(1), (3), & (b), 3.4(a) & (b), 8.4(c) & (f)
DR 1-102(A)(5)	Rules 3.1, 3.2, 3.3(a) & (b), 3.4, 8.4(d) & (f)
DR 1-102(A)(6)	Rules 3.4(b), 8.4(b) & (f)
DR 1-103(A)	Rules 5.1(c), 8.3
DR 1-103(B)	Rule 8.1(b)

Canon 2: Making Counsel Available

EC 2-1	Rules 6.1, 6.2(a), 7.2(a), 7.2(c)
EC 2-2	Rules 6.1, 7.2(a)
EC 2-3	Rules 4.3, 7.3
EC 2-4	Rule 7.3
EC 2-5	None
EC 2-6	Rule 7.2(a)
EC 2-7	Rules 7.2(a), 7.2(c)
EC 2-8	Rules 7.1, 7.2(a) & (b), 7.4
EC 2-9	Rule 7.1
EC 2-10	Rule 7.1
EC 2-11	Rule 7.1 (Comment)
EC 2-12	Rule 7.1 (Comment)
EC 2-13	Rule 7.1 (Comment)
EC 2-14	Rule 7.2(c)
EC 2-15	Rule 7.2(a) & (b)
EC 2-16	Rules 1.5(a), 6.1, 6.2(b)

** Table B provides cross-references to related provisions, but only in the sense that the provisions consider substantially similar subject matter or reflect similar concerns. A cross-reference does not indicate that a provision of the ABA Model Code of Professional Responsibility has been incorporated by the provision of a Model Rule. The Canons of the Code are not cross-referenced.

ABA MODEL CODE	ABA MODEL RULES
EC 2-17	Rule 1.5(a)
EC 2-18	Rule 1.5(a)
EC 2-19	Rule 1.5(b)
EC 2-20	Rule 1.5(c) & (d)
EC 2-21	Rules 1.7(a), 1.8(f)
EC 2-22	Rule 1.5(e)
EC 2-23	None
EC 2-24	Rule 6.1
EC 2-25	Rules 6.1, 6.2
EC 2-26	None
EC 2-27	Rule 6.2(a) & (c)
EC 2-28	Rule 6.2(a)
EC 2-29	Rule 6.2
EC 2-30	Rules 1.16(a)(1) & (2), 1.16(b)(4), 4.2, 6.2(b) & (c)
EC 2-31	Rules 1.3, 1.16(a) & (b)
EC 2-32	Rule 1.16
EC 2-33	Rules 5.4, 6.3, 6.4
DR 2-101(A)	Rule 7.1
DR 2-101(B)	Rules 7.1, 7.2(a)
DR 2-101(C)	Rule 7.1
DR 2-101(D)	None
DR 2-101(E)	Rule 7.1
DR 2-101(F)	Rule 7.1
DR 2-101(G)	Rule 7.1
DR 2-101(H)	Rule 7.2
DR 2-101(I)	Rule 7.2(b)
DR 2-102(A)	Rules 7.2(a), 7.2(c)
DR 2-102(B)	Rules 7.2(a), 7.1 (Comment)
DR 2-102(C)	Rule 7.1 (Comment)
DR 2-102(D)	Rule 7.1 (Comment)
DR 2-102(E)	Rules 7.1, 7.2(c)
DR 2-103(A)	Rule 7.3
DR 2-103(B)	Rule 7.2(a) & (b)
DR 2-103(C)	Rules 5.4(a), 7.2(b), 7.3
DR 2-103(D)	Rules 1.16(a)(1), 5.4(a), 7.2(b), 7.3
DR 2-103(E)	Rules 1.16(a), 7.2(a), 7.3
DR 2-104	Rules 1.16(a), 7.3
DR 2-105	Rule 7.2(c)
DR 2-106(A)	Rule 1.5(a)

ABA MODEL CODE	ABA MODEL RULES
DR 2-106(B)	Rule 1.5(a)
DR 2-106(C)	Rule 1.5(d)
DR 2-107(A)	Rule 1.5(e)
DR 2-107(B)	Rule 5.4(a)(1)
DR 2-108(A)	Rule 5.6
DR 2-108(B)	Rule 5.6
DR 2-109(A)	Rules 1.16(a)(1), 3.1
DR 2-110(A)	Rule 1.16(b)(1), (c), & (d)
DR 2-110(B)	Rules 1.16(a), 3.1, 4.4(a)
DR 2-110(C)	Rules 1.4(a)(5), 1.16(a) & (b)

Canon 3: Unauthorized Practice

EC 3-1	None
EC 3-2	None
EC 3-3	Rule 8.4(e)
EC 3-4	None
EC 3-5	None
EC 3-6	Rule 5.3(a)
EC 3-7	None
EC 3-8	Rule 5.4(a), (b), & (d)
EC 3-9	Rule 8.4(d)
DR 3-101(A)	Rule 5.5(a)
DR 3-101(B)	Rules 5.5(a), 8.4(d)
DR 3-102	Rule 5.4(a)
DR 3-103	Rule 5.4(b)

Canon 4: Confidences and Secrets

EC 4-1	Rules 1.6(a), 1.18
EC 4-2	Rules 1.6(a) & (b)(1), 5.3(a)
EC 4-3	Rule 1.6(a)
EC 4-4	Rules 1.6(a), 1.13(g)
EC 4-5	Rules 1.8(b), 1.9(b), 1.10(a) & (b), 5.1(a) & (c), 5.3(a)
EC 4-6	Rule 1.9(b)
DR 4-101(A)	Rule 1.6(a)
DR 4-101(B)	Rules 1.6(a), 1.8(b), 1.9(b)
DR 4-101(C)	Rule 1.6(a) & (b)
DR 4-101(D)	Rules 5.1(a) & (b), 5.3(a) & (b)

ABA MODEL CODE	ABA MODEL RULES
Canon 5: Independent Judgment	
EC 5-1	Rules 1.7(a), 1.8(c), (d), (e), (f), (g), & (i)
EC 5-2	Rules 1.7(a), 1.8(c)
EC 5-3	Rules 1.7, 1.8(a), (d), & (e)
EC 5-4	Rule 1.8(d)
EC 5-5	Rule 1.8(a) & (c)
EC 5-6	Rules 1.8(c), 7.3
EC 5-7	Rules 1.5(c), 1.8(e) & (i), 1.15
EC 5-8	Rule 1.8(e)
EC 5-9	Rules 1.7(a), 3.7
EC 5-10	Rule 3.7(a)
EC 5-11	Rules 1.7(a), 2.1
EC 5-12	Rule 1.2(a)
EC 5-13	Rule 1.7(a)
EC 5-14	Rule 1.7(a)
EC 5-15	Rule 1.7
EC 5-16	Rules 1.7(b), 1.13(f) & (g)
EC 5-17	Rule 1.7
EC 5-18	Rule 1.13(a), (b), & (c)
EC 5-19	Rule 1.7(b)
EC 5-20	Rules 1.12(a) & (b), 2.4
EC 5-21	Rule 1.7
EC 5-22	Rule 1.7
EC 5-23	Rules 1.7(a), 1.8(f), 5.4(c)
EC 5-24	Rules 1.13(a), (b), & (c), 5.4(a)
DR 5-101(A)	Rules 1.7, 1.8(i), 6.3, 6.4
DR 5-101(B)	Rules 1.7, 3.7
DR 5-102(A)	Rules 1.7, 3.7
DR 5-102(B)	Rules 1.7(b), 3.7
DR 5-103(A)	Rules 1.8(i), 1.15
DR 5-103(B)	Rule 1.8(e)
DR 5-104(A)	Rules 1.7, 1.8(a)
DR 5-104(B)	Rule 1.8(d)
DR 5-105(A)	Rules 1.7, 1.10(c)
DR 5-105(B)	Rules 1.7, 1.13(g)
DR 5-105(C)	Rules 1.7(b), 1.13(g), 1.9(a)
DR 5-105(D)	Rules 1.10(a), 1.12(c), 1.13(c)
DR 5-106	Rule 1.8(g)
DR 5-107(A)	Rules 1.7(b), 1.8(f)

ABA MODEL CODE	ABA MODEL RULES
DR 5-107(B)	Rules 1.7(a), 1.8(f), 1.13(b) & (c), 2.1, 5.4(c)
DR 5-107(C)	Rule 5.4(a) & (d)

Canon 6: Competence

EC 6-1	Rule 1.1
EC 6-2	Rules 1.1, 5.1(a) & (b), 6.1
EC 6-3	Rule 1.1
EC 6-4	Rules 1.1, 1.3
EC 6-5	Rule 1.1
EC 6-6	Rule 1.8(h)
DR 6-101	Rules 1.1, 1.3, 1.4(a)
DR 6-102	Rule 1.8(h)

Canon 7: Zeal Within the Law

EC 7-1	Rules 1.2(d), 1.3, 3.1
EC 7-2	Rule 1.2(d)
EC 7-3	Rule 2.1
EC 7-4	Rules 3.1, 3.3(a)(1)
EC 7-5	Rules 1.2(d), 3.1, 3.3(a)(3) & (b), 4.1
EC 7-6	Rule 3.4(a) & (b)
EC 7-7	Rule 1.2(a)
EC 7-8	Rules 1.2(a) & (c), 1.4, 2.1
EC 7-9	Rule 1.2(c)
EC 7-10	Rule 4.4(a)
EC 7-11	Rules 1.14(a), 3.8(a), (b), (c), & (d), 3.9
EC 7-12	Rule 1.14
EC 7-13	Rule 3.8
EC 7-14	Rules 3.1, 3.8(a) & (f), 4.4(a)
EC 7-15	Rule 3.9
EC 7-16	Rule 3.9
EC 7-17	Rule 1.2(b)
EC 7-18	Rules 3.8(c), 4.2, 4.3
EC 7-19	None
EC 7-20	Rules 3.2, 3.5(a) & (d)
EC 7-21	Rule 4.4(a)
EC 7-22	Rules 1.2(d), 3.4(c)
EC 7-23	Rule 3.3(a)(2)
EC 7-24	Rules 3.3(d), 3.4(e)
EC 7-25	Rules 3.1, 3.4(c) & (e), 3.5(d), 3.6, 4.4(a)
EC 7-26	Rule 3.3(a)(3) & (b)

ABA MODEL CODE	ABA MODEL RULES
EC 7-27	Rules 3.3(b) & (d), 3.4(a) & (f)
EC 7-28	Rules 3.4(b), 5.3(a)
EC 7-29	Rules 3.5(a) & (c), 4.4(a)
EC 7-30	Rules 3.5(c), 4.4(a)
EC 7-31	Rule 3.5(a) & (c)
EC 7-32	Rules 3.3(a)(1) & (b), 3.5(a) & (c)
EC 7-33	Rule 3.6
EC 7-34	Rules 3.5(a), 8.4(f)
EC 7-35	Rule 3.5(b)
EC 7-36	Rule 3.5(d)
EC 7-37	Rules 3.5(d), 4.4(a)
EC 7-38	Rules 1.3, 3.4(c)
EC 7-39	None
DR 7-101(A)	Rules 1.2(a), 1.3, 3.2, 3.5(d), 4.4(a)
DR 7-101(B)	Rules 1.2(b), 1.16(b)
DR 7-102(A)(1)	Rules 3.1, 4.4(a)
DR 7-102(A)(2)	Rule 3.1
DR 7-102(A)(3)	Rules 3.3(a)(1), (a)(3), & (b), 4.1
DR 7-102(A)(4)	Rules 3.3(a) & (b), 4.1
DR 7-102(A)(5)	Rules 3.3(a)(1), 4.1
DR 7-102(A)(6)	Rules 1.2(d), 3.3(b), 3.4(b)
DR 7-102(A)(7)	Rules 1.2(d), 3.3(a)(3) & (b), 4.1
DR 7-102(A)(8)	Rules 1.2(d), 8.4(a) & (b)
DR 7-102(B)	Rules 1.6(b)(1), 3.3(b) & (c), 4.1
DR 7-103(A)	Rule 3.8(a)
DR 7-103(B)	Rule 3.8(d)
DR 7-104	Rules 3.4(f), 4.2, 4.3
DR 7-105	None
DR 7-106(A)	Rules 1.2(d), 3.4(c) & (d), 3.5(a)
DR 7-106(B)	Rules 3.3(a)(2), 3.9
DR 7-106(C)	Rules 3.4(a), (c), (d), & (e), 3.5(d), 4.4(a)
DR 7-107(A)–(I)	Rule 3.6
DR 7-107(D)–(F)	Rule 4.4(a)
DR 7-107(J)	Rules 5.1(a) & (b), 5.3(a) & (b)
DR 7-108(A)	Rule 3.5(a), (b), & (c)
DR 7-108(B)	Rules 3.5(a), (b), & (c), 5.3(b)
DR 7-108(C)	Rule 3.5(a), (b), & (c)
DR 7-108(D)	Rules 3.5(c)(3), 4.4(a)
DR 7-108(E)	Rules 3.5(a), (b), & (c), 4.4(a), 5.1(c), 5.3(b)

ABA MODEL CODE	ABA MODEL RULES
DR 7-108(F)	Rules 3.5(a), (b), & (c), 4.4(a)
DR 7-108(G)	Rules 3.3(b), 3.5(c)
DR 7-109(A)	Rules 3.3(a)(1), (a)(3), & (b), 3.4(a)
DR 7-109(B)	Rules 3.3(b), 3.4(a) & (f)
DR 7-109(C)	Rule 3.4(b)
DR 7-110(A)	Rules 3.5(a), 8.4(f)
DR 7-110(B)	Rule 3.5(a) & (b)

Canon 8: Improving Legal System

EC 8-1	Rule 6.1
EC 8-2	Rule 6.1
EC 8-3	Rules 6.1, 6.2(a), 8.4(d)
EC 8-4	Rule 3.9
EC 8-5	Rules 3.3(a)(1), (a)(3), & (b), 3.9
EC 8-6	Rule 8.2(a)
EC 8-7	Rule 6.1
EC 8-8	Rule 1.11(d)
EC 8-9	Rule 6.1
DR 8-101	Rules 3.5, 8.4(b), (c), & (f)
DR 8-102	Rule 8.2(a)
DR 8-103	Rule 8.2(b)

Canon 9: Appearance of Impropriety

EC 9-1	Rule 8.4(f)
EC 9-2	Rules 1.4(a), 8.4(e)
EC 9-3	Rules 1.11(a), 1.12(a) & (b)
EC 9-4	Rule 8.4(c) & (e)
EC 9-5	Rule 1.15
EC 9-6	Preamble, Rule 8.4(e)
EC 9-7	Rule 1.15
DR 9-101(A)	Rule 1.12(a) & (b)
DR 9-101(B)	Rules 1.11(a), 1.12(a) & (b)
DR 9-101(C)	Rules 1.4(a)(5), 3.9, 8.4(e)
DR 9-102	Rules 1.4(a), 1.15

ABA STANDING COMMITTEE ON ETHICS AND PROFESSIONAL RESPONSIBILITY

COMPOSITION AND JURISDICTION

The Standing Committee on Ethics and Professional Responsibility, which consists of ten members, may:

(1) by the concurrence of a majority of its members, express its opinion on proper professional or judicial conduct, either on its own initiative or when requested to do so by a member of the bar or the judiciary;

(2) periodically publish its issued opinions to the profession in summary or complete form and, on request, provide copies of opinions to members of the bar, the judiciary and the public;

(3) provide under its supervision informal responses to ethics inquiries the answers to which are substantially governed by applicable ethical codes and existing written opinions;

(4) on request, advise or otherwise assist professional organizations and courts in their activities relating to the development, modification and interpretation of statements of the ethical standards of the profession such as the Model Rules of Professional Conduct, the predecessor Model Code of Professional Responsibility and the Model Code of Judicial Conduct;

(5) recommend amendments to or clarifications of the Model Rules of Professional Conduct or the Model Code of Judicial Conduct; and

(6) adopt rules relating to the procedures to be used in issuing opinions, effective when approved by the Board of Governors.

[The above Composition and Jurisdiction statement is found at §31.7 of the Bylaws of the Association. The Rules of Procedure are not incorporated into the Bylaws.]

RULES OF PROCEDURE

1. The Committee may express its opinion on questions of proper professional and judicial conduct. The Model Rules of Professional Conduct and the Model Code of Judicial Conduct, as they may be amended or superseded, contain the standards to be applied. For as long as a significant number of jurisdictions continue to base their professional standards on the predecessor Model Code of Professional Responsibility, the Committee will continue to refer also to the Model Code in its opinions.

2. The Committee may issue an opinion on its own initiative or upon a request from a member of the bar or the judiciary or from a professional organization or a court.

3. The Committee may issue opinions of two kinds: Formal Opinions and Informal Opinions. Formal Opinions are those upon subjects the Committee determines to be of widespread interest or unusual importance. Other opinions are Informal Opinions. The Committee will assign to each opinion a non-duplicative identifying number, with distinction between Formal Opinions and Informal Opinions.

4. The Committee will not usually issue an opinion on a question that is known to be pending before a court in a proceeding in which the requestor is involved. The Committee's published opinions will not identify the person who was the requestor or whose conduct is the subject of the opinion. The Committee will not issue an opinion on a question of law.

5. The Committee may invite or accept written information relevant to a particular opinion from a person or persons interested in such an opinion before the Committee begins its work on an opinion. Ordinarily, the Committee will not invite anyone to make an oral presentation or argument in support of that position.

6. When a Committee or staff member receives an inquiry about the status of a draft opinion from anyone outside the Committee, the member may inform the inquirer that the Committee is considering the question. Draft opinions may, in appropriate circumstances, be shown to other interested ABA Committees and entities. Committee and staff members shall not, absent unusual circumstances, discuss the substance of pending opinions with the public, but may mention topics related to pending opinions in a general fashion.

7. Before issuing an opinion with respect to judicial conduct the Committee will submit the proposed opinion to the Judges' Advisory Committee and consider any objection or comment from the Judges' Advisory

Committee and any member of it. The Committee may assume that the Judges' Advisory Committee and its members have no objection or comment if none is received by the Committee within 30 days after the submission.

8. If the Committee decides not to issue a requested opinion the requestor will be promptly notified.

9. The Committee will issue an opinion only with the concurrence of six members in a vote taken at a meeting or in a telephone conference call. When a Committee member votes against a position declaring a Committee policy, that vote may be recorded in the minutes, which may include the name of the dissenting Committee member. The minutes shall not reflect the names of Committee members voting for or against any non-Committee policy question except that a member's vote shall be recorded and identified at the member's request. When drafting an opinion, policy statement or other document to be publicly disseminated, the Committee shall make every effort to reach a consensus. When, after a full examination of the issue and an exchange of views, the Committee cannot reach a consensus, a dissenting opinion may be appropriate to express the views of a Committee member or members. A member may place a statement of dissent in the Committee file or request that the dissent be published with the opinion.

10. The Chair may assign to one or more members the responsibility of preparing a proposed opinion for consideration by the Committee. The Committee will issue a requested opinion as promptly as feasible.

11. A Formal Opinion overrules an earlier Formal Opinion or Informal Opinion to the extent of conflict. An Informal Opinion overrules an earlier Informal Opinion to the extent of conflict but does not overrule an earlier Formal Opinion.

12. Opinions of the Committee issued before the effective dates of the Model Rules of Professional Conduct, the predecessor Model Code of Professional Responsibility and the Model Code of Judicial Conduct continue in effect to the extent not inconsistent with those standards and not overruled or limited by later opinions.

13. The Committee will make opinions and/or summaries of opinions available for publication in the American Bar Association journal. The Committee will cause Formal Opinions and Informal Opinions to be published in looseleaf form.

14. The Committee may through its staff arrange to provide informal responses to ethics inquiries the answers to which are substantially gov-

erned by applicable ethical codes and opinions of this Committee or other ethics committees. The staff will maintain a log of such inquiries that will periodically be reviewed by the Committee.

15. Information contained in Committee files relating to requests for opinions that would disclose the identity of the inquirer or the person whose conduct is the subject of the opinion will not voluntarily be disclosed by the Association without the consent of the affected persons.

ABA SPECIAL COMMITTEE ON IMPLEMENTATION OF THE MODEL RULES OF PROFESSIONAL CONDUCT (1983–1987)

MICHAEL FRANCK, *Chair*
Lansing, Michigan

EDWARD L. BENOIT
Twin Falls, Idaho

W. STELL HUIE
Atlanta, Georgia

ROGER BROSNAHAN
Minneapolis, Minnesota

JAMES T. JENNINGS
Roswell, New Mexico

WAYNE A. BUDD
Boston, Massachusetts

CAROLYN B. LAMM
Washington, D.C.

RICHARD M. COLEMAN
Los Angeles, California

LLOYD LOCHRIDGE
Austin, Texas

JOHN C. ELAM
Columbus, Ohio

LEON SILVERMAN
New York, New York

JOSEPH E. GALLAGHER
Scranton, Pennsylvania

E.C. WARD
Natchez, Mississippi

ROBERT O. HETLAGE
St. Louis, Missouri

BEN J. WEAVER
Indianapolis, Indiana

AMENDMENTS TO THE MODEL RULES OF PROFESSIONAL CONDUCT (BY RULE)

Preamble
Amended 2002 per Midyear Meeting Report 401.

Scope
Amended 2002 per Midyear Meeting Report 401.

Rule 1.0
Amended 2002 per Midyear Meeting Report 401.
Amended 2009 per Midyear Meeting Report 109.
Amended 2012 per Annual Meeting Report 105A.

Rule 1.1
Amended 2002 per Midyear Meeting Report 401.
Amended 2012 per Annual Meeting Reports 105A and C.

Rule 1.2
Amended 2002 per Midyear Meeting Report 401.

Rule 1.3
Amended 2002 per Midyear Meeting Report 401.

Rule 1.4
Amended 2002 per Midyear Meeting Report 401.
Amended 2012 per Annual Meeting Report 105A.

Rule 1.5
Amended 2002 per Midyear Meeting Report 401.

Rule 1.6
Amended 2002 per Midyear Meeting Report 401.
Amended 2003 per Annual Meeting Report 119A.
Amended 2012 per Annual Meeting Reports 105A and F.

Rule 1.7
Amended 1987 per Midyear Meeting Report 121.
Amended 2002 per Midyear Meeting Report 401.

Rule 1.8
Amended 1987 per Midyear Meeting Report 121.
Amended 2002 per Midyear Meeting Report 401.
Amended 2020 per Annual Meeting Report 107.

Rule 1.9
Amended 1987 per Midyear Meeting Report 121.
Amended 1989 per Midyear Meeting Report 120A.
Amended 2002 per Midyear Meeting Report 401.

Rule 1.10
Amended 1989 per Midyear Meeting Report 120A.
Amended 2002 per Midyear Meeting Report 401.
Amended 2009 per Midyear Meeting Report 109.
Amended 2009 per Annual Meeting Report 109.

Rule 1.11
Amended 1987 per Midyear Meeting Report 121.
Amended 2002 per Midyear Meeting Report 401.

Rule 1.12
Amended 1987 per Midyear Meeting Report 121.
Amended 2002 per Midyear Meeting Report 401.

Rule 1.13
Amended 2002 per Midyear Meeting Report 401.
Amended 2003 per Annual Meeting Report 119B.

Rule 1.14
Amended 1997 per Midyear Meeting Report 113.
Amended 2002 per Midyear Meeting Report 401.

Rule 1.15
Amended 2002 per Midyear Meeting Report 401.

Rule 1.16
Amended 2002 per Midyear Meeting Report 401.

Rule 1.17
Added 1990 per Midyear Meeting Report 8A.
Amended 2002 per Midyear Meeting Report 401.
Amended 2012 per Annual Meeting Report 105F.

Rule 1.18
Added 2002 per Midyear Meeting Report 401.
Amended 2012 per Annual Meeting Report 105B.

Rule 2.1
Amended 2002 per Midyear Meeting Report 401.

Rule 2.2
Deleted 2002 per Midyear Meeting Report 401.

Rule 2.3
Amended 2002 per Midyear Meeting Report 401.

Rule 2.4
Added 2002 per Midyear Meeting Report 401.

Rule 3.1
Amended 2002 per Midyear Meeting Report 401.

Rule 3.2
Amended 2002 per Midyear Meeting Report 401.

Rule 3.3
Amended 2002 per Midyear Meeting Report 401.

Rule 3.4
Amended 2002 per Midyear Meeting Report 401.

Rule 3.5
Amended 2002 per Midyear Meeting Report 401.

Rule 3.6
Amended 1994 per Annual Meeting Report 100.
Amended 2002 per Midyear Meeting Report 401.

Rule 3.7
Amended 2002 per Midyear Meeting Report 401.

Rule 3.8
Amended 1990 per Midyear Meeting Report 118.
Amended 1994 per Annual Meeting Report 100.
Amended 1995 per Annual Meeting Report 101.
Amended 2002 per Midyear Meeting Report 401.
Amended 2008 per Midyear Meeting Report 105B.

Rule 3.9
Amended 2002 per Midyear Meeting Report 401.

Rule 4.1
Amended 2002 per Midyear Meeting Report 401.

Rule 4.2
Amended 1995 per Annual Meeting Report 100.
Amended 2002 per Midyear Meeting Report 401.

Rule 4.3
Amended 2002 per Midyear Meeting Report 401.

Rule 4.4
Amended 2002 per Midyear Meeting Report 401.
Amended 2012 per Annual Meeting Report 105A.

Rule 5.1
Amended 2002 per Midyear Meeting Report 401.

Rule 5.3
Amended 2002 per Midyear Meeting Report 401.
Amended 2012 per Annual Meeting Report 105C.

Rule 5.4
Amended 1990 per Midyear Meeting Report 8A.
Amended 2002 per Midyear Meeting Report 401.

Rule 5.5
Amended 2002 per Annual Meeting Report 201B.
Amended 2007 per Midyear Meeting Report 104.
Amended 2012 per Annual Meeting Reports 105 B and C.
Amended 2013 per Midyear Meeting Report 107A.
Amended 2016 per Midyear Meeting Report 103.

Rule 5.6
Amended 1990 per Midyear Meeting Report 8A.
Amended 2002 per Midyear Meeting Report 401.

Rule 5.7
Added 1994 per Midyear Meeting Report 113.
Amended 2002 per Midyear Meeting Report 401.

Rule 6.1
Amended 1993 per Midyear Meeting Report 8A.
Amended 2002 per Midyear Meeting Report 401.

Rule 6.3
Amended 1987 per Midyear Meeting Report 121.

Rule 6.5
Added 2002 per Midyear Meeting Report 401.

Rule 7.1
Amended 2002 per Midyear Meeting Report 401.
Amended 2012 per Annual Meeting Report 105B.
Amended 2018 per Annual Meeting Report 101.

Rule 7.2
Amended 1989 per Midyear Meeting Report 120B.
Amended 1990 per Midyear Meeting Report 8A.
Amended 2002 per Midyear Meeting Report 401.
Amended 2002 per Annual Meeting Report 114.
Amended 2012 per Annual Meeting Report 105B.
Amended 2018 per Annual Meeting Report 101.

Rule 7.3
Amended 1989 per Midyear Meeting Reports 115 and 120B.
Amended 2002 per Midyear Meeting Report 401.
Amended 2012 per Annual Meeting Report 105B.
Amended 2018 per Annual Meeting Report 101.

Rule 7.4
Deleted 2018 per Annual Meeting Report 101.

Rule 7.5
Deleted 2018 per Annual Meeting Report 101.

Rule 7.6
Added 2000 per Midyear Meeting Report 110.

Rule 8.1
Amended 2002 per Midyear Meeting Report 401.

Rule 8.3
Amended 1991 per Midyear Meeting Report 108C.
Amended 2002 per Midyear Meeting Report 401.

Rule 8.4
Amended 1998 per Annual Meeting Report 117.
Amended 2002 per Midyear Meeting Report 401.
Amended 2016 per Annual Meeting Report 109.

Rule 8.5
Amended 1993 per Annual Meeting Report 114.
Amended 2002 per Annual Meeting Report 201C.
Amended 2013 per Midyear Meeting Report 107D.

AMENDMENTS TO THE MODEL RULES OF PROFESSIONAL CONDUCT (BY DATE)

1987 Midyear Meeting
Rules 1.7, 1.8, 1.9, 1.11, 1.12 and 6.3

1989 Midyear Meeting
Rules 1.9, 1.10, 7.2, 7.3 and 7.4

1990 Midyear Meeting
Rules 1.17, 3.8, 5.4, 5.6 and 7.2

1991 Midyear Meeting
Rule 8.3

1992 Annual Meeting
Rule 7.4

1993 Midyear Meeting
Rule 6.1

1993 Annual Meeting
Rule 8.5

1994 Midyear Meeting
Rule 5.7

1994 Annual Meeting
Rules 3.6, 3.8 and 7.4

1995 Annual Meeting
Rules 3.8 and 4.2

1997 Midyear Meeting
Rule 1.14

1998 Annual Meeting
Rule 8.4

2000 Midyear Meeting
Rule 7.6

APPENDIX E: AMENDMENTS TO THE MODEL RULES

2002 Midyear Meeting
Preamble, Scope, Rules 1.0, 1.1, 1.2, 1.3, 1.4, 1.5, 1.6, 1.7, 1.8, 1.9, 1.10, 1.11, 1.12, 1.13, 1.14, 1.15, 1.16, 1.17, 1.18, 2.1, 2.2, 2.3, 2.4, 3.1, 3.2, 3.3, 3.4, 3.5, 3.6, 3.7, 3.8, 3.9, 4.1, 4.2, 4.3, 4.4, 5.1, 5.3. 5.4, 5.6, 5.7, 6.1, 6.5, 7.1, 7.2, 7.3, 7.4, 7.5, 8.1, 8.3 and 8.4

2002 Annual Meeting
Rules 5.5, 7.2, 7.5 and 8.5

2003 Annual Meeting
Rules 1.6 and 1.13

2007 Midyear Meeting
Rule 5.5

2008 Midyear Meeting
Rule 3.8

2009 Midyear Meeting
Rules 1.0 and 1.10

2009 Annual Meeting
Rule 1.10

2012 Annual Meeting
Rules 1.0, 1.1, 1.4, 1.6, 1.17, 1.18, 4.4, 5.3, 5.5, 7.1, 7.2 and 7.3

2013 Midyear Meeting
Rules 5.5 and 8.5

2016 Midyear Meeting
Rule 5.5

2016 Annual Meeting
Rule 8.4

2018 Annual Meeting
Rules 7.1, 7.2, 7.3, 7.4, and 7.5

2020 Annual Meeting
Rule 1.8

FORMAL ETHICS OPINIONS

AMERICAN BAR ASSOCIATION
STANDING COMMITTEE ON ETHICS AND PROFESSIONAL RESPONSIBILITY

Formal Opinion 490   March 24, 2020

Ethical Obligations of Judges in Collecting Legal Financial Obligations and Other Debts

Summary

This opinion addresses the ethical requirement of judges under the Model Code of Judicial Conduct, Rules 1.1 and 2.6, to undertake a meaningful inquiry into a litigant's ability to pay court fines, fees, restitution, other charges, bail, or civil debt before using incarceration as punishment for failure to pay, as inducement to pay or appear, or as a method of purging a financial obligation whenever state or federal law so provides. Meaningful inquiry is also required by Rules 1.2, 2.2, and 2.5 as a fundamental element of procedural justice necessary to maintain the integrity, impartiality, and fairness of the administration of justice and the public's faith in it. According to the same Rules, a judge may not set, impose, or collect legal financial obligations under circumstances that give the judge an improper incentive either to multiply legal financial obligations or to fail to inquire into a litigant's ability to pay. The opinion also discusses innovative guidance on best practices for making ability to pay inquiries, including model bench cards, methods of notice, and techniques for efficiently eliciting relevant financial information from litigants.[1]

I. Introduction

Local, municipal, state, and federal trial court judges do essential work administering justice day in and day out with the utmost integrity, fairness, and dedication. It has long been said that "[f]our things belong to a judge; to hear courteously; to answer wisely; to consider soberly and to decide impartially."[2] Every day, in courtrooms all around the country, trial judges display these and other qualities essential to the administration of justice.

---

1. This opinion is based on the Model Code of Judicial Conduct as amended by the House of Delegates through February 2019. Individual jurisdictions' court rules, laws, opinions, and rules of judicial conduct control. The Committee expresses no opinion on the applicable law or constitutional interpretation in a particular jurisdiction.

2. Leon R. Yankwich, *The Art of Being A Judge*, 105 U. PENN. L. REV. 374, 385 (1957) (quoting Socrates).

They do so both on and off the bench and despite managing heavy dockets, shrinking budgets, and other constraints.

This opinion is addressed to one important area of procedural justice in which the high standard consistently set by so many judges has not been met in some jurisdictions. There is evidence that judges in some jurisdictions have repeatedly failed to inquire into litigants' ability to pay financial obligations prior to incarceration for nonpayment. Inquiry into a litigant's ability to pay before resorting to incarceration—either as punishment for failure to pay, as a means of purging or inducing payment of a financial obligation (whether civil or criminal), or as leverage to demand bail in amounts unconnected to public safety—is a core ethical obligation of the judiciary. Failure to inquire in the circumstances described in this opinion can violate not only settled law requiring such inquiry, and thus violate Rules 1.1 and 2.6 of the Model Code of Judicial Conduct, (MCJC) but also Rules 1.2, 2.2, and 2.5. The duty to inquire is foundational not just to the constitutional rights of litigants but to the integrity of the judicial process and public confidence in it.[3]

In Section II this opinion describes specific evidence of failures to make legally required inquiries into litigants' ability to pay, as well as the background budget constraints, expansion of court fines, fees, and other legal financial obligations, and the standards relating to judicial discipline. In Section III the opinion analyzes the standards for discipline and presents innovative guidance on best practices for making ability-to-pay inquiries developed by judges and flagship organizations such as the National Center for State Courts and the Conference of State Court Administrators.

II. Background

The U.S. Department of Justice investigation of Ferguson, Missouri, found in 2015 that the city's "municipal court does not act as a neutral arbiter of the law or a check on unlawful police conduct. Instead, the court primarily uses its judicial authority as the means to compel the payment of fines and fees that advance the City's financial interests."[4] The Report concluded that the court's method of collecting legal financial obligations violated the Due Process and the Equal Protection Clauses of the Fourteenth Amendment,

---

3. *See* ABA Standards for Criminal Justice Special Functions of the Trial Judge 6-1.1(a) (Am. Bar Ass'n 3d ed. 2000) ("The trial judge has the responsibility for safeguarding both the rights of the accused and the interests of the public in the administration of criminal justice."); *see also* Model Code of Judicial Conduct pmbl.¶ 1 (Am. Bar Ass'n 2011) ("Inherent in all the Rules contained in this Code are the precepts that judges, individually and collectively, must respect and honor the judicial office as a public trust and strive to maintain and enhance confidence in the legal system.").

4. Civil Rights Div., U.S. Dep't of Justice, Investigation of the Ferguson Police Department 3 (2015).

"impose[d] unnecessary harm, overwhelmingly on African-American individuals, and [ran] counter to public safety."[5]

Ferguson is a particularly egregious example, unrepresentative of the integrity and care regularly shown by fair and dedicated judges in local, municipal, state, and federal courts. But there is evidence that problems with debt collection procedures extend to other jurisdictions. The problems include:

- Threatening to incarcerate or incarcerating individuals for failure to pay legal financial obligations without inquiry into their ability to pay;[6]
- Ordering individuals to pay legal financial obligations with disability benefits, welfare benefits, or money borrowed from family members as a condition of avoiding incarceration and without inquiring into ability to pay;[7]
- Making payment of legal financial obligations a condition of probation and subsequently failing to determine ability to pay before revoking probation for failure to pay either the underlying legal fi-

---

5. *Id.* at 3, 57-58; *see also* Fant v. City of Ferguson, 107 F. Supp. 3d 1016, 1030–32 (E.D. Mo. 2015), *amended by* Fant v. City of Ferguson, No. 4:15-CV-00253-AGF, 2015 WL 4232917, at *3–4 (E.D. Mo. July 13, 2015); ALICIA BANNON ET AL., BRENNAN CTR. FOR JUSTICE, CRIMINAL JUSTICE DEBT: A BARRIER TO REENTRY 4 (2010) (describing racially disproportionate effects of fines, fees, and other charges).

6. *See* West v. City of Santa Fe, No. 3:16-CV-00309, 2018 WL 5276264, at *1 (S.D. Tex. Sept. 19, 2018) (denying defendants' motion to dismiss complaint alleging *Bearden* violations), adopting report and recommendation of Magistrate Judge, West v. City of Santa Fe, 2018 WL 4047115, at *10 (S.D. Tex. Aug. 16, 2018)]; Brown v. Lexington Cty., No. 3:17-cv-1426-MBS, 2018 WL 1556189, at *2–3,*14–15 (D.S.C. Mar. 29, 2018) (plaintiffs alleged incarceration for failing to pay legal financial obligations occurred without inquiry into ability to pay; denying defendants' motion for summary judgment on ground that there are genuine issues of material fact on judicial immunity claims); Cain v. City of New Orleans, 281 F. Supp. 3d 624, 632–33, 647–52 (E.D. La. 2017) ("There is no evidence that the Judges now consider, or have ever considered, ability to pay before imprisoning indigent criminal defendants for failure to pay" unless "the issue is brought to their attention."), *aff'd sub nom.*, Cain v. White, 937 F.3d 446, 448 (5th Cir. 2019); Doe v. Angelina Cty., 733 F. Supp 245, 253–54 (E.D. Tex. 1990); *see also* Campbell Robertson, *Missouri City to Pay $4.7 Million to Settle Suit Over Jail Practices*, N.Y. TIMES (July 15, 2016), https://www.nytimes.com/2016/07/16/us/missouri-city-to-pay-4-7-million-to-settle-suit-over-jailing-practices.html (describing settlement of suit against City of Jennings for practices similar to those in Ferguson); *id.* ("Many of the 90 cities around [St. Louis County] were generating substantial proportions of their revenues by aggressively charging fines and fees for violations as minor as broken taillights. Warrants were issued for those who could not or did not pay, and jail time for unpaid traffic tickets was routine."); *id.* (noting the suit's allegation that many of those jailed were "poor and black").

7. *See* Joseph Shapiro, *Supreme Court Ruling Not Enough to Prevent Debtors Prisons*, NPR (May 21, 2014, 5:01 AM), https://www.npr.org/2014/05/21/313118629/supreme-court-ruling-not-enough-to-prevent-debtors-prisons (noting that even when inquiry into ability to pay occurs it is frequently informal and subjective).

nancial obligations or new obligations associated with the costs of administering probation;[8]

- Linking warrants, bonds, and arrest for accused persons, probationers, and others not already serving a prison sentence, in ways that either result in incarceration without inquiry into ability to pay the bond, or result in payment under threat of incarceration;[9]

- Using the contempt power to collect unpaid civil debt by jailing or threatening to jail individuals without inquiry into their ability to pay, or using the contempt power to punish failure to appear at judgment debtor examinations by incarceration where bail on the warrant for contempt of court is set without inquiry into ability to pay and bail is automatically applied to satisfy the civil judgment.[10]

- Maintaining an improper pecuniary interest in the setting, imposition, or enforcement of legal financial obligations, or outsourcing these functions to private entities that have an improper pecuniary interest.[11]

---

8. *See Cain*, 281 F. Supp. 3d at 629–31; HUMAN RIGHTS WATCH, PROFITING FROM PROBATION: AMERICA'S "OFFENDER-FUNDED" PROBATION INDUSTRY 1–5 (2014) [hereinafter PROFITING FROM PROBATION].

9. *See* O'Donnell v. Harris Cty., 892 F.3d 147, 152 (5th Cir. 2018) (affirming preliminary injunction granted by the district court on claim that county bail policies violated due process); McNeil v. Cmty. Prob. Services, LLC, No. 1:18-cv-00033, 2019 WL 633012, at *2-7, 16 (M.D. Tenn. Feb. 14, 2019) (granting preliminary injunction against issuing arrest warrants with secured bail amounts set without inquiry into ability of misdemeanor probationers' ability to pay as a condition of avoiding jail pending probation revocation hearing), *aff'd*, 945 F.3d 991 (6th Cir. 2019); Rodriguez v. Providence Cmty. Corrs., Inc., 155 F. Supp. 3d 758 (M.D. Tenn. 2015) (granting preliminary injunction against issuing arrest warrants with secured bail amounts absent inquiry into a probationers' ability to pay when only alleged probation violation was nonpayment); Jones v. City of Clanton, No. 2:15cv34-MHT, 2015 WL 5387219, at *2 (M.D. Ala. Sept. 14, 2015) (same); *cf.* Walker v. City of Calhoun, 901 F.3d 1245, 1266 (11th Cir. 2018) (concluding that a forty-eight-hour hearing requirement for bail hearings for accused persons is presumptively constitutional).

10. *See* Turner v. Rogers, 564 U.S. 431 (2011) (vacating judgment of civil contempt and remanding for an ability to pay inquiry); *see also* ACLU, A POUND OF FLESH: THE CRIMINALIZATION OF PRIVATE DEBT 6 (2018) (noting that forty-four states allow judges to issue arrest warrants for contempt for failure to appear at post-judgment proceedings or failing to otherwise provide financial information); *id.* ("Judges sometimes set bail at the exact amount of the judgment. And the bail money is often turned over to the debt collector or creditor as payment against the judgment.").

11. *See* Caliste v. Cantrell, 937 F.3d 525, 530–31 (5th Cir. 2019) (setting bond without inquiry into ability to pay where court generates significant revenue from bonds for salaries of court staff violates due process); *Cain*, 281 F. Supp. 3d at 655–56 (concluding that an unconstitutional conflict of interest arises when a court's "funding structure puts the Judges in the difficult position of not having sufficient funds to staff their offices unless they impose and collect sufficient fines and fees from a largely indigent population of criminal defendants"); *id.*("[T]he Judges' practice of failing to inquire into ability to pay is itself indicative of their conflict of interest."); PROFITING FROM PROBATION, *supra* note 8, at 1-7.

In addition to the cases and materials cited in notes 6–10 and this note other cases have resulted in judgments, injunctive relief, or settlement agreements requiring compli-

The Committee recognizes that courts across the country have faced *severe* budget crises over the last few decades as a result of recessions and cuts in traditional sources of state and local funding.[12] To address these significant deficits, many courts have increased legal fines, fees, and other charges.[13] Over the same period, misdemeanor enforcement grew and a movement to require criminal defendants to pay restitution and other costs of administering the criminal justice system expanded (including costs related to appointment of counsel, bail, probation, and jury trial).[14] Furthermore, in some jurisdictions, elements of the administration of criminal justice have been outsourced to private contractors whose compensation may be linked to fines, fees, and other charges assessed against defendants. Overall, the effect is that a person can incur substantial legal financial obligations for conviction of a petty or juvenile offense or even a non-criminal code violation.[15]

---

ance with *Bearden. See* Edwards v. Cofield, No. 3:17-CV-321-WKW, 2017 WL 2255775 (M.D. Ala. May 18, 2017); Bell v. City of Jackson, No. 3:15-cv-00732-TSL-RHW, 2016 WL 6405833 (S.D. Miss. June 20, 2016); Kennedy v. City of Biloxi, No. 1:15cv348-HSO-JCG, 2016 WL 4425862 (S.D. Miss. Mar. 7, 2016); Snow v. Lambert, No. 15-567-SDD-RLB, 2015 WL 5071981 (M.D. La. Aug. 27, 2015); Pierce v. City of Velda City, No. 4:15-cv-570-HEA, 2015 WL 10013006 (E.D. Mo. June 3, 2015); Powell v. City of St. Ann, No. 4:15-cv-00840 (E.D. Mo. May 27, 2015); Edwards v. Red Hills Cmty. Prob., No. 1:15-cv-00067-LJA (M.D. Ga. Apr. 10, 2015); Jenkins v. City of Jennings, No. 4:15-cv-00252 (E.D. Mo. Feb. 8, 2015); Burks v. Scott Cty., No 3:14-cv-00745-HTW-LRA (S.D. Miss. Sept. 23, 2014); Fuentes v. Benton Cty., No. 15-2-02976-1 (Sup. Ct. Wash. Yakima Cty. Oct. 6, 2015).

12. John T. Matthias & Laura Klaversma, Nat'l Ctr. For State Courts, Current Practices in Collecting Fines and Fees in State Courts: A Handbook of Collection Issues and Solutions 3, 8 (2d ed. 2009) [hereinafter NCSC Handbook] (describing fiscal crises).

13. *See* Alexes Harris et al., *Drawing Blood from Stones: Legal Debt and Social Inequality in the Contemporary United States*, 115 Am. J. Soc. 1753, 1769 fig. 1 (2010); Bannon et al., *supra* note 5, at 7.

14. In the area of bail, for instance, see Press Release, U.S. Dep't of Justice, Fact Sheet on White House and Justice Dep't Convening — A Cycle of Incarceration: Prison, Debt and Bail Practices (Dec. 3, 2015) (The "rising use of bail payments has contributed to a 60 percent increase in the number of un-convicted inmates in jails between 1996 and 2014 . . . . [I]n New York City in 2010, nearly 80 percent of arrestees failed to make bail at arraignment for bail amounts less than $500."). On changes in misdemeanor enforcement, see Alexandra Natapoff, Punishment Without Crime: How Our Massive Misdemeanor System Traps the Innocent and Makes America More Unequal (2018).

15. *See* State v. Blazina, 344 P.3d 680, 683–84 (Wash. 2015) (en banc) (summarizing data); Claire Greenberg et al., *The Growing and Broad Nature of Legal Financial Obligations: Evidence from Alabama Court Records*, 48 Conn. L. Rev. 1079 (2016); ACLU of Wash. & Columbia Legal Services, Modern-Day Debtors' Prisons: The Ways Court-Imposed Debts Punish People for Being Poor (2014); Juleyka Lantigua-Williams, *How Prison Debt Ensnares Offenders*, The Atlantic (June 2, 2016), https://www.theatlantic.com/politics/archive/2016/06/how-prison-debt-ensnares-offenders/484826/; Monica Llorente, *Criminalizing Poverty Through Fines, Fees, and Costs*, Am. Bar Ass'n (Oct. 3, 2016), https://www.americanbar.org/groups/litigation/committees/childrens-rights/articles/2016/criminalizing-poverty-fines-fees-costs/ (describing a range of legal financial obligations associated with juvenile cases and adult criminal cases; reporting that Illinois charges a fifteen

Enforcement policies for legal financial obligations have shifted as well. The traditional view that judicial independence and impartiality demand restraint in the collection of legal financial obligations[16] gave way over the last three decades to more vigorous collection policies adopted on the view that prompt collection is necessary to "encourage[] personal responsibility by those assessed," to "maintain [the] credibility" and "authority" of courts in the eyes of the public and litigants, and to "increase[] revenue" in the face of "[t]ight operating budgets."[17] These are important state interests as long as the person who faces legal financial obligations is not indigent or otherwise unable to pay. In endorsing this shift in enforcement policy a decade ago, the National Center for State Courts ("NCSC") Handbook admonished that courts should still "pay attention to defendants' perceptions of procedural fairness . . . ."[18] The Handbook added that serving warrants and incarcerating people is not only "expensive ... [t]he defendant often fails once again to appear or pay, and the process starts over . . . ."[19] Incarceration for failure to pay legal financial obligations should therefore be "a last resort."[20]

III. Analysis

The key MCJC Rules that apply to procedural justice are Rule 1.1 ("a judge shall comply with the law); Rule 1.2 ("a judge shall act at all times in a manner that promotes public confidence in the independence, integrity and impartiality of the judiciary"); Rule 2.2 ("a judge shall uphold the law and shall perform all duties of judicial office fairly and impartially"); Rule 2.5 ("a judge shall perform judicial and administrative duties, competently and diligently" and "shall cooperate with other judges and court officials in the administration of court business"); and Rule 2.6 (a judge shall "accord every person who has a legal interest in a proceeding, or that person's lawyer, the right to be heard according to law"). These rules make clear that "[c]onduct that compromises or appears to compromise the independence, integrity, and impartiality of a judge undermines public confidence in the judiciary."[21]

---

percent penalty on unpaid balances and a thirty percent collection fee); Joseph Shapiro, *As Court Fees Rise, the Poor Are Paying the Price*, NPR (May 19, 2014, 4:02 PM), https://www.npr.org/2014/05/19/312158516/increasing-court-fees-punish-the-poor (noting an increase in court fees over time in forty-eight states); *State-by-State Court Fees*, NPR (May 19, 2014, 4:02 PM), https://www.npr.org/2014/05/19/312455680/state-by-state-court-fees (survey of the types of legal financial obligations imposed in each state); NATAPOFF, *supra* note 14, at 125–26.

16. *See* NCSC HANDBOOK, *supra* note 12, at 20.

17. *Id.* at 3, 6, 12.

18. *Id.* at 1.

19. *Id.* at 31.

20. *Id.*

21. MODEL CODE OF JUDICIAL CONDUCT R. 1.2 cmt. 3 (AM. BAR ASS'N 2011).

Judges must also "seek the necessary docket time, court staff, expertise, and resources to discharge all adjudicative and administrative responsibilities."[22]

As discussed below, the right to procedural justice addressed in this opinion derives from several sources: state and federal constitutional guarantees of due process of law, statutory prescriptions, and a judge's ethical responsibility to ensure the integrity and fairness of proceedings before the judge.

The Committee recognizes and concurs that "[i]mposing discipline upon a judge for an incorrect legal ruling is an extremely sensitive issue because of the potential impact on judicial independence."[23] For this reason, ordinary legal errors that can be corrected on appeal are not generally subject to discipline. However, "egregious legal error, legal error motivated by bad faith, or a continuing pattern of legal error may well violate several provisions of the Code of Judicial Conduct."[24] A "pattern of repeated legal error obviously is more serious than an isolated instance," and there is consensus among courts and disciplinary bodies "that legal error is egregious when judges deny individuals their basic or fundamental procedural rights."[25] Significantly, for present purposes, in contexts where the *pro se* status of litigants or the relatively modest amount of the money owed makes appeal unlikely or too costly, discipline is one of the only methods to ensure that violations of fundamental rights are prevented.[26]

A. The Right to an Inquiry into Ability to Pay

This Committee does not opine on questions of substantive law, but in interpreting the model rules of judicial conduct that apply to procedural justice we observe the distinctive significance of the right to be heard prior to facing incarceration for failure to pay.[27] As the Supreme Court held decades ago in *Bearden v. Georgia*, a defendant cannot be incarcerated for failure to

---

22. *Id.* R. 2.5 cmt. 2.

23. CHARLES GEYH ET AL., JUDICIAL CONDUCT AND ETHICS § 2.02, 2-5 (5th ed. 2013).

24. *Id.* at 2-7; *see also* State v. Blazina, 344 P.3d 680, 682–84 (Wash. 2015) (describing barriers to appeal of legal financial obligations).

25. GEYH, *supra* note 23, at 2-8; *see also In re* Aucoin, 767 So. 2d 30 (La. 2000) (trying defendants immediately after arraignment merited public censure); *In re* Scott, 386 N.E.2d 218, 222 (Mass. 1979) (denying counsel to juveniles and invoking nonexistent law merited prohibition on criminal and juvenile sittings); *In re* McGee, 452 N.E.2d 1258, 1259 (N.Y. 1983) (coercing guilty pleas merited removal).

26. *See In re* Piraino, Determination, 2014 WL 3889892, at *6 (N.Y. Comm'n Jud. Conduct, July 30, 2014) ("We reject respondent's argument that such sentencing errors are properly addressed by an appellate court, not in a disciplinary setting. Since most of the overpayments in this case involved relatively small amounts, it is unrealistic to expect that the defendants would expend the resources necessary to pursue an appellate remedy.").

27. MODEL CODE OF JUDICIAL CONDUCT pmbl. ¶5 ("The Rules . . . are rules of reason that should be applied consistent with constitutional requirements, statutes, other court rules, and decisional law, and with due regard for all relevant circumstances.").

pay absent an opportunity to be heard on the question whether the failure to pay is "willful," whether "bona fide" efforts have been made to acquire the resources to pay, and whether there are alternatives to incarceration that would meet the state's interests.[28] As long as a defendant's failure to pay is due to genuine financial incapacity, alternatives to incarceration must be explored.[29] More recently, the Supreme Court extended the *Bearden* framework for inquiry into ability to pay to contempt proceedings in *civil* debt collection cases that rely on incarceration to induce payment.[30] Finally, some states have adopted an ability-to-pay requirement via their state's constitutional guarantee of due process of law, by statute, or both.[31]

Thus although the outer limits of *Bearden* may vary from jurisdiction to jurisdiction,[32] the fundamental right to be heard on one's ability to pay rests

---

28. Bearden v. Georgia, 461 U.S. 660, 668–69 (1983) (revocation of probation of defendant required to pay fine and restitution was unconstitutional absent inquiry into ability to pay).

29. *Id.* at 668–69 ("[I]t is fundamentally unfair to revoke probation automatically without considering whether adequate alternative methods of punishing the defendant are available").

30. *See* Turner v. Rogers, 564 U.S. 431, 435 (2011) (holding that while there is no per se right to counsel in civil contempt proceedings leading to incarceration for failure to pay child support, "the State must nonetheless have in place alternative procedures that ensure a fundamentally fair determination of the critical incarceration-related question, whether the supporting parent is able to comply with the support order"); *id.* at 435 (citing Moseley v. Mosier, 306 S.E.2d 624, 626 (S.C. 1983) for the state's rule that a parent unable to make the required payments is not in contempt under *Bearden*). Neither *Bearden* nor *Turner* addresses a judge's discretion to waive a legal financial obligation under either state or federal law, though that discretion sometimes exists. This opinion does not address waiver of legal financial obligations. *See also* Timbs v. Indiana, 139 S.Ct. 682 (2019) (holding excessive fines clause of the Eight Amendment applies to the states).

31. *See, e.g.,* Del Valle v. State, 80 So. 3d 999, 1005–06, 1012 (Fla. 2011); State v. Blazina, 344 P.3d 680, 685 (Wash. 2015) (en banc); ARTHUR W. PEPIN, CONFERENCE OF STATE COURT ADMINISTRATORS, THE END OF DEBTORS' PRISONS: EFFECTIVE COURT POLICIES FOR SUCCESSFUL COMPLIANCE WITH LEGAL FINANCIAL OBLIGATIONS 19, n.97 (2015–2016) (citing Ohio Admin. Code, § 5120:1-1-02(K); Va. Code Annot., § 19.2-305 (2012)).

32. Some jurisdictions, for instance, have (a) distinguished bail for arrestees who could be charged with crimes from bail on arrest in post-judgment contexts, *see* Walker v. City of Calhoun, 901 F.3d 1245, 1266 (11th Cir. 2018) (holding that forty-eight-hour period of detention before conducting a hearing on indigency, probable cause, and bail for arrestees who may be charged with criminal offenses is consistent with due process principles of *Bearden*); (b) upheld the constitutionality of probation revocation hearings where the willfulness determination required by *Bearden* is not explicitly made by the trial court, but is implicit in record evidence, *see* State v. Brady, 300 P.3d 778, 780–81 (Utah Ct. App. 2013); (c) placed the burden of proving that failure to pay was not willful and that bona fide efforts have been made on the probationer once failure to pay has been established at a hearing, *see* Winbush v. State, 433 P.3d 1275, 1278 (Okla. Crim. App. 2018) (gathering other authorities); and (d) declined to apply *Bearden* to plea bargains in which the defendant specifically agreed to pay restitution in exchange for a reduced sentence under circumstances suggesting bad faith, *see* State v. Nordahl, 680 N.W.2d 247, 252 (N.D. 2004) (relying on U.S. v. Mitchell, 51 M.J. 490 (C.A.A.F. 1999)); *see also* U.S. v. Johnson, 767 F. Supp. 243, 248 (N.D. Ala. 1991) (*Bearden* does

upon a clearly established principle for the fair administration of justice[33]—
one that resonates with the abolition of debtor's prisons for private debts in
the 19th century.[34] The Supreme Court of Maine stated the principle in a judicial discipline case decided shortly after *Bearden*:

> The most basic right of citizens in this country is to be at liberty
> in society. That right is so essential to our way of life that it may
> only be taken away by the courts following carefully prescribed
> procedures.[35]

Procedural regularity in this setting is essential. Failure to adopt and
consistently follow "carefully prescribed procedures" in proceedings that
could result in incarceration for failure to pay strikes at the very roots of the
fair and impartial administration of justice and poses a direct threat to public
faith in the legitimacy of the judicial process. As the Georgia Supreme Court
observed in a disciplinary case involving other serious procedural irregulari-
ties at the trial level, trial judges *"are* the judicial system"[36] for many litigants.

> [T]heir initial, possibly only, contact of any serious nature with our
> judicial system occurs in the [local state court]. These individuals'
> experiences may constitute the sole basis for their personal impres-
> sion of our judicial system, and for their respect, or lack thereof, for
> the judiciary of this State. ... *Nowhere is the community more sensitive
> to the regularities, or irregularities, of judicial conduct than at the local
> level.* ... The state court judge plays a crucial role in achieving even-

---

not apply to plea-bargained probation terms); Wright v. State, 610 So. 2d 1187, 1189 (Ala.
Crim. App. 1992) (same); Dickey v. State, 570 S.E. 2d 634, 636 (Ga. Ct. App. 2002) (same);
Gamble v. Commonwealth, 293 S.W.3d 406, 411–12 (Ky. Ct. App. 2009) (same); Commonwealth v. Payne, 602 N.E.2d 594, 597 (Mass. App. Ct. 1992). *But see* Dirico v. State, 728 So. 2d
763, 767 (Fla. Dist. Ct. App. 1999) (plea bargain that included waiver of defense of inability
to pay invalid); State v. Myles, 882 So. 2d 1254, 1257 (La. Ct. App. 2004) (holding *Bearden* applies to plea bargained probation terms).

33. *Bearden* relied on a series of earlier cases in which the Supreme Court held that a
prison term cannot be imposed or extended beyond the statutory maximum term of im-
prisonment merely for failure to pay a fine, and that the right to appeal cannot be denied
merely for inability to pay a fee for a trial transcript. *See* Tate v. Short, 401 U.S. 395 (1971);
Williams v. Illinois, 399 U.S. 235 (1970); Griffin v. Illinois, 351 U.S. 12 (1956).

34. On the efforts to abolish debtors' prison for private debts in the 19th century, see
BRUCE H. MANN, REPUBLIC OF DEBTORS: BANKRUPTCY IN THE AGE OF AMERICAN INDEPEN-
DENCE (2002).

35. *In re* Benoit, 487 A.2d 1158, 1165 (Me. 1985); *see also* Foucha v. Louisiana, 504 U.S. 71,
80 (1992) ("Freedom from bodily restraint has always been at the core of the liberty protected by the Due Process Clause . . . .").

36. *In re* Inquiry Concerning a Judge, 462 S.E.2d 728, 733 (Ga. 1995).

handed and just results, particularly because litigants of widely disparate backgrounds, resources and abilities are involved.[37]

Procedural irregularity regarding incarceration for failure to pay is, therefore, a serious breach of a judge's Rule 1.1 duty "to comply with the law."[38] Indeed, discipline has been imposed for procedural irregularity of this kind for decades as a violation of clearly established law, and, in at least one jurisdiction, years before *Bearden* was decided.[39]

B. The Integrity and Fairness of the Judicial Process, Public Confidence in the Judiciary, and Inquiry into a Litigant's Ability to Pay

Procedural irregularity regarding incarceration for failure to pay directly implicates other fundamental rule of law values—values the courts are bound by other provisions of the MCJC to protect. Without meaningful inquiry into a litigant's ability to pay, public confidence in the independence, integrity, and impartiality of the judiciary is not "promoted" within the meaning of Rule 1.2. It is compromised. This is particularly true in circumstances where the court, the municipal government, or private contractors seek financial gain through incarceration or the threat of it, and there is no genuine public safety justification supporting incarceration.[40] The fairness and impartiality required by Rules 1.2 and 2.2 are compromised by bail requirements and collection methods that affect low income litigants while litigants of means can simply pay to avoid incarceration. Procedural irregularity

---

37. *Id.* at 733 (emphasis added); *see In re* Bailey, 541 So. 2d 1036, 1039 (Miss. 1989) ("[M]ost of our citizens have their primary, if not their only, direct contact with the law through the office of the justice court judge."); *see also In re* Restaino, 890 N.E.2d 224, 230 (N.Y. 2008) (when "tools of judicial administration are abused as punitive instruments to deprive a person of his or her liberty—a right of the most fundamental order—such conduct is inexcusable and does violence to the court's integrity and the inviolable public trust").

38. *See also* MODEL CODE OF JUDICIAL CONDUCT R. 2.6(A) (AM. BAR ASS'N 2011) (duty to "accord to every person who has a legal interest in a proceeding, or that person's lawyer, the right to be heard according to law"). See also discussion in the text, *supra*, at p. 6.

39. *See In re* Aucoin, 767 So.2d 30 (La. 2000) (public censure); *In re* Benoit, 487 A.2d 1158 (Me. 1985) (censure and suspension); *In re* Roberts, 689 N.E.2d 911 (N.Y. 1997) (removal); *In re* Skinner, 690 N.E.2d 484 (N.Y. 1997) (censure); *In re* Hammel, 668 N.E.2d 390 (N.Y. 1996) (removal); *In re* Nichols, Determination, (N.Y. Com'n Jud. Conduct, Nov. 19, 2001) (admonition); *In re* Bartie, 138 S.W.3d 81 (Tex. 2004) (removal); *see also In re* Scott, 386 N.E.2d 218, 227 (Mass. 1979) (barred from criminal and juvenile sittings for a year).

40. The Conference of State Court Administrators has warned that "funding courts through fines and fees that flow to the local town or county that pays court staff and judges creates at least the perception that judicial independence is diminished." PEPIN, *supra* note 31, at 9 (quoting earlier report); *see infra*, note 46.

in the use of a court's contempt power also directly compromises the fairness and impartiality required by these Rules.[41]

Significantly, the Comments to Rule 2.2 invite courts to show particular solicitude to those who cannot afford counsel in order to ensure that they have "the opportunity to have their matters fairly heard" by making "reasonable accommodations."[42] Incarcerating *pro se* litigants for failure to pay legal financial obligations without inquiring into their ability to pay directly undermines their opportunity to be heard on issues as to which they may most need accommodation. Finally, to the extent that courts do not have "carefully prescribed procedures" in place to prevent incarceration for failure to pay and do not provide training to judges, court staff, prosecutors, and public defenders on proper procedures, the competent and diligent performance of "judicial and administrative duties" as well as the "cooperat[ion] with other judges and court officials in the administration of court business" required by Rule 2.5 is compromised.[43]

Accordingly, a judge's uncertainty regarding whether inquiry into a litigant's ability to pay in a particular circumstance is necessary under binding precedent should be resolved in favor of making the inquiry.[44] And where a

---

41. *See* Comm'n on Judicial Performance v. Willard, 788 So. 2d 736 (Miss. 2001) (removing judge for, among other things, misuse of contempt process to collect civil debt); *In re* Pizzi, 617 A.2d 663 (N.J. 1993) (mem.) (reprimand of judge who failed to give defendant notice of a contempt charge and sentenced defendant without receiving evidence); *In re* Hammel, 668 N.E.2d 390, 391 (N.Y. 1996) (removing judge who failed to follow procedures for summary contempt and incarcerated defendants without inquiry into ability to pay legal financial obligations); Public Admonition of Kennedy (Tex. Com. Jud. Conduct, July 12, 1996) (admonishing judge for using arrest warrant incident to contempt in order to enforce civil judgment). Setting bail after arrest for allegedly contumacious failure to appear at a civil post-judgment debtor examination in the amount dedicated to satisfaction of the judgment deprives the defendant of both the opportunity to be heard on whether her failure to appear is in fact punishable as contempt and whether she has the means to satisfy the judgment. *See supra* note 10. Procedural irregularity in entering an underlying default judgment can also result in discipline. *See In re* Landry, 789 So. 2d 1271 (La. 2001).

42. Model Code of Judicial Conduct R. 2.2, cmt. [4].

43. *In re* Benoit, 487 A.2d 1158, 1165 (Me. 1985) (emphasizing the importance of "carefully prescribed procedures"). The above referenced Rules protecting the integrity and fairness of the judicial process along with public confidence in the administration of justice warrant particular attention in the handful of jurisdictions that expressly limit the circumstances in which discipline can be imposed for legal error under Rules 1.1 and 2.6. *See* Cynthia Gray, *The Line Between Judicial Error and Judicial Misconduct: Balancing Judicial Independence and Accountability*, 32 Hofstra L. Rev. 1245, 1278–79 (2004) (describing relevant limitations in these jurisdictions).

44. *See In re* Aucoin, 767 So. 2d 30, 31–33 (La. 2000) (judge censured for "grossly negligent disregard for procedural due process" for using "instanter trial" procedure seventeen times after appellate court had reversed a conviction on instanter trial; discipline appropriate even though judge understood the reversal to concern whether he was required to allow defendants to obtain evidence and call witnesses at instanter trials, *not* whether the trials themselves violated due process, and even though judge's conduct followed "long-

litigant is unrepresented or the matter is civil, doubts about ability to pay, the willfulness of a litigant's failure to pay, the bona fide efforts of the litigant to secure the means to pay, and the viability of alternatives to incarceration, should generally be resolved against incarceration in the absence of circumstances indicating that the litigant poses a threat to public safety. Whatever the status of the litigant, inquiry into ability to pay should be grounded in objective financial data to the extent such information can reasonably be ascertained.[45] Judges must also avoid conflicts of interest that arise from setting, imposing, or enforcing legal financial obligations to fund the court on terms that give judges a direct incentive either to increase these obligations or to avoid inquiring into ability to pay.[46]

To comply with these obligations, courts should adopt policies, practices, and procedures to efficiently and accurately determine a litigant's ability to pay, to divide administrative tasks to guard against even the appearance of impropriety in the setting and enforcement of legal financial obligations, and to provide training to judges, court staff, prosecutors, and defense attorneys. Innovative options and comprehensive guidance on how to design and implement these policies, practices, and procedures may be found in materials recently published by the Conference of State Court Administrators, the National Center for State Courts, and other organizations.[47] Ways to ensure

---

standing" practice in that district); *id.* (although "not an excuse for respondent's failure to recognize the constitutional infirmity in the procedure," judge's misapprehension and the fact that he was following local practice "mitigate to some extent against a finding of willful misconduct"); *cf. In re* Gremillion, 204 So. 3d 183, 194 (La. 2016) (discipline is warranted for legal error where a ruling is "made contrary to clear and determined law about which there is no confusion or question as to its interpretation and . . . [the error is] egregious, made in bad faith, or made as part of a pattern or practice of legal error") (quoting *In re* Quirk, 705 So.2d 172, 180–81 (La. 1997)).

45. *See* Turner v. Rogers, 564 U.S. 431, 447–48 (2011); Commonwealth v. Henry, 55 N.E.3d 943, 953 (Mass. 2016) ("In determining the defendant's ability to pay, the judge must consider the financial resources of the defendant, including income and net assets, and the defendant's financial obligations, including the amount necessary to meet minimum basic human needs such as food, shelter, and clothing for the defendant and his or her dependents.").

46. *See In re* Storie, 574 S.W.2d 369 (Mo. 1978) (en banc) (judge suspended for personally administering a law "library fund" from charges assessed in guilty pleas where funds were spent on law books, wages, court furnishings, and court maintenance); *see also* Brown v. Vance, 637 F.2d 272 (5th Cir. 1981); Brucker v. City of Doraville, 391 F. Supp. 3d 1207 (N.D. Ga. 2019); Augustus v. Roemer, 771 F. Supp. 1458, 1473 (E.D. La. 1991).

47. *See* Harvard Law School Criminal Justice Policy Program, Confronting Criminal Justice Debt: A Guide for Policy Reform (2016); National Center for State Courts, Missouri Municipal Courts: Best Practice Recommendations (2015); Roopal Patel & Meghna Philip, Brennan Ctr. for Justice, Criminal Justice Debt: A Toolkit for Action (2012), https://www.brennancenter.org/sites/default/files/2019-08/Report_Criminal%20Justice%20Debt.pdf; Arthur Pepin, Conference of State Court Administrators, Four Essential Elements Required to Deliver Justice in Limited Jurisdiction Courts in the 21st Century (2013–2014); Roopal Patel & Meghna Philip, *A*

observance of basic procedural safeguards include, for example, (i) using a "bench card" that provides judges and other staff relevant instructions on ability-to-pay inquiries, including a workable definition of indigence and alternatives to incarceration,[48] (ii) providing advance notice to litigants of their ability-to-pay hearing and emphasizing that financial means will be "a critical issue" covered at the hearing, (iii) distributing a form "to elicit relevant financial information," and (iv) providing a meaningful opportunity to address questions about the litigant's "financial status" at the hearing.[49]

IV. Conclusion

The liberty interests protected by the duty to inquire into ability to pay prior to incarceration for failure to pay are fundamental to litigants and to the rule of law itself. Courts have an ethical duty not only to comply with the law insofar as it requires inquiry into ability to pay but to protect the integrity, fairness, and impartiality of the judicial process by ensuring that compliance is robust and consistent with legitimate state interests in public safety. See Rules 1.1, 1.2, 2.2, 2.5, and 2.6. Courts should therefore adopt carefully prescribed procedures to prevent incarceration where a litigant lacks the resources to pay legal financial obligations or private civil debts.

Abstaining: Hon. Goodwin Liu.

Legislative Model for Dismantling Debtors' Prisons, BRENNAN CTR. FOR JUSTICE (Aug. 7, 2012), https://www.brennancenter.org/our-work/analysis-opinion/legislative-model-dismantling-debtors-prisons (describing Illinois statute); PEPIN, *supra* note 31.

48. The Task Force on Fines, Fees and Bail Practices of the Conference of Chief Justices, a joint effort of the Conference of State Court Administrators, the State Justice Institute, the Bureau of Justice Assistance, and the National Center for State Courts, has published a model "bench card." *See* NATIONAL TASK FORCE ON FINES, FEES AND BAIL PRACTICES, LAWFUL COLLECTION OF LEGAL FINANCIAL OBLIGATIONS (2017), https://www.ncsc.org/~/media/Images/Topics/Fines%20Fees/BenchCard_FINAL_Feb2_2017.ashx.

49. *See Turner*, 564 U.S. at 447–48.

AMERICAN BAR ASSOCIATION
STANDING COMMITTEE ON ETHICS AND PROFESSIONAL RESPONSIBILITY

Formal Opinion 491   **April 29, 2020**

Obligations Under Rule 1.2(d) to Avoid Counseling or Assisting in a Crime or Fraud in Non-Litigation Settings

Model Rule 1.2(d) prohibits a lawyer from advising or assisting a client in conduct the lawyer "knows" is criminal or fraudulent. That knowledge may be inferred from the circumstances, including a lawyer's willful blindness to or conscious avoidance of facts. Accordingly, where facts known to the lawyer establish a high probability that a client seeks to use the lawyer's services for criminal or fraudulent activity, the lawyer has a duty to inquire further to avoid advising or assisting such activity. Even if information learned in the course of a preliminary interview or during a representation is insufficient to establish "knowledge" under Rule 1.2(d), other rules may require the lawyer to inquire further in order to help the client avoid crime or fraud, to avoid professional misconduct, and to advance the client's legitimate interests. These include the duties of competence, diligence, communication, and honesty under Rules 1.1, 1.3, 1.4, 1.13, 1.16, and 8.4. If the client or prospective client refuses to provide information necessary to assess the legality of the proposed transaction, the lawyer must ordinarily decline the representation or withdraw under Rule 1.16. A lawyer's reasonable evaluation after inquiry and based on information reasonably available at the time does not violate the rules. This opinion does not address the application of these rules in the representation of a client or prospective client who requests legal services in connection with litigation.[1]

---

1. This opinion is based on the ABA Model Rules of Professional Conduct as amended by the ABA House of Delegates through August 2019. The laws, court rules, regulations, rules of professional conduct, and opinions promulgated in individual jurisdictions are controlling.

236

I. Introduction

In the wake of media reports,[2] disciplinary proceedings,[3] criminal prosecutions,[4] and reports on international counter-terrorism enforcement and efforts to combat money-laundering, the legal profession has become increasingly alert to the risk that a client or prospective client[5] might try to retain a lawyer for a transaction or other non-litigation matter that could be legitimate but which further inquiry would reveal to be criminal or fraudulent.[6] For example, a client might seek legal assistance for a series of purchases and sales of properties that will be used to launder money. Or a client might propose an all-cash deal in large amounts and ask that the proceeds be deposited in a bank located in a jurisdiction where transactions of this kind are commonly used to conceal terrorist financing or other illegal activities.[7] On the other hand, further inquiry may dispel the lawyer's concerns.

This opinion addresses a lawyer's obligation to inquire when faced with a client who may be seeking to use the lawyer's services in a transaction to commit a crime or fraud. Ascertaining whether a client seeks to use the lawyer's services for prohibited ends can be delicate. Clients are generally entitled to be believed rather than doubted, and in some contexts investigations can be both costly and time-consuming. At the same time, clients ben-

---

2. *See* Debra Cassens Weiss, *Group Goes Undercover at 13 Law Firms to Show How U.S. Laws Facilitate Anonymous Investment*, A.B.A. J. (Feb. 1, 2016), https://www.abajournal.com/news/article/group_goes_undercover_at_13_law_firms_to_show_how_us_laws_facilitate; *see also* Louise Story & Stephanie Saul, *Stream of Foreign Wealth Flows to Elite New York Real Estate*, N.Y. TIMES (Feb. 7, 2015), https://www.nytimes.com/2015/02/08/nyregion/stream-of-foreign-wealth-flows-to-time-warner-condos.html.

3. *In re* Albrecht, 42 P.3d 887, 898–900 (Or. 2002) (disbarment for assisting client in money laundering).

4. *See, e.g.*, United States v. Farrell, 921 F.3d 116 (4th Cir. 2019) (affirming conviction for money laundering); United States v. Blair, 661 F.3d 755 (4th Cir. 2011) (same); Laura Ende, *Escrow, Money Laundering Cases Draw Attention to the Perils of Handling Client Money*, STATE BAR OF CAL. (Feb. 2017), http://www.calbarjournal.com/February2017/TopHeadlines/TH1.aspx (lawyer sentenced "to five years in prison after being convicted of felonies related to a money laundering scheme").

5. "Client" refers hereinafter to "client and prospective client" unless otherwise indicated.

6. Hereinafter, "transaction" refers both to transactions and other non-litigation matters unless otherwise indicated. This opinion does not address the application of rules triggering a duty to inquire where a client requests legal services in connection with litigation. ABA Comm. on Ethics & Prof'l Responsibility, Informal Op. 1470 (1981), discusses how a lawyer *not* involved in the past misconduct of a client should handle the circumstance of a proposed transaction arising from or relating to the past misconduct.

7. *See* AM. BAR ASS'N TASK FORCE ON GATEKEEPER REGULATION AND THE PROFESSION, VOLUNTARY GOOD PRACTICES GUIDANCE FOR LAWYERS TO DETECT AND COMBAT MONEY LAUNDERING AND TERRORIST FINANCING 15–16 (2010) [hereinafter GOOD PRACTICES GUIDANCE] (describing institutions, such as the United Nations, the World Bank, the International Monetary Fund, and the U.S. Department of State, believed to be "credible sources" for information regarding risks in different jurisdictions; *id.* at 24 (noting the "higher risk situation" when a client offers to pay in cash).

efit greatly from having informed assistance of counsel. A lawyer's obligation to inquire when faced with circumstances addressed in this opinion is well-grounded in authority interpreting Rule 1.2(d) and in the rules on competence, diligence, communication, honesty, and withdrawal.

As set forth in Section II of this opinion, a lawyer who has knowledge of facts that create a high probability that a client is seeking the lawyer's services in a transaction to further criminal or fraudulent activity has a duty to inquire further to avoid assisting that activity under Rule 1.2(d). Failure to make a reasonable inquiry is willful blindness punishable under the actual knowledge standard of the Rule. Whether the facts known to the lawyer require further inquiry will depend on the circumstances. As discussed in Section III, even where Rule 1.2(d) does not require further inquiry, other Rules may. These Rules include the duty of competence under Rule 1.1, the duty of diligence under Rule 1.3, the duty of communication under Rule 1.4, the duty to protect the best interests of an organizational client under Rule 1.13, the duties of honesty and integrity under Rules 8.4(b) and (c), and the duty to withdraw under Rule 1.16(a). Further inquiry under these Rules serves important ends. It ensures that the lawyer is in a position to provide the informed advice and assistance to which the client is entitled, that the representation will not result in professional misconduct, and that the representation will not involve counseling or assisting a crime or fraud. Section IV addresses a lawyer's obligations in responding to a client who either agrees or does not agree to provide information necessary to satisfy the duty to inquire. Finally, Section V examines hypothetical scenarios in which the duty to inquire would be triggered, as well as instances in which it would not.

II. The Duty to Inquire Under Rule 1.2(d)

Rule 1.2(d) states that a lawyer "shall not counsel a client to engage, or assist a client, in conduct that the lawyer knows is criminal or fraudulent." A duty to inquire to avoid knowingly counseling or assisting a crime or fraud may arise under this Rule in two ways. First, Rule 1.0(f) states that to "know[]" means to have "actual knowledge of the fact in question." When facts already known to the lawyer are so strong as to constitute "actual knowledge" of criminal or fraudulent activity, the lawyer must "consult with the client regarding the limitations on the lawyer's conduct."[8] This consultation will ordinarily include inquiry into whether there is some misapprehension regarding the relevant facts. If there is no misunderstanding and the client persists, the lawyer must withdraw.[9]

---

8. MODEL RULES OF PROF'L CONDUCT R. 1.2 cmt. [13] [hereinafter MODEL RULES].

9. *See* MODEL RULES R. 1.16(a)(1); Section IV, *infra*. Rule 1.2(d) nevertheless permits a lawyer to "discuss the legal consequences of any proposed course of conduct with a client and may counsel or assist a client to make a good faith effort to determine the validity, scope, meaning or application of the law."

In *In re Blatt*,[10] for example, the New Jersey Supreme Court disciplined a lawyer for participation in a real estate transaction where *"[o]n their face* the [transaction] documents suggest[ed] impropriety if not outright illegality."[11] Addressing the lawyer's duties, the court wrote:

> A lawyer may not follow the directions of a client without first satisfying himself that the latter is seeking a legitimate and proper goal and intends to employ legal means to attain it. . . . The propriety of any proposed course of action must be initially considered by the attorney, and it may be thereafter pursued only if the lawyer is completely satisfied that it involves no ethical compromise. . . . [The lawyer's] duty, upon being requested to draft the aforementioned agreements, was to learn all the details of the proposed transaction. Only then, upon being satisfied that he had indeed learned all the facts, and that his client's proposed course of conduct was proper, would he have been at liberty to pursue the matter further.[12]

Additionally, if facts before the lawyer indicate a high probability that a client seeks to use the lawyer's services for criminal or fraudulent activity, a lawyer's conscious, deliberate failure to inquire amounts to knowing assistance of criminal or fraudulent conduct. Rule 1.0(f) refers to "actual knowledge" and provides that "[a] person's knowledge may be inferred from circumstances." Substantial authority confirms that a lawyer may not ignore the obvious.[13]

The obligation to inquire is well established in ethics opinions. Nearly forty years ago, prior to the adoption of the Model Rules, ABA Informal Opinion 1470 (1981) declared that "a lawyer should not undertake represen-

---

10. 324 A.2d 15 (N.J. 1974).

11. *Id.* at 18 (emphasis added).

12. *Id.* at 18–19; *see also In re* Evans, 759 N.E.2d 1064 (Ind. 2001) (mem.) (three-year suspension for filing fraudulent federal tax returns knowingly misrepresenting sale proceeds from real estate transaction); *In re* Harlow, 2004 WL 5215045, at *2 (Mass. State Bar Disciplinary Bd. 2004) (suspending lawyer for violation of 1.2(d) for assisting client in knowing manipulation of state licensing agency's escrow account requirements); State *ex rel.* Counsel for Discipline of Nebraska Supreme Court v. Mills, 671 N.W.2d 765 (Neb. 2003) (two-year suspension for participating in illegal scheme to avoid estate taxes by knowingly backdating and preparing false documents); *accord* N.C. State Bar, Formal Op. 12, 2001 WL 1949450 (2001).

13. In the words of Charles Wolfram, "as in the criminal law, a lawyer's studied ignorance of a readily ascertainable fact by consciously avoiding it is the functional equivalent of knowledge of the fact. . . . As a lawyer, one may not avoid the bright light of a clear fact by averting one's eyes or turning one's back." CHARLES W. WOLFRAM, MODERN LEGAL ETHICS 696 (1986); *see also* ELLEN J. BENNETT & HELEN W. GUNNARSSON, ANNOTATED MODEL RULES OF PROFESSIONAL CONDUCT 47 (9th ed. 2019) ("[a] lawyer's assistance in unlawful conduct is not excused by a failure to inquire into the client's objectives"); *id.* (gathering cases).

tation in disregard of facts *suggesting* that the representation might aid the client in perpetrating a fraud or otherwise committing a crime . . . . A lawyer cannot escape responsibility by avoiding inquiry. A lawyer must be satisfied, on the facts before him and readily available to him, that he can perform the requested services without abetting fraudulent or criminal conduct . . . ."[14]

Relying on ABA Informal Opinion 1470, the Legal Ethics Committee of the Indiana State Bar Association concluded in 2001 that "[a] lawyer should not undertake representation without making further inquiry if the facts presented by a prospective client suggest that the representation might aid the client in perpetrating a fraud or otherwise committing a crime."[15] The opinion reasoned that an attorney asked to create a "new" sole power of attorney for a prospective client on behalf of her wealthy grandfather in matters concerning his estate has a duty to inquire further. The opinion emphasized the possibility that the granddaughter could fraudulently use the power of attorney to benefit herself rather than serve the interests of her grandfather, whom the attorney had not consulted, the possibility that the grandfather would not wish to grant sole power of attorney to his granddaughter, and the possibility that the grandfather might lack the capacity to consent to such an arrangement (made likely by the fact that the lawyer's paralegal observed the grandfather's deteriorated condition). Thus, although it is possible that the granddaughter's representation of the facts was accurate and therefore consistent with Rule 1.2(d), "the fact that a proposed client in drafting a power of attorney was the agent and not a frail principal should have suggested to [the lawyer] the possibility that the client's real objective might be fraud. [The lawyer] then *had an ethical responsibility to find out whether the proposal was above-board* before performing the services. By failing to make further inquiry, [the lawyer] violated Rule 1.2."[16]

Similarly, New York City Ethics Opinion 2018-4 concluded that lawyers must inquire when "retained to assist an individual client in a transaction that appears to the lawyer to be suspicious."[17] The opinion explains that "[i]n general, assisting in a suspicious transaction is not competent where a reasonable lawyer prompted by serious doubts would have refrained from providing assistance or would have investigated to allay suspicions before rendering or continuing to render legal assistance. . . . What constitutes a

---

14. ABA Comm. on Ethics & Prof'l Responsibility, Informal Op. 1470 (1981) (emphasis added) (interpreting the analogous ABA Model Code provision 7-102(A)(7), which provides that a lawyer must not "[c]ounsel or assist his client in conduct that the lawyer knows to be illegal or fraudulent").

15. Ind. State Bar Ass'n Comm. on Legal Ethics, Op. 2, at 4 (2001).

16. *Id.* at 4 (emphasis added). The Opinion reaches the same conclusion if the grandfather is considered to be the true client. *Id.* at 6–7. *Accord* N.C. State Bar Ass'n, Formal Op. 7 (2003).

17. N.Y.C. Bar Ass'n Comm. on Prof'l Ethics, Formal Op. 2018-4, at 2 (2018); *see also* Conn. Bar Ass'n Standing Comm. on Prof'l Ethics, Informal Op. 91-22 (1991).

suspicion sufficient to trigger inquiry will depend on the circumstances."[18] Failure to inquire may constitute "conscious avoidance" when, for example, "the lawyer is aware of serious questions about the legality of the transaction and renders assistance without considering readily available facts that would have confirmed the wrongfulness of the transaction."[19]

Courts imposing discipline are generally in accord. When a lawyer deliberately or consciously avoids knowledge that a client is or may be using the lawyer's services to further a crime or fraud, discipline is imposed.[20] Some courts have applied the even broader standard set out in Comment [13] to Rule 1.2, which requires a lawyer to consult with the client when the lawyer "comes to know or *reasonably should know* that [the] client expects assistance not permitted by the Rules of Professional Conduct . . . ." (Emphasis added.) For example, in *In re Dobson*,[21] the South Carolina Supreme Court identified facts showing that the lawyer "knew" or "*should have known*" that he was furthering a client's illegal scheme, and added, "[w]e also find that respondent *deliberately evaded* knowledge of facts which tended to implicate him in a fraudulent scheme. This Court will not countenance the conscious avoidance of one's ethical duties as an attorney."[22]

---

18. N.Y.C Bar Ass'n Comm. on Prof'l Ethics, Formal Op. 2018-4, at 3 (2018).

19. *Id.* Hypotheticals in Section V of this opinion, *infra*, identify circumstances that should prompt further inquiry.

20. *See In re* Bloom, 745 P.2d 61 (Cal. 1987) (affirming disbarment of lawyer who assisted client in sale and transport of explosives to Libya; categorically rejecting lawyer's defense that he believed in good faith that transaction was authorized by national security officials); *In re* Albrecht, 42 P.3d 887, 898–99 (Or. 2002) ("suspicious nature" of transactions, combined with other facts, support inference that lawyer must have known his participation in scheme constituted money laundering; upholding disbarment for knowingly assisting crime or fraud and rejecting defense that lawyer was "an unwitting dupe to a talented con man"); *see also* ELLEN BENNETT & HELEN GUNNARSSON, ANNOTATED MODEL RULES OF PROFESSIONAL CONDUCT 47 (9th ed.) ("[a] lawyer's assistance in unlawful conduct is not excused by a failure to inquire into the client's objectives"). *But see* Iowa Supreme Court Att'y Disciplinary Bd. v. Ouderkirk, 845 N.W. 2d 31, 45–48 (Iowa 2014) (declining to infer knowledge of client's fraud despite what disciplinary counsel argued were "highly suspicious" circumstances where sophisticated, longstanding client who typically relied on the lawyer exclusively to prepare final paperwork deceived the lawyer about a fraudulent transfer to avoid creditors).

21. 427 S.E.2d 166 (S.C. 1993).

22. *Id.* at 427 (emphasis added); *see also* Florida Bar v. Brown, 790 So.2d 1081, 1088 (Fla. 2001) (suspension for soliciting illegal campaign contributions from employees and others for political candidates viewed as favorable to business interests of major client of firm; lawyer "should have known" conduct was criminal or fraudulent under Florida version of Rule 1.2(d) which expressly incorporates this standard); *In re* Siegel, 471 N.Y.S. 2d 591, 592 (N.Y. App. Div. 1984) (attorney "knew *or should have known* that at the very least, his conduct was a breach of trust, if not illegal") (emphasis added). Other jurisdictions have rejected a negligence standard for Rule 1.2(d). *See In re* Tocco, 984 P.2d 539, 543 (Ariz. 1999) (en banc) (declining to read a should have known standard into Arizona Rule 1.2(d); "While actual knowledge can be proven by circumstantial evidence, a mere showing that the attorney reasonably *should have known* her conduct was in violation of the rules, without more, is insuf-

Criminal cases treat deliberate ignorance or willful blindness as equivalent to actual knowledge.[23] As the Supreme Court recently summarized:

> The doctrine of willful blindness is well established in criminal law. Many criminal statutes require proof that a defendant acted knowingly or willfully, and courts applying the doctrine of willful blindness hold that defendants cannot escape the reach of these statutes by deliberately shielding themselves from clear evidence of critical facts that are strongly suggested by the circumstances. . . . [The Model Penal Code defines] "knowledge of the existence of a particular fact" to include a situation in which "a person is aware of a *high probability* of [the fact's] existence, unless he actually believes that it does not exist." Our Court has used the Code's definition as a guide . . . [a]nd every Court of Appeals—with the possible exception of the District of Columbia Circuit—has fully embraced willful blindness, applying the doctrine to a wide range of criminal statutes.[24]

A lawyer may accordingly face criminal charges or civil liability, in addition to bar discipline, for deliberately or consciously avoiding knowledge that a client is or may be using the lawyer's services to further a crime or fraud.[25] To prevent these outcomes, a lawyer must inquire further when the

---

ficient."); *accord* Iowa Supreme Court Bd. of Prof'l Ethics and Conduct v. Jones, 606 N.W.2d 5, 7–8 (Iowa 2000).

The Committee acknowledges the tension between the "actual knowledge" standard of Model Rule 1.2(d), on the one hand, and those authorities applying a reasonably should know standard. This opinion concludes only that the standard of actual knowledge set out in the text of Model Rules 1.2(d) and 1.0(f) is met by appropriate evidence of willful blindness. When the Model Rules intend a lower threshold of scienter, such as "reasonably should know," the text generally makes this explicit. *See, e.g.*, MODEL RULES R. 2.3(b), 2.4(b), 4.3.

23. United States v. Ramsey, 785 F.2d 184, 189 (7th Cir. 1986) ("[A]ctual knowledge and deliberate avoidance of knowledge are the same thing.").

24. Global-Tech Appliances, Inc. v. SEB USA, 563 U.S. 754, 767 (2011) (emphasis added) (citations omitted) (applying willful blindness standard to statute prohibiting knowing inducement of patent infringement).

25. *See* United States v. Cavin, 39 F.3d 1299, 1310 (5th Cir. 1994) (upholding deliberate ignorance jury instruction in prosecution of a lawyer); United States v. Scott, 37 F.3d 1564, 1578 (10th Cir. 1994) (affirming use of deliberate ignorance instruction against an attorney convicted of conspiracy to defraud the IRS); Wyle v. R.J. Reynolds Indus., Inc., 709 F.2d 585, 590 (9th Cir. 1983) (upholding deliberate ignorance finding against law firm in antitrust suit because firm was aware of high probability that client made illegal payments and failed to investigate); United States v. Benjamin, 328 F.2d 854, 862 (2d Cir. 1964) (a lawyer may be held liable in a securities fraud suit if the lawyer has "deliberately closed his eyes to the facts he had a duty to see"); Harrell v. Crystal, 611 N.E. 2d 908, 914 (Ohio Ct. App. 1992) (affirming finding of liability in malpractice action for lawyer's failure to investigate sham tax shelters); Pa. Bar Ass'n Comm. on Legal Ethics & Prof'l Responsibility, Informal Op. 2003-104 (2003) (where facts suggested property transfer to client from relative was to con-

facts before the lawyer create a high probability that a client seeks to use the lawyer's services for criminal or fraudulent activity.[26]

III. The Duty To Inquire Under Other Rules

Rule 1.2(d) is not the only source of a lawyer's duty to inquire. A lawyer may be obliged to inquire further in order to meet duties of competence, diligence, communication, honesty, and withdrawal under Rules 1.1, 1.3, 1.4, 1.13, 1.16, and 8.4. The kinds of facts and circumstances that would trigger a duty to inquire under these rules include, for example, (i) the identity of the client, (ii) the lawyer's familiarity with the client, (iii) the nature of the matter (particularly whether such matters are frequently associated with criminal or fraudulent activity), (iv) the relevant jurisdictions (especially whether any jurisdiction is classified as high risk by credible sources), (v) the likelihood and gravity of harm associated with the proposed activity, (vi) the nature and depth of the lawyer's expertise in the relevant field of practice, (vii) other facts going to the reasonableness of reposing trust in the client,[27] and (viii)

---

ceal assets from creditors, lawyer handling sale of property to a third party "must evaluate whether the transfer of realty to your client was 'fraudulent'" under state law); *cf.* RESTATE-MENT (THIRD) OF THE LAW GOVERNING LAWYERS § 94, Reporter's Note, cmt. g. at 17 (AM. LAW INST. 2000) ("the preferable rule is that proof of a lawyer's conscious disregard of facts is relevant evidence which, together with other evidence bearing on the question, may warrant a finding of actual knowledge").

26. As the authorities and analysis in this Section make clear, the duty to inquire under Model Rule 1.2(d) is tied to the circumstances and the lawyer's state of knowledge. It is *not* a freestanding, blanket obligation to scrutinize every client for illicit ends irrespective of the nature of the specific matter and the attorney-client relationship. *See* United States v. Sarantos, 455 F.2d 877, 881 (2d Cir. 1972) ("Construing 'knowingly' in a criminal statute to include willful blindness . . . is no radical concept in the law," but the standard does not mean that an attorney has a general duty to "investigate 'the truth of his client's assertions' or risk going to jail"; upholding criminal conviction of lawyer who actively aided in immigration related marriage fraud); Pa. Bar Ass'n Comm. on Legal Ethics & Prof'l Responsibility, Informal Op. 2001-26 ("*Generally*, a lawyer has no obligation to inquire or otherwise uncover facts that are not necessary to enable the lawyer to fulfill his or her obligations with respect to the representation"; warning nevertheless that Rule 1.2(d) applies to filing of worker's compensation claims and leaving attorney to determine relevance of client's fatal condition to client's specific claim) (emphasis added). However, the Committee rejects the view that the actual knowledge standard of Rule 1.2(d) relieves the lawyer of a duty to inquire further where the lawyer is aware of facts creating a high probability that the representation would further a crime or fraud. *Cf.* RESTATEMENT (THIRD) OF THE LAW GOVERNING LAWYERS § 94 cmt. g. at 11 ("Under the actual knowledge standard . . . a lawyer is not required to make a particular kind of investigation in order to ascertain more clearly what the facts are, although it will often be prudent for the lawyer to do so."); *id.* § 51 cmt. h., ill. 6 at 366; George M. Cohen, *The State of Lawyer Knowledge Under the Model Rules of Professional Conduct*, 3 AM. U. BUS. L. REV. 115, 116 (2014) (discussing association of willful blindness with recklessness, without citing to *Global-Tech Appliances*, and analyzing assumption that "the actual knowledge standard aims to exclude a duty to inquire").

27. For facts that can undermine the reasonableness of reposing trust, see the discussion of "risk categories" provided by the GOOD PRACTICES GUIDANCE, *supra* note 7, at 15–36.

any other factors traditionally associated with providing competent representation in the field.

First, Rule 8.4(b) makes it professional misconduct for a lawyer to "commit a criminal act that reflects adversely on the lawyer's honesty, trustworthiness or fitness as a lawyer in other respects." Rule 8.4(c) makes it professional misconduct for a lawyer to "engage in conduct involving dishonesty, fraud, deceit or misrepresentation." Providing legal services could violate Rules 8.4(b) and (c) where the relevant law on criminal or fraudulent conduct defines the lawyer's state of mind as culpable even without proof of actual knowledge.[28] In such a situation, the lawyer must conduct further investigation to protect the client, advance the client's legitimate interests, and prevent the crime or fraud.

Second, and more broadly, the lawyer's duty of competence, diligence, and communication under Rules 1.1, 1.3, and 1.4 may require the lawyer, prior to advising or assisting in a course of action, to develop sufficient knowledge of the facts and the law to understand the client's objectives, identify means to meet the client's lawful interests, to probe further, and, if necessary, persuade the client not to pursue conduct that could lead to criminal liability or liability for fraud. Comment [5] of Rule 1.1 states that "[c]ompetent handling of a particular matter requires inquiry into and analysis of the factual and legal elements of the problem."[29] The duty of diligence under Rule 1.3 requires that a lawyer ascertain the relevant facts and law in a timely and appropriately thorough manner.[30] Rule 1.4(a)(5), which requires consultation with the client regarding "any relevant limitation on the lawyer's conduct" arising from the client's expectation of assistance that is not permitted by the Rules of Professional Conduct or other law, may require investigation of the relevant facts and law. Rule 1.4(b) requires the lawyer to give the client explanations sufficient to enable the client to make informed decisions about the representation.

---

28. *See In re* Berman, 769 P.2d 984, 989 (Cal. 1989) (en banc) (holding, in disciplinary proceeding for aiding a money laundering scheme, that attorney's "*belief*" that the financial statements contained false information reflects sufficient indicia of fraudulent intent to constitute moral turpitude"). The same conduct would require the lawyer's withdrawal under Rule 1.16(a)(1).

29. *See also* Iowa Supreme Court Att'y Disciplinary Bd. v. Wright, 840 N.W.2d 295, 301 (Iowa 2013) (failure to conduct even preliminary research on overseas internet scam violates Rule 1.1); *In re* Winkel, 577 N.W.2d 9 (Wis. 1998) (failure to obtain information on trust funds of clients' business prior to surrendering clients' assets to bank). *See also* RESTATEMENT (THIRD) OF THE LAW GOVERNING LAWYERS § 52 cmt. c at 377 ("[A] lawyer must perform tasks reasonably appropriate to the representation, including, where appropriate, inquiry into the facts.").

30. *See In re* Konnor, 694 N.W. 2d 376 (Wis. 2005) (failure to investigate concern that rents owed to estate were being misappropriated).

Rule 1.13 imposes a duty to inquire in entity representations. Rule 1.13(a) provides that a lawyer "employed or retained by the organization represents the organization acting through its duly authorized constituents." Determining the interests of the organization will often require further inquiry to clarify any ambiguity about who has authority and what the organization's priorities are. Under Rule 1.13(b), once the lawyer learns of action, omission, or planned activity on the part of an "officer, employee, or other person associated with the organization . . . that is a violation of a legal obligation to the organization, and that is likely to result in substantial injury to the organization, then the lawyer shall proceed as is reasonably necessary in the best interests of the organization." Even if the underlying facts regarding the violation or potential violation are already well established and require no additional inquiry, determining what is "reasonably necessary" and in the "best interest of the organization" will commonly involve additional communication and investigation.[31]

Recent ABA guidance and opinions support this approach. Concern that individuals might use the services of U.S. lawyers for money-laundering and terrorist financing prompted the ABA House of Delegates to adopt in 2010 the *ABA Voluntary Good Practices Guidance for Lawyers to Detect and Combat Money Laundering and Terrorist Financing* ("Good Practices Guidance"). The Good Practices Guidance advocates a "risk-based approach" to avoid assisting in money laundering or terrorist financing, according to guidelines developed by the Financial Action Task Force on Money Laundering ("FATF").[32] Recommended measures include "examining the nature of the legal work involved, and where the [client's] business is taking place."[33]

---

31. *See* MODEL RULES R. 1.13 cmts. [3] & [4]. Rule 1.13(b) was added after a series of high profile financial accounting scandals in the early 2000s. AM. BAR ASS'N TASK FORCE ON CORPORATE RESPONSIBILITY (2003), *reprinted in* 59 BUS. LAW. 145, 166–70 (2003). Other law may also create a duty to inquire. The Sarbanes-Oxley Act of 2002 creates a duty for the "chief legal officer" to conduct an "appropriate" investigation in response to another lawyer's report of "evidence of a material violation" by the company. 17 C.F.R. § 205.3(b)(2) (2012); *see also In re* Kern, 816 S.E. 2d 574 (S.C. 2018) (discussing obligations of securities lawyers); U.S. DEP'T OF JUSTICE, PRINCIPLES OF FEDERAL PROSECUTION OF BUSINESS ORGANIZATIONS § 9-28.720 (quality of internal investigation can affect eligibility for "cooperation credit"); Cohen, *supra* note 26, at 129–30 (discussing obligations of securities lawyers).

32. *See* GOOD PRACTICES GUIDANCE, *supra* note 7, at 2. A "risk-based approach" is generally "intended to ensure that measures to prevent or mitigate money laundering and terrorist financing are commensurate with the risks identified . . . [H]igher risk areas should be subject to enhanced procedures, such as enhanced client due diligence ("CDD") . . . ." *Id.* at 8. The report continues: "This paper [identifies] the risk categories and offer[s] voluntary good practices designed to assist lawyers in detecting money laundering while satisfying their professional obligations." *Id.*

33. ABA Standing Comm. on Ethics & Prof'l Responsibility, Formal Op. 463, at 2 (2013) (summarizing GOOD PRACTICES GUIDANCE).

ABA Formal Opinion 463 addresses efforts to require U.S. lawyers to perform "gatekeeping" duties to protect the international financing system from criminal activity arising out of worldwide money-laundering and terrorist financing activities. Observing that "the Rules do not mandate that a lawyer perform a 'gatekeeper' role," especially in regards to "mandatory reporting" to public authorities "of suspicion about a client," Opinion 463 nevertheless identifies the Good Practices Guidance as a resource "consistent with the Model Rules" and with Informal Opinion 1470.[34] It also reinforces the duty to investigate in appropriate circumstances. Specifically, Opinion 463 states that "[i]t would be prudent for lawyers to undertake Client Due Diligence ("CDD") in appropriate circumstances to avoid facilitating illegal activity or being drawn unwittingly into a criminal activity. . . . [P]ursuant to a lawyer's ethical obligation to act competently, a duty to inquire further may also arise. An appropriate assessment of the client and the client's objectives, and the means for obtaining those objectives, are essential prerequisites for accepting a new matter or continuing a representation as new facts unfold."[35]

A lawyer's reasonable judgment under the circumstances presented, especially the information known and reasonably available to the lawyer at the time, does not violate the rules. Nor should a lawyer be subject to discipline because a course of action, objectively reasonable at the time it was chosen, turned out to be wrong with hindsight.[36]

---

34. *Id.*

35. *Id.* at 2–3 (emphasis added); *see also id.* at 2 n.10 ("The Good Practices Guidance encourages all lawyers to perform basic CDD by (1) identifying and verifying the identity of each client; (2) identifying and verifying the identity of any 'beneficial owner' of the client, defined as the natural person(s) with ultimate control of a client, when such an analysis is warranted from a risk-based standpoint; and (3) obtaining enough information to understand a client's circumstances, business, and objectives.").

36. In numerous contexts of evaluating attorney conduct, courts and regulators have warned against hindsight bias. *See* Woodruff v. Tomlin, 616 F.2d 924, 930 (6th Cir. 1980) ("[E]very losing litigant would be able to sue his attorney if he could find another attorney who was willing to second guess the decisions of the first attorney with the advantage of hindsight."); *In re* Claussen, 14 P.3d 586, 593–94 (Or. 2000) (en banc) (declining to discipline lawyer who aided client in converting insurance policy to cash while client's bankruptcy petition was pending; lawyer did not know client would abscond with money and cannot be judged by a standard of "clairvoyance" that reflects the knowledge of "hindsight"); N.Y.C. Bar Ass'n Comm. on Prof'l Ethics, Formal Op. 2018-4 (2018) ("Under the knowledge standard of Rule 1.2(d), a lawyer is not deemed to 'know' facts, or the significance of facts, that become evident only with the benefit of hindsight."); N.Y.C. Bar Ass'n Comm. on Prof'l Ethics, Formal Op. 2005-05 (2005) (in handling of "'thrust upon' concurrent client conflicts a lawyer who does balance the relevant considerations in good faith should not be subject to discipline for getting it wrong in hindsight"); Pa. Bar Ass'n Comm. on Legal Ethics & Prof'l Responsibility, Formal Op. 2001-100 (2001) (the propriety of accepting stock as payment of legal fees for a start-up "should be made based on the information available at the time of the transaction and not with the benefit of hindsight").

IV. Other Obligations Incident to the Duty to Inquire

If the client refuses to provide information or asks the lawyer not to evaluate the legality of a transaction the lawyer should explain to the client that the lawyer cannot undertake the representation unless an appropriate inquiry is made. If the client does not agree to provide information, then the lawyer must decline the representation or withdraw.[37] If the client agrees, but then temporizes and fails to provide the requested information, or provides incomplete information, the lawyer must remonstrate with the client. If that fails to rectify the information deficit, the lawyer must withdraw. Indeed, proceeding in a transaction without the requested information may, depending on the circumstances, be evidence of the lawyer's willful blindness under Rule 1.2(d).[38] If the client agrees, provides additional information, and the lawyer concludes that the requested services would amount to assisting in a crime or fraud, the lawyer must either discuss the matter further with the client, decline the representation, or seek to withdraw under Rule 1.16(a).[39]

In general, a lawyer should not assume that a client will be unresponsive to remonstration. However, if the client insists on proceeding with the proposed course of action despite the lawyer's remonstration, the lawyer must decline the representation or withdraw.[40] The lawyer may have discretion to disclose information relating to the representation under Model Rule 1.6(b)(1)-(3).[41]

If the lawyer needs information from sources other than the prospective client and can obtain that information without disclosing information protected by Rules 1.6 and 1.18, the information should be sought. If the lawyer needs to disclose protected information in order to analyze the transaction,

---

37. As discussed below, under Rule 1.2(c) a lawyer cannot assent to an unreasonable limitation on the representation even if the client seeks or insists upon such a limitation and offers consent.

38. *See also* N.Y.C. Bar Ass'n Comm. on Prof'l Ethics, Formal Op. 2018-4 at 5 ("[A] client's refusal to authorize and assist in an inquiry into the lawfulness of the client's proposed conduct will ordinarily constitute an additional, and very significant, 'red flag.'").

39. MODEL RULES R. 1.2 cmt. [13] ("If a lawyer comes to know or reasonably should know that a client expects assistance not permitted by the Rules of Professional Conduct or other law . . . the lawyer must consult with the client regarding the limitations on the lawyer's conduct.").

40. *See also* N.Y.C. Bar Ass'n Comm. on Prof'l Ethics, Formal Op. 2018-4 at 6 ("If it becomes clear during a lawyer's representation that the client has failed to take necessary corrective action, and the lawyer's continued representation would assist client conduct that is illegal or fraudulent, Rule 1.16(b)(1) mandates that the lawyer withdraw from representation."). For a discussion of the obligation to withdraw upon learning that a lawyer's services have been used to further a fraud, see ABA Standing Comm. on Ethics and Prof'l Responsibility, Formal Op. 92-366 (1992).

41. N.Y.C. Bar Ass'n Comm. on Prof'l Ethics, Formal Op. 2018-4 at 6.

the lawyer must seek the client's informed consent in advance. [42] If the client will not consent or the lawyer believes that seeking consent will lead to criminal or fraudulent activity, the lawyer must decline the representation or withdraw.[43]

If an inquiry would result in expenses that the client refuses to pay, the lawyer may choose to conduct the inquiry without payment or to decline or discontinue the representation.

Overall, as long as the lawyer conducts a reasonable inquiry, it is ordinarily proper to credit an otherwise trustworthy client where information gathered from other sources fails to resolve the issue, even if some doubt remains.[44] This conclusion may be reasonable in a variety of circumstances. For example, the lawyer may have represented the client in many other matters. The lawyer may know the client personally, professionally, or socially. The business arrangements and other individuals or parties involved in the transaction may be familiar to the lawyer.

Finally, Rule 1.2(c) permits a lawyer to "limit the scope of [a] representation if the limitation is reasonable under the circumstances and the client gives informed consent." Permitted scope limitations include, for example, that the client has limited but lawful objectives for the representation, or that certain available means to accomplish the client's objectives are too costly for the client or repugnant to the lawyer.[45] Any limitation, however, must "accord with the Rules of Professional Conduct and other law," including the lawyer's duty to provide competent representation.[46] In the circumstances addressed by this opinion, a lawyer may not agree to exclude inquiry into the legality of the transaction.

V. Hypotheticals

The following hypotheticals are intended to clarify when circumstances might require further inquiry because of risk factors known to the lawyer.

---

42. MODEL RULES R. 1.0(e) ("'Informed consent' denotes the agreement by a person to a proposed course of conduct after the lawyer has communicated adequate information and explanation about the material risks of and reasonably available alternatives to the proposed course of conduct.").

43. MODEL RULES R. 1.16(c)(2).

44. *See* N.Y.C. Bar Ass'n Comm. on Prof'l Ethics, Formal Op. 2018-4 at 5.

45. *See* MODEL RULES R. 1.2 cmt. [6] ("A limited representation may be appropriate because the client has limited objectives for the representation. In addition, the terms upon which representation is undertaken may exclude specific means that might otherwise be used to accomplish the client's objectives. Such limitations may exclude actions that the client thinks are too costly or that the lawyer regards as repugnant or imprudent.")

46. *See id.* cmt. [7] ("an agreement for a limited representation does not exempt a lawyer from the duty to provide competent representation"); *id.* cmt. [8] ("All agreements concerning a lawyer's representation of a client must accord with the Rules of Professional Conduct and other law.").

Some are drawn from the Good Practices Guidance, an important resource for transactional lawyers detailing how to conduct proper due diligence as well as how to identify and address risk factors in the most common scenarios in which a lawyer's assistance might be sought in criminal or fraudulent transactions.[47]

Further inquiry would be required in the first two examples because the combination of risk factors known to the lawyer creates a high probability that the client is engaged in criminal or fraudulent activity.

#1: A prospective client has significant business connections and interests abroad. The client has received substantial payments from sources other than his employer. The client holds these funds outside the US and wants to bring them into the US through a transaction that minimizes US tax liability. The client says: (i) he is "employed" outside the US but will not say how; (ii) the money is in a "foreign bank" in the name of a foreign corporation but the client will not identify the bank or the corporation; (iii) he has not disclosed the payments to his employer or any governmental authority or to anyone else; and (iv) he has not included the amounts in his US income tax returns.[48]

#2: A prospective client tells a lawyer he is an agent for a minister or other government official from a "high risk" jurisdiction[49] who wishes to remain anonymous and would like to purchase an expensive property in the United States. The property would be owned through corporations that have undisclosed beneficial owners. The prospective client says that large amounts of money will be involved in the purchase but is vague about the source of the funds, or the funds appear to come from "questionable" sources.[50]

If, on the same facts as #2, the client assures the lawyer that information will be provided but does not follow through, the lawyer must either withdraw or again discuss with the client the need for the information to continue

---

47. The analysis of the hypotheticals that follows draws on the GOOD PRACTICES GUIDANCE but should not be read to support the conclusion that any isolated risk factor identified in the GOOD PRACTICES GUIDANCE necessarily creates a duty to inquire in all matters in which it may be present. The question is whether a reasonable lawyer under the specific circumstances would be obliged to conduct further inquiry. The Committee further cautions that circumstances that render a specific jurisdiction or other factor "high risk" can change. On the one hand, if new circumstances presenting a greater risk arise the lawyer should take appropriate action, and may need to seek advice on what, if any, action is required. On the other hand, new circumstances may support acceptance or continuation of the representation by showing that, upon inquiry, the high-risk designation is inaccurate or inapplicable to the matter.

48. This hypothetical is drawn from ABA Comm. on Ethics & Prof'l Responsibility, Informal Opinion 1470, which concludes that a lawyer must conduct further inquiry.

49. For information about "high risk" jurisdictions, see GOOD PRACTICES GUIDANCE, *supra* note 7, at 15–16.

50. This hypothetical is based on *In re* Jankoff, 81 N.Y.S.3d 733, 734 (N.Y. App. Div. 2018) (public censure imposed on stipulated facts), and *In re* Koplik, 90 N.Y.S.3d 187 (N.Y. App. Div. 2019) (same).

in the representation, seek an explanation for the delay, and withdraw if the explanation the client offers is unsatisfactory. If the information provided is incomplete — e.g., information that leaves the identity of the actual funding sources opaque — the lawyer must follow the same course: withdraw or again discuss with the client the need for the information to continue in the representation, seek an explanation for the delay, and withdraw if the explanation offered is unsatisfactory.[51]

In examples #3 through #5 below, the duty to inquire depends on contextual factors, most significantly, the lawyer's familiarity with the client and the jurisdiction.

#3: A general practitioner in rural North Dakota receives a call from a long-term client asking her to form a limited liability company for the purpose of buying a ranch.[52]

#4: The general practitioner in rural North Dakota receives a call from a new and unknown prospective client saying that the client just won several million dollars in Las Vegas and needs the lawyer to form a limited liability company to buy a ranch.[53]

#5: A prospective client in New York City asks a general practitioner in a mid-size town in rural Georgia to provide legal services for the acquisition of several farms in rural Georgia. The prospective client tells the lawyer that he has made a lot of money in hedge funds and now wants to diversify his investments by purchasing these farms but says he doesn't want his purchases to cause a wave of land speculation and artificially inflate local prices. He wants to wire money into the law firm's trust account over time for the purchases. He asks the lawyer to create a series of LLCs to make strategic (and apparently unrelated) acquisitions.[54]

VI. Conclusion

Model Rule 1.2(d) prohibits a lawyer from advising or assisting a client in a transaction or other non-litigation matter the lawyer "knows" is criminal or fraudulent. That knowledge may be inferred from the circumstances, including a lawyer's willful blindness or conscious disregard of available facts. Accordingly, where there is a high probability that a client seeks to use the lawyer's services for criminal or fraudulent activity, the lawyer must in-

---

51. *See supra*, Section IV.

52. This hypothetical is drawn from Good Practices Guidance, *supra* note 7, at 8, and should not require further inquiry regarding the legitimacy of the transaction assuming prior matters have not involved abuse of the attorney-client relationship on the part of the client. It is likely, of course, that some inquiry into other details will be necessary to handle the transaction competently.

53. This hypothetical is drawn from Good Practices Guidance, *supra* note 7, at 8, and requires further inquiry.

54. This hypothetical is drawn from American Law Institute, Anti-Money Laundering Rules and Other Ethics Issues 450-51 (2017) and requires further inquiry.

quire further to avoid advising or assisting such activity. Even if information learned in the course of a preliminary interview or during a representation is insufficient to establish "knowledge" under Rule 1.2(d), other rules may require further inquiry to help the client avoid crime or fraud, to advance the client's legitimate interests, and to avoid professional misconduct. These include the duties of competence, diligence, communication, and honesty under Rules 1.1, 1.3, 1.4, 1.13, 1.16, and 8.4. If the client or prospective client refuses to provide information necessary to assess the legality of the proposed transaction, the lawyer must ordinarily decline the representation or withdraw under Rule 1.16. A lawyer's reasonable evaluation after that inquiry based on information reasonably available at the time does not violate the rules.

AMERICAN BAR ASSOCIATION
STANDING COMMITTEE ON ETHICS AND PROFESSIONAL RESPONSIBILITY
321 N. Clark Street, Chicago, Illinois 60654-4714 Telephone (312) 988-5328
CHAIR: Barbara S. Gillers, New York, NY
■ Lonnie T. Brown, Athens, GA ■ Robert Hirshon, Ann Arbor, MI ■ Hon. Goodwin Liu, San Francisco, CA
■ Thomas B. Mason, Washington, DC ■ Michael H. Rubin, Baton Rouge, LA
■ Lynda Shely, Scottsdale, AZ ■ Norman W. Spaulding, Stanford, CA
■ Elizabeth Clark Tarbert, Tallahassee, FL ■ Lisa D. Taylor, Parsippany, NJ

CENTER FOR PROFESSIONAL RESPONSIBILITY

Formal Opinion 492   June 9, 2020

Obligations to Prospective Clients: Confidentiality, Conflicts and "Significantly Harmful" Information

A prospective client is a person who consults a lawyer about the possibility of forming a client-lawyer relationship. Model Rule 1.18 governs whether the consultation limits the lawyer or the lawyer's firm from accepting a new client whose interests are materially adverse to the prospective client in a matter that is the same or substantially related to the subject of the consultation, even when no client-lawyer relationship results from the consultation. Under Model Rule 1.18 a lawyer is prohibited from accepting a new matter if the lawyer received information from the prospective client that could be significantly harmful to the prior prospective client in the new matter. Whether information learned by the lawyer could be significantly harmful is a fact-based inquiry depending on a variety of circumstances including the length of the consultation and the nature of the topics discussed. The inquiry does not require the prior prospective client to reveal confidential information. Further, even if the lawyer learned information that could be significantly harmful to the prior prospective client in the new matter, the lawyer's firm can accept the new matter if the lawyer is screened from the new matter or the prospective client provides informed consent, as set forth in Model Rule 1.18(d)(1) and (2).[1]

I. Introduction

Prospective clients often consult with a lawyer in anticipation of forming a client-lawyer relationship. These consultations give clients and lawyers an opportunity to get to know one another, to ascertain whether they will like working together, and to discuss preliminary matters like conflicts, fee arrangements, and the client's legal needs. During these consultations it is likely that the prospective client will reveal information necessary for each to decide whether to proceed. Some of that information could create a con-

---

1. This opinion is based on the ABA Model Rules of Professional Conduct as amended by the ABA House of Delegates through August 2019. The laws, court rules, regulations, rules of professional conduct and opinions promulgated in individual jurisdictions are controlling.

flict of interest that would prevent the lawyer from undertaking a future representation.

This opinion provides guidance on the types of information that could give rise to such disqualifying conflicts, what the prospective client should be asked to demonstrate in support of a claim that the lawyer has a conflict of interest in a subsequent matter, what precautions the lawyer and the lawyer's firm might take to avoid receiving disqualifying information during an initial consultation with a prospective client, and how to minimize the consequences of receiving such information.[2]

Prior to 2002, the Model Rules did not address obligations owed to individuals who consulted with a lawyer but never established a client-lawyer relationship with the lawyer.[3] In 2002, as part of the Ethics 2000 amendments, the ABA adopted Model Rule 1.18, which establishes a lawyer's obligations to a "prospective client."[4] Earlier, the ABA had provided guidance on ethical obligations to prospective clients in Formal Opinion 90-398 (1990).[5]

II. Analysis

A. Who is a "Prospective Client"?

Under Model Rule 1.18(a), a "prospective client" is "[a] person who consults with a lawyer about the possibility of forming a client-lawyer relationship with respect to a matter."[6] Comment [2] to Model Rule 1.18 explains:

A person becomes a prospective client by consulting with a lawyer about the possibility of forming a client-lawyer relationship with re-

---

2. Unless otherwise indicated, "prospective client" (sometimes referred to in case law as a "former prospective client") refers to an individual who has consulted with the lawyer about the possibility of forming a client-lawyer relationship with respect to a matter, but no client-lawyer relationship is subsequently established.

3. *See, e.g.,* Art Garwin, A Legislative History: The Development of the ABA Model Rules of Professional Conduct, 1982-2013 (2013).

4. *Id.* at 397-406. The only change to Rule 1.18 after 2002 was made in 2012, when the word "consults" was substituted for "discusses" in Rule 1.18(a) and in the Comments. This was not intended as a substantive change. The amendment clarified that communications that could constitute a "discussion" or a "consultation" could be written, oral or electronic. *See* Model Rules of Prof'l Conduct R. 1.18 cmt. [2] (2019) [hereinafter Model Rules]; Ellen J. Bennett & Helen W. Gunnarsson, Annotated Model Rules of Professional Conduct 309 (9th ed. 2019).

5. *See* ABA Comm. on Ethics & Prof'l Responsibility, Formal Op. 90-358 (1990) ("Information imparted to a lawyer by a would-be client seeking legal representation is protected from revelation or use under Model Rule 1.6 even though the lawyer does not undertake representation of or perform legal work for the would-be client.").

6. Model Rules R. 1.18 (2019). As discussed below a client-lawyer relationship may be formed during the consultation. The lawyer should take the precautions discussed in this opinion to avoid that result if that is not the lawyer's intention.

spect to a matter. Whether communications, including written, oral, or electronic communications, constitute a consultation depends on the circumstances. For example, a consultation is likely to have occurred if a lawyer, either in person or through the lawyer's advertising in any medium, specifically requests or invites the submission of information about a potential representation without clear and reasonably understandable warnings and cautionary statements that limit the lawyer's obligations, and a person provides information in response.[7]

Comment [2] clarifies, however, that not every contact between a lawyer and an individual regarding legal services makes that individual a "prospective client:"

[A] consultation does not occur if a person provides information to a lawyer in response to advertising that merely describes the lawyer's education, experience, areas of practice, and contact information, or provides legal information of general interest. Such a person communicates information unilaterally to a lawyer, without any reasonable expectation that the lawyer is willing to discuss the possibility of forming a client-lawyer relationship, and is thus not a "prospective client." Moreover, a person who communicates with a lawyer for the purpose of disqualifying the lawyer is not a "prospective client."[8]

Thus, a person who communicates information unilaterally to a lawyer after reviewing the lawyer's website or other advertising describing the lawyer's education and experience does not *for that reason alone* become a "prospective client" within the meaning of Model Rule 1.18.[9] Additionally, as the

---

7. MODEL RULES R. 1.18(b) cmt. [2].

8. *Id.*

9. *See* ABA Comm. on Ethics & Prof'l Responsibility, Formal Op. 10-457 (2010) ("not all initial communications from persons who wish to be prospective clients" result in such status); Ariz. State Bar, Advisory Op. 02-04 (2002) (no duty of confidentiality owed to person who unilaterally sends unsolicited information to a lawyer); Fla. Bar, Advisory Op. 07-3 (2009) (a person seeking legal services who sends information unilaterally to a lawyer has no reasonable expectation of confidentiality regarding that information); San Diego County Bar Ass'n, Advisory Op. 2006-1 (2006) (no duty of confidentiality owed to someone who sends information to a lawyer after obtaining the email address of the lawyer from a state bar website); Va. State Bar Op. 1842 (2008) (lawyer has no duty of confidentiality to person who unilaterally transmits unsolicited information in voice mail or email); Wis. State Bar Prof'l Ethics Comm., Formal Op. EF-11-03 (2011) (person seeking representation who sends unsolicited confidential information through email to a lawyer does not thereby establish a client-lawyer relationship or a duty of confidentiality).

last sentence of Comment [2] notes, if the person consulting with the lawyer does not have a reasonable intent to retain the lawyer, but instead is merely attempting to disqualify the lawyer from representing anyone else in the matter, the person is not a "prospective client."[10]

B. The Obligation to Protect Confidential Information

Model Rule 1.18(b) imposes a duty of confidentiality with respect to information learned during a consultation, even when no client-lawyer relationship ensues. It provides:

> Even when no client-lawyer relationship ensues, a lawyer who has learned information from a prospective client shall not use or reveal that information, except as Rule 1.9 would permit with respect to information of a former client."[11]

This duty includes protecting all information learned during the consultation, unless the lawyer has the informed consent of the prospective client to condition the consultation on the lawyer *not* maintaining the confidentiality of the information communicated. As stated by Comment [5] to Model Rule 1.18, "[a] lawyer may condition a consultation with a prospective client on the person's informed consent that no information disclosed during the consultation will prohibit the lawyer from representing a different client in the matter."[12] Model Rule 1.0(e) defines "informed consent."[13]

---

10. Bernacki v. Bernacki, 1 N.Y.S.3d 761, 764 (Sup. Ct. 2015) (husband in a divorce sent an email to his wife titled "Attorneys Which [sic] Whom I Have Sought Legal Advice" and then listed "twelve of the most experienced matrimonial attorneys in the county," each of whom the husband asserted "would conflict themselves out" or be subject to disqualification); RESTATEMENT OF THE LAW (THIRD), THE LAW GOVERNING LAWYERS § 15 cmt. c [hereinafter RESTATEMENT THIRD] ("a tribunal may consider whether the prospective client disclosed confidential information to the lawyer for the purpose of preventing the lawyer or the lawyer's firm from representing an adverse party rather than in a good faith endeavor to determine whether to retain the lawyer").

11. MODEL RULES R. 1.18(b). *See also* N.Y.C. Bar Ass'n Comm. on Prof'l Ethics, Formal Op. 2013-1 (2013) (discussing the scope of protected information under Rule 1.18(b)); D.C. Bar Op. 374 (2018) (information from prospective client is protected from disclosure to the same extent as client information is protected by D.C. Rule 1.6)); RESTATEMENT THIRD, *supra* note 10, § 59 cmt. c (2000) ("Information acquired during the representation or before or after the representation is confidential so long as it is not generally known . . . and relates to the representation. Such information, for example, might be acquired by the lawyer in considering whether to undertake a representation.").

12. MODEL RULES R. 1.18 cmt. [5].

13. MODEL RULES R. 1.0(e).

C. Disqualifying Conflicts Based on the Acquisition of "Significantly Harmful" Information

Model Rule 1.18(c) provides for potential disqualification arising out of the consultation:

A lawyer subject to paragraph (b) shall not represent a client with interests materially adverse to those of a prospective client in the same or a substantially related matter *if the lawyer received information from the prospective client that could be significantly harmful to that person in the matter* . . . . [14]

The phrase "significantly harmful" qualifies the lawyer's duties toward prospective clients where no client-lawyer relationship is established and distinguishes these duties from duties owed to clients. Comment [1] explains:

Prospective clients, like clients, may disclose information to a lawyer, place documents or other property in the lawyer's custody, or rely on the lawyer's advice. A lawyer's consultations with a prospective client usually are limited in time and depth and leave both the prospective client and the lawyer free (and sometimes required) to proceed no further. Hence, *prospective clients should receive some but not all of the protection afforded clients.*[15]

The notion that "prospective clients" receive "some but not all of the protections afforded clients" can be illustrated by comparing the application of Model Rule 1.9 with Model Rule 1.18 with respect to possible conflicts of interests. Under Model Rule 1.9, "[a] lawyer who has formerly represented a client in a matter shall not thereafter represent another person in the same or substantially related matter in which that person's interest are materially adverse to the interests of the former client" unless certain conditions are met.[16] As Comment [3] to Model Rule 1.9 explains, for former clients the question is whether confidential information *could have been* shared, not whether confi-

---

14. MODEL RULES R. 1.18(c) (emphasis added).

15. MODEL RULES R. 1.18 cmt. [1] (emphasis added). *See also* Wis. State Bar Prof'l Ethics Comm., Formal Op. EI-10-03 (2011) (the "more lenient standard [in Rule 1.18] reflects the attenuated relationship with prospective clients"); N.Y.C. Bar Ass'n Comm. on Prof'l Ethics, Formal Op. 2013-1, *supra* note 11 ("The 'significantly harmful' test makes the [Rule 1.18(c)] restriction less exacting than the corresponding restriction on representations that are materially adverse to a former client."). A person and a lawyer may, of course, have as many consultations and discussions as they mutually find beneficial in order to determine whether to enter into a client-lawyer relationship. In such circumstances, however, the lawyer is more likely to receive information that could be "significantly harmful" in a later representation adverse to the prospective client.

16. MODEL RULES R. 1.9(a).

dences were in fact shared, regardless of the harmful quality of the information. The Comment reads, in part,

> A former client is not required to reveal the confidential information learned by the lawyer in order to establish a substantial risk that the lawyer has confidential information to use in a subsequent matter. A conclusion about the possession of such information may be based on the nature of the services the lawyer provided the former client and the information that would in ordinary practice be learned by a lawyer providing such services.[17]

A former client need not reveal confidential information to satisfy the "substantial relationship" test. "Matters are 'substantially related' for purposes of [Model Rule 1.9] if they involve the same transaction or legal dispute or *if there otherwise is a substantial risk* that confidential factual information as would normally have been obtained in the prior representation would materially advance the client's position in the subsequent matter."[18] As described by Judge Posner in in *Analytica v. NPD Research*:

> [A] lawyer may not represent an adversary of his former client if the subject matter of the two representations is "substantially related," which means: if the lawyer *could have obtained confidential information* in the first representation that would have been relevant in the second. It is irrelevant whether he actually obtained such information and used it against his former client . . . .[19]

Model Rule 1.18 is different than Model Rule 1.9 because it imposes the additional requirement, not found in Model Rule 1.9, that the prospective client have communicated information that "could be significantly harmful" in a subsequent matter. As a result, the mere fact that a prospective client consulted with a lawyer in a substantially related matter is not sufficient, alone, to disqualify the lawyer from a later matter.[20] Nor is it sufficient to conclude

---

17. MODEL RULES R. 1.9 cmt. [3]. *See also* N.Y.C. Bar Ass'n Comm. on Prof'l Ethics, Formal Op. 2013-1, *supra* note 11, at 5 ("Under Rule 1.9(a), the bar against adverse representation is automatic; if the relevant parties' interests are materially adverse and the matters are the same or substantially related, the bar applies whether or not the lawyer received any information, harmful or otherwise from the former client.") (footnote omitted); Analytica Inc. v. NPD Research, 708 F.2d 1263, 1267 (7th Cir. 1983) ("If the 'substantial relationship' test applies . . . it is not appropriate for the court to inquire into whether actual confidences were disclosed [by the former client].").

18. MODEL RULES R. 1.9 cmt. [3] (emphasis added) .

19. *Analytica, Inc.*, 708 F.2d at 1266 (emphasis added).

20. Bernacki v. Bernacki, 1 N.Y.S.3d 761, 764 (Sup. Ct. 2015) (prospective client's "reference to the information as 'confidential' without more is insufficient"); RESTATEMENT THIRD,

that a conflict exists merely because a prospective client volunteers information to a lawyer because, as noted above, the unilateral transmission of information to a lawyer does not create a Model Rule 1.18 duty, nor will Model Rule 1.18 protect someone who contacts a lawyer with the intent to disqualify the lawyer from representing other parties in the matter.[21]

With respect to what must be shown to establish that a person is entitled to the protections of Model Rule 1.18, evidence beyond the mere fact of a consultation is generally required.[22] The fact that the prospective client must come forward with some evidence concerning the contents of the consultation with the lawyer does not mean, however, that the prospective client must disclose confidential information or detail the substance of the discussions. The cases and other authorities support the conclusion that only certain disclosures are required, for example, the date, duration and manner of communication (*i.e.*, in person, email, over the phone, etc.), and a summary description of the topics discussed.[23]

With respect to the "significantly harmful" test, information disclosed by the person invoking the protection of Model Rule 1.18 need not demonstrate that the harm is certain to occur in order to demonstrate a conflict. Instead, the Model Rule addresses information that "could be significantly harmful,"

---

supra note 10, § 15, cmt. c (after a consultation with a prospective client, "a lawyer is not always prohibited from representing a client with interests adverse to those of the prospective client in the same or a substantially related matter").

21. *See* MODEL RULES R. 1.18 cmt. [2]. *See also supra* note 9 (collecting opinions).

22. *See* Thomson v. Duker, 346 S.W.3d 390, 396 (Mo. Ct. App. 2011) (Rule 1.18 requires "at least some disclosure, either by the objecting prospective client or by the lawyer, of the scope of information discussed" during the consultation) (cites omitted); RESTATEMENT THIRD, *supra* note 10, § 15(c) (the prospective client "bears the burden of persuading the tribunal that the lawyer received information "that could be significantly harmful to the prospective client in the matter"); *but see* ABA Comm. on Ethics & Prof'l Responsibility, Formal Op. 10-457, *supra* note 9 (a lawyer's website that "specifically encourages a website visitor to submit a personal inquiry about a proposed representation on a conveniently provided electronic form" may be deemed to invite the submission of confidential information and therefore provide information to the lawyer that could be "significantly harmful" to the prospective client in a subsequent adverse representation).

23. The format could be similar to what is known as a "privilege log," submitted to a court in connection with a claim of privilege. The information which is the subject of the privilege claim is not disclosed. Rather information sufficient to establish the claim of privilege is ordinarily all that is required. Federal Rule of Civil Procedure 26(b)(5) (requiring that privilege logs "describe the nature of the documents, communications, or tangible things not produced or disclosed --- and do so in a manner that, without revealing information itself privileged or protected will enable other parties to assess the claim [of privilege or other protection]." In appropriate instances, protected information can be disclosed to courts *in camera*. *See* O Builders Associates, Inc. v. Yuna Corp. of N.J., 19 A.3d 966, 978 (N.J. 2011) ("the parties may protect the confidentiality of their information by, among other means, requesting that the record be subject to a protective order . . . and the movant may further request that the application be considered *in camera*") (cites omitted); Keith v. Keith, 140 So.3d 1202, 1211-1212 (La. Ct. App. 2014) (discussing the use of *in camera* proceedings in Rule 1.18 decisions).

a standard that "focuses on the *potential* use of the information."[24] Post-hoc promises by the lawyer not to use the information do not change the standard from one of potential use or harm to a standard that requires actual use or harm.[25]

Information that is typically viewed as "significantly harmful" includes, for instance, "views on various settlement issues including price and timing"; "personal accounts of each relevant event [and the prospective client's] strategic thinking concerning how to manage the situation"; an "18-minute phone call" with a "prospective client-plaintiff [during which a firm] 'had 'outlined potential claims'" against defendant and "'discussed specifics as to amount of money needed to settle the case'"; and a presentation by a corporation seeking to bring an action of "the underlying facts and legal theories about its proposed lawsuit."[26] Other recognized categories of significantly harmful information include: "sensitive personal information" in a divorce case; "premature possession of the prospective client's financial information"; knowledge of "settlement position"; a "prospective client's personal thoughts and impressions regarding the facts of the case and possible litigation strategies,"[27] and "the possible terms and structure of a proposed bid" by one corporation to acquire another.[28]

The Restatement also offers helpful guidance. Section 15(2) of the Restatement provides for disqualification of a lawyer who, in discussing "the possibility of . . . forming a client-lawyer relationship" received "from the prospective client confidential information that could be significantly harmful to the prospective client" in a matter."[29] Further, in the words of the North Dakota Supreme Court:

> Information may be "significantly harmful" if it is sensitive or privileged information that the lawyer would not have received in the ordinary course of due diligence; or if it is information that has long-term significance or continuing relevance to the matter, such as motives, litigation strategies or potential weakness. "Significantly harmful" may also be the premature possession of information that could have a substantial impact on settlement proposals and trial

---

24. N.Y.C. Bar Ass'n Comm. on Prof'l Ethics, Formal Op. 2013-1, *supra* note 11, at 5 (emphasis in original).

25. *Id.*

26. *Id.* at 8, note 9 (cites omitted).

27. Wis. State Bar Prof'l Ethics Comm., Formal Op. EI-10-03, *supra* note 15, at 4-5 (cites omitted).

28. *See* N.Y.C. Bar Ass'n Comm. on Prof'l Ethics, Formal Op. 2013-1, *supra* note 11, at 7 (discussion of "Scenario 3").

29. RESTATEMENT THIRD, *supra* note 10, § 15 (2000). The language "information that could be significantly harmful to that person" in Rule 1.18(c) tracks the Restatement's language.

strategy; the personal thoughts and impression about the facts of the case; or information that is extensive, critical, or of significant use.[30]

As an illustration, the Restatement discusses an initial meeting between a lawyer and a prospective client seeking a divorce. The prospective client and the lawyer have an hour-long conversation in which they discuss the prospective client's "reasons for seeking a divorce and the nature and extent of his and Spouse's property interests." The prospective client decides not to retain the lawyer because "the suggested fee [is] too high." Thereafter, the spouse seeks to hire the lawyer. The Restatement concludes that the lawyer received "significantly harmful information" from the prospective client and cannot represent the opposing spouse.[31]

On the other hand, and as the New Jersey Supreme Court explained in *O Builders & Associates v. Yuna Corp*, "significantly harmful" information under Rule 1.18 "cannot be simply detrimental in general to the former prospective client, but the harm suffered must be prejudicial in fact to the former prospective client within the confines of the specific matter in which disqualification is sought, a determination that is exquisitely fact-sensitive and -specific."[32]

So, for example, information that causes embarrassment or inconvenience "does not seem to be '*significant*'" while information relating to "[c]ivil or criminal liability would seem to easily qualify."[33] Specific instances in which information was deemed *not* to be "significantly harmful" include: a lawyer who "avoided learning the details of the case in half-hour consultation"; a brief consultation that occurred ten years earlier and concerned a "tenuously related matter"; and a one-day "'beauty contest'" consultation where the prospective client's in-house lawyer "regulated disclosures and

---

30. Kuntz v. Disciplinary Bd. of Supreme Court of North Dakota, 869 N.W.2d 117, 125 (N.D. 2015) (comparing duties under North Dakota Rule 1.18 with duties under North Dakota Rule 1.9, which are analogous to the corresponding Model Rules) (cites omitted). *See also In re* Carpenter, 863 N.W.2d 223 (N.D. 2015) ([a] lawyer can also violate Rule 1.18(b) if the lawyer misuses information gathered in connection with a consultation with a prospective client; discipline imposed for using information about owners of mineral rights learned as part of a consultation with a prospective client for the benefit of a subsequent client in a substantially related matter).

31. RESTATEMENT THIRD, *supra* note 10, § 15(2), at 142 (2000). *See also* Sturdivant v. Sturdivant, 241 S.W.3d 740, 742 (Ark. 2006) (prospective client provided "significantly harmful information" when he told divorce attorney "everything he knew regarding the children and his concerns about his former wife"). *See also* Wis. State Bar Prof'l Ethics Comm., Formal Op. EI-10-03, *supra* note 15, at 4-5 (collecting cases); N.Y.C. Bar Ass'n Comm. on Prof'l Ethics, Formal Op. 2013-1, *supra* note 11, at note 9 (collecting cases).

32. O Builders Associates, Inc. v. Yuna Corp. of N.J., 19 A.3d 966, 978 (N.J. 2011) (cites omitted). *See also Kuntz*, 869 N.W.2d at 125.

33. John M. Burman, *Waiving a Conflict of Interest and Revoking That Waiver Part III – Conflicts Involving Prospective and Former Clients*, 34 WYO. LAW. 45, note 53 (2011) (emphasis added).

there was no showing that confidential information disclosed could be detrimental to client."[34]

Context is important. In *Marriage of Perry*, for instance, the court concluded that information had been disclosed during the consultation but did not disqualify the lawyer pursuant to Montana's Rule 1.18 because the prospective client "did not establish that any information [she disclosed to the challenged counsel] in telephone calls several years earlier could have any impact on the proceeding, particularly since [the challenged counsel] "was not associated as counsel until three years into the proceeding, by which time substantially more information had been disclosed."[35] Further, information that may be on its face "significantly harmful," may not be such if the court determines that it was generally known by the parties.[36]

D. Limiting Information During an Initial Consultation and Avoiding Imputation of Conflicts.

In order to avoid receiving "significantly harmful information" from a prospective client, lawyers should warn prospective clients against disclosing detailed information. Comment [4] to Model Rule 1.18 states that a lawyer "should limit the initial consultation [with a prospective client] to only such information as reasonably appears necessary" for the purpose of "considering whether or not to undertake a new matter."[37] This caution, however, is not intended to discourage lawyers from engaging in a thorough discussion with prospective clients in order to ascertain whether the lawyer wants to take on the representation. It is simply a reminder that the more information learned in a consultation, the more likely that the lawyer may be precluded from representing other parties in a substantially related matter. Comment [5] provides that a lawyer "may condition a consultation with a prospective client on the person's informed consent that no information disclosed during the consultation will prohibit the lawyer from representing a different client in the matter."[38] If an agreement between the lawyer and the prospective cli-

---

34. RESTATEMENT THIRD, *supra* note 10, § 15 cmt. c, Reporters Note (cites omitted).

35. *Marriage of Perry*, 293 P.3d 170, 176 (Mont. 2013) *but see* Wis. State Bar Prof'l Ethics Comm., Formal Op. EI-10-03, *supra* note 15 ("the fact that information may be discoverable at some point in current or future litigation, does not by itself mean that the information should not be considered significantly harmful. [It] may be a factor in the analysis, but is not . . . determinative.").

36. Mayers v. Stone Castle Partners, 1 N.Y.S.3d 58, 62 (1st Dept. 2015) (information not significantly harmful because it was generally known, the adversary was aware of some of the details of the relevant transaction, and the motion to disqualify opposing counsel was made "a year into the litigation").

37. MODEL RULES R. 1.18 cmt. [4].

38. MODEL RULES R. 1.18 cmt. [5]. With prospective clients who are inexperienced in legal matters, the burden will be on the lawyer to demonstrate that the discussions conformed to the agreed limitations or that the prospective client provided informed consent to the use of the information provided during the consultation. How the lawyer meets this

ent *"expressly so provides,* the prospective client may also consent to the lawyer's subsequent use of information received from the prospective client."[39] This may include, for example, an explicit caution on a website intake link saying that sending information to the firm will not create a client-lawyer relationship and the information may not be kept privileged or confidential.

Once a lawyer receives confidential information from a prospective client that disqualifies the lawyer from future adverse representations imputation of the conflict to other lawyers in a firm may be avoided through screening, in some circumstances. Model Rule 1.18(d) reads:

> When the lawyer has received disqualifying information as defined in paragraph (c), representation is permissible if: (1) both the affected client and the prospective client have given informed consent, confirmed in writing; *or:* (2) the lawyer who received the information took reasonable measures to avoid exposure to more disqualifying information than was reasonably necessary to determine whether to represent the prospective client; and (i) the disqualified lawyer is timely screened from any participation in the matter and is apportioned no part of the fee therefrom; and (ii) written notice is promptly given to the prospective client.[40]

---

burden depends on the circumstances. N.Y.C. Bar Ass'n Comm. on Prof'l Ethics, Formal Op. 2013-1, *supra* note 11 ("the adequacy [of the lawyer's explanation and disclosure] will depend on the relevant facts, particularly the sophistication of the consenting party and [the party's] familiarity with the retention of legal representation and conflict waivers. For example, if the prospective client is an organization that frequently retains lawyers, particularly one with in-house legal advisors, it may need to be told little more than that the law firm would be free to use or reveal information received in the consultation or to represent others with materially adverse interests in the same or any related matter . . . in the event the organization does not retain the firm.").

39. MODEL RULES R. 1.18 cmt. [5] (emphasis added). *See also* N.Y.C. Bar Ass'n Comm. on Prof'l Ethics, Formal Op. 2013-1, *supra* note 11, at 5 (noting that the consent must be informed and confirmed in writing and recommending other steps to ensure the effectiveness of the waiver); MODEL RULES R. 1.0 cmt. [6] (discussing how adequacy of disclosure and explanation by the lawyer may depend on the sophistication of the client); Wis. State Bar Prof'l Ethics Comm., Formal Op. EI-10-03, *supra* note 15, at 6 (discussing how to avoid later disqualification through informed consent of the prospective client).

40. MODEL RULES R. 1.18(d) (emphasis added). For the requirements of informed consent see Model Rule 1.0(e) and Comments [6] and [7] to Rule 1.0. Informed consent under Rule 1.18 may occur in different contexts. "Informed consent" may be obtained at the outset of a consultation containing a condition that any information provided by the prospective client "will not be disqualifying," as set forth in Comment [5] to Model Rule 1.18. "Informed consent" may also allow a lawyer who has received "significantly harmful" information from a prospective client to represent an adverse party pursuant to Model Rule 1.18(d) above. In the former scenario, providing adequate disclosure at the outset of a consultation with a prospective client poses challenges for the lawyer who may not know much about the prospective client's matter and may know even less about the opposing party's potential claims.

E. Resolving Disputes Related to "Significantly Harmful" Information

Finally, when the basic facts are contested, courts or disciplinary authorities may benefit from reviewing documents and/or holding a hearing to assess the facts and, if necessary, determine the credibility of the lawyer and of the person invoking Model Rule 1.18.[41] However, evidentiary hearings may not be necessary and, when conducted, should avoid forcing the prospective client to reveal confidential information.[42]

IV. Conclusion

A lawyer who receives information that "could be significantly harmful" from a prospective client and then represents a client in the same or a substantially related matter where that client's interests are materially adverse to those of the prospective client violates Model Rule 1.18(c) unless the conflict is waived by the prospective client. Whether information that "could be significantly harmful" has been disclosed by a prospective client is a fact-specific inquiry and determined on a case-by-case basis. The test focuses on the potential harm in the new matter. The prospective client must provide some details about the time, manner and duration of communications with the lawyer and also some description of the topics discussed, but need not disclose the contents of the discussion or confidential information. Whether information conveyed is "significantly harmful" in the subsequent matter will depend on, for example, the duration of the discussion, the topics discussed, whether the lawyer reviewed documents, and whether the information conveyed is known by other parties, as well as the relationship between the information and the issues in the subsequent matter.

---

41. *See, e.g.,* Marriage of Perry, 293 P.3d 170, 176-77 (Mont. 2013) (trial court held an evidentiary hearing and examined notes taken by the lawyer concerning the communications with the prospective client before ruling on whether "significantly harmful information" had been disclosed).

42. *See* Richman v. Eighth Judicial Dist. Court, No. 60676, 2013 WL 3357115 at *6 (Nev. May 31, 2013) (trial court did not abuse its discretion by ruling on affidavits and documents without an evidentiary hearing).

AMERICAN BAR ASSOCIATION
STANDING COMMITTEE ON ETHICS AND PROFESSIONAL RESPONSIBILITY
321 N. Clark Street, Chicago, Illinois 60654-4714 Telephone (312) 988-5328
CHAIR: Barbara S. Gillers, New York, NY
■ Lonnie T. Brown, Athens, GA ■ Robert Hirshon, Ann Arbor, MI ■ Hon. Goodwin Liu, San Francisco, CA
■ Thomas B. Mason, Washington, DC ■ Michael H. Rubin, Baton Rouge, LA
■ Lynda Shely, Scottsdale, AZ ■ Norman W. Spaulding, Stanford, CA
■ Elizabeth Clark Tarbert, Tallahassee, FL ■ Lisa D. Taylor, Parsippany, NJ

CENTER FOR PROFESSIONAL RESPONSIBILITY

AMERICAN BAR ASSOCIATION
STANDING COMMITTEE ON ETHICS AND PROFESSIONAL RESPONSIBILITY

Formal Opinion 493   **July 15, 2020**

Model Rule 8.4(g): Purpose, Scope, and Application

This opinion offers guidance on the purpose, scope, and application of Model Rule 8.4(g). The Rule prohibits a lawyer from engaging in conduct related to the practice of law that the lawyer knows or reasonably should know is harassment or discrimination on the basis of various categories, including race, sex, religion, national origin, and sexual orientation. Whether conduct violates the Rule must be assessed using a standard of objective reasonableness, and only conduct that is found harmful will be grounds for discipline. [1]

Rule 8.4(g) covers conduct related to the practice of law that occurs outside the representation of a client or beyond the confines of a courtroom. In addition, it is not restricted to conduct that is severe or pervasive, a standard utilized in the employment context. However, and as this opinion explains, conduct that violates paragraph (g) will often be intentional and typically targeted at a particular individual or group of individuals, such as directing a racist or sexist epithet towards others or engaging in unwelcome, nonconsensual physical conduct of a sexual nature.

The Rule does not prevent a lawyer from freely expressing opinions and ideas on matters of public concern, nor does it limit a lawyer's speech or conduct in settings unrelated to the practice of law. The fact that others may personally disagree with or be offended by a lawyer's expression does not establish a violation. The Model Rules are rules of reason, and whether conduct violates Rule 8.4(g) must necessarily be judged, in context, from an objectively reasonable perspective.

Besides being advocates and counselors, lawyers also serve a broader public role. Lawyers "should further the public's understanding of and confidence in the rule of law and the justice system because legal institutions in a constitutional democracy depend on popular participation and support to maintain their authority." [2] *Discriminatory and harassing conduct, when engaged in by lawyers in connection with the practice of law, engenders skepticism and distrust of those charged with ensuring*

---

1. This opinion is based on the ABA Model Rules of Professional Conduct as amended by the ABA House of Delegates through August 2019. The laws, court rules, regulations, rules of professional conduct, and opinions promulgated in individual jurisdictions are controlling.

2. MODEL RULES OF PROF'L CONDUCT Scope [14] (2019) [hereinafter MODEL RULES].

justice and fairness. Enforcement of Rule 8.4(g) is therefore critical to maintaining the public's confidence in the impartiality of the legal system and its trust in the legal profession as a whole.[3]

I. Introduction

In August 2016, the ABA House of Delegates adopted Model Rule 8.4(g).[4] The Rule prohibits a lawyer from "engag[ing] in conduct that the lawyer knows or reasonably should know is harassment or discrimination on the basis of race, sex, religion, national origin, ethnicity, disability, age, sexual orientation, gender identity, marital status or socioeconomic status in conduct related to the practice of law."[5] Adoption of paragraph (g) followed years of study and debate within the ABA. This opinion offers guidance on the Rule's purpose, scope, and application.

The conduct addressed by Rule 8.4(g) harms the legal system and the administration of justice. As one court emphasized in sanctioning a male lawyer for disparagingly referring to his female adversary as "babe" and making other derogatory, sexual comments during a deposition,

> [The lawyer's] behavior . . . was a crass attempt to gain an unfair advantage through the use of demeaning language, a blatant example of "sexual [deposition] tactics." . . . "These actions . . . have no place in our system of justice and when attorneys engage in such actions they do not merely reflect on their own lack of professionalism but they disgrace the entire legal profession and the system of justice that provides a stage for such oppressive actors."[6]

---

3. As explained in this opinion, events in the legal profession and in the broader community influenced the development of Rule 8.4(g) and demonstrated the necessity for its adoption. The police-involved killing of George Floyd and the unprecedented social awareness generated by it and other similar tragedies have brought the subject of racial justice to the forefront, further underscoring the importance of Rule 8.4(g) and this opinion.

4. *See Annual Meeting 2016: ABA Amends Model Rules to Add Anti-Discrimination, Anti-Harassment Provision* (Aug. 8, 2016),

https://www.americanbar.org/groups/professional_responsibility/committees_commissions/ethicsandprofessionalresponsibility/ (summarizing events at the House of Delegates meeting). The provision was adopted by voice vote, with no one speaking in opposition. *See* Stephen Gillers, *A Rule to Forbid Bias and Harassment in Law Practice: A Guide for State Courts Considering Model Rule 8.4(g)*, 30 GEO. J. LEGAL ETHICS 195, 197 (2017).

5. MODEL RULES R. 8.4(g).

6. Mullaney v. Aude, 730 A.2d 759, 767 (Md. Ct. Spec. App. 1999) (quoting trial judge in the case); *see also* Principe v. Assay Partners, 586 N.Y.S.2d 182, 185 (Sup. Ct. 1992) ("[D] iscriminatory conduct on the part of an attorney is inherently and palpably adverse to the goals of justice and the legal profession. . . . 'The continued existence of a free and democratic society depends upon recognition of the concept that justice is based upon the rule of law grounded in respect for the dignity of the individual. . . . Law so grounded makes justice possible, for only through such law does the dignity of the individual attain respect

Comment [3] to the prior version of Rule 8.4 explained that some of the same behavior subjected a lawyer to discipline when the behavior was prejudicial to the administration of justice.[7] Other rules prohibit similar conduct in contexts related to the representation of a client.[8] Rule 8.4(g) is

---

and protection. . . .' While the conduct here falls under the heading of sexist, the same principle applies to any professional discriminatory conduct involving any of the variations to which human beings are subject, whether it be religion, sexual orientation, physical condition, race, nationality or any other difference.") (quoting Preamble to the Code of Professional Responsibility)); Cruz-Aponte v. Caribbean Petroleum Corp., 123 F. Supp. 3d 276, 280 (D.P.R. 2015) ("When an attorney engages in discriminatory behavior, it reflects not only on the attorney's lack of professionalism, but also tarnishes the image of the entire legal profession and disgraces our system of justice."); *In re* Thomsen, 837 N.E.2d 1011, 1012 (Ind. 2005) ("Interjecting race into proceedings where it is not relevant is offensive, unprofessional and tarnishes the image of the profession as a whole."); *In re* Charges of Unprofessional Conduct, 597 N.W.2d 563, 568 (Minn. 1999) (maintaining that "it is especially troubling" when a lawyer engages in "race-based misconduct" and, if not addressed, "undermines confidence in our system of justice").

On June 4, 2020, the Washington Supreme Court issued an open letter regarding the issues raised by the George Floyd situation, forcefully embracing the cause of racial justice: "We call on every member of our legal community to reflect on this moment and ask ourselves how we may work together to eradicate racism. . . . We go by the title of "Justice" and we reaffirm our deepest level of commitment to achieving justice by ending racism. We urge you to join us in these efforts. This is our moral imperative." Supreme Court of Washington, *Open Letter to the Judiciary and the Legal Community* (June 4, 2020), https://www.courts. wa.gov/content/publicUpload/Supreme%20Court%20News/Judiciary%20Legal%20Community%20 SIGNED%20060420.pdf.

7. MODEL RULES R. 8.4(d) cmt. [3] (1998). In particular, the Comment stated:

A lawyer who, in the course of representing a client, knowingly manifests by words or conduct, bias or prejudice based upon race, sex, religion, national origin, disability, age, sexual orientation or socioeconomic status, violates paragraph (d) *when such actions are prejudicial to the administration of justice*. Legitimate advocacy respecting the foregoing factors does not violate paragraph (d). A trial judge's finding that peremptory challenges were exercised on a discriminatory basis does not alone establish a violation of this rule.

Id. (emphasis added).

8. *See, e.g.,* MODEL RULES R. 3.5(d) (prohibits "conduct intended to disrupt a tribunal"); MODEL RULES R. 4.4(a) (prohibits using "means that have no substantial purpose other than to embarrass, delay, or burden a third person" when "representing a client").

The Model Code of Judicial Conduct has long contained a provision prohibiting judges from engaging in this sort of discriminatory and harassing conduct and requiring that judges ensure that lawyers appearing before them adhere to the same restrictions. MODEL CODE OF JUDICIAL CONDUCT R. 2.3 (2011). The pertinent portion of the Rule provides:

(B) A judge shall not, in the performance of judicial duties, by words or conduct manifest bias or prejudice, or engage in harassment, including but not limited to bias, prejudice, or harassment based upon race, sex, gender, religion, national origin, eth-

more expansive, also forbidding harassment and discrimination in practice-related settings beyond the courtroom and in contexts that may not be connected to a specific client representation.[9] Such breadth was necessitated by evidence that sexual harassment, in particular, occurs outside of court-related and representational situations—for example, in non-litigation matters or at law firm social events or bar association functions.[10]

---

nicity, disability, age, sexual orientation, marital status, socioeconomic status, or political affiliation, and shall not permit court staff, court officials, or others subject to the judge's direction and control to do so.

(C) A judge shall require lawyers in proceedings before the court to refrain from manifesting bias or prejudice, or engaging in harassment, based upon attributes including but not limited to race, sex, gender, religion, national origin, ethnicity, disability, age, sexual orientation, marital status, socioeconomic status, or political affiliation, against parties, witnesses, lawyers, or others.

Model Rules R. 2.3(B) & (C); *see also* Gillers, *supra* note 4, at 209-11 (discussing adoption of CJC Rule 2.3 and its relationship to Model Rule 8.4(g)). In addition, in 2015, the ABA revised its *Standards for Criminal Justice: Prosecutorial Function and Defense Function* to add anti-bias provisions for both prosecutors and defense counsel. For example, the Defense Function standard provides:

(a) Defense counsel should not manifest or exercise, by words or conduct, bias or prejudice based upon race, sex, religion, national origin, disability, age, sexual orientation, gender identity, or socioeconomic status. Defense counsel should strive to eliminate implicit biases, and act to mitigate any improper bias or prejudice when credibly informed that it exists within the scope of defense counsel's authority.

(b) Defense counsel should be proactive in efforts to detect, investigate, and eliminate improper biases, with particular attention to historically persistent biases like race, in *all of counsel's work*. A public defense office should regularly assess the potential for biased or unfairly disparate impacts of its policies on communities within the defense office's jurisdiction, and eliminate those impacts that cannot be properly justified.

Criminal Justice Standards for the Defense Function, Std. 4-1.6 (4th ed. 2017) (emphasis added). *See also* Criminal Justice Standards for the Prosecution Function, Std. 3-1.6 (4th ed. 2017) (setting forth the same standard for prosecutors).

9. Some jurisdictions have limited their antidiscrimination and anti-harassment rules to conduct related to the representation of a client. *See, e.g.*, Colo. Rules of Prof'l Conduct R. 8.4(g) (2020) (conduct "in the representation of a client"); Mass. Rules of Prof'l Conduct R. 3.4(i) (2020) (conduct "in appearing in a professional capacity before a tribunal"); Mo. Rules of Prof'l Conduct R. 4-8.4(g) (2020) (conduct "in representing a client"); Neb. Rules of Prof'l Conduct § 3-508.4(d) (2020) (conduct when "a lawyer is employed in a professional capacity").

10. *See generally* Wendy N. Hess, *Addressing Sexual Harassment in the Legal Profession: The Opportunity to Use Model Rule 8.4(g) to Protect Women from Harassment*, 96 U. Det. Mercy L. Rev. 579 (2019). *See also* Standing Committee on Ethics & Prof'l Responsibility, et al., Report to the House of Delegates on Revised Resolution 109, at 10 (Aug. 2016); *infra* note 31 and accompanying text; *Standing Committee on Ethics and Professional Responsibility*

Furthermore, Rule 8.4(g) prohibits conduct that is not covered by other law, such as federal proscriptions on discrimination and harassment in the workplace.[11] Although conduct that violates Title VII of the Civil Rights Act of 1964 would necessarily violate paragraph (g),[12] the reverse may not be true. For example, a single instance of a lawyer making a derogatory sexual comment directed towards another individual in connection with the practice of law would likely not be severe or pervasive enough to violate Title VII, but would violate Rule 8.4(g).[13] The isolated nature of the conduct, however, could be a mitigating factor in the disciplinary process.[14]

Rule 8.4(g) does not regulate conduct unconnected to the practice of law, as do some other rules of professional conduct.[15] Nevertheless, it does im-

---

Hearing on Model Rule 8.4(g), at 39, 61-62 (Feb. 2016) (Wendy Lazar testifying that "so much sexual harassment and bullying against women actually takes place on the way home from an event or in a limo traveling on the way back from a long day of litigation"; former ABA president Laura Bellows testifying about anecdotal evidence of sexual harassment, such as, at a "Christmas party"), https://www.americanbar.org/content/dam/aba/administrative/professional_responsibility/aba_model_rule%208_4_comments/february_2016_public_hearing_transcript.pdf.

11. *See* Title VII of the Civil Rights Act of 1964, 42 U.S.C. § 2000 *et seq.* (2019). *See also* Bostock v. Clayton County, 590 U.S. ___ (2020) (recognizing that discrimination and harassment based on sexual orientation and gender identity are prohibited by Title VII as components of "sex," one of the protected categories listed in the statute). Sexual orientation and gender identity are expressly included among Model Rule 8.4(g)'s categories.

12. *See* MODEL RULES R. 8.4(g) cmt. [3] (noting that "[t]he substantive law of antidiscrimination and anti-harassment statutes and case law may guide application of paragraph (g)").

13. *See* Harris v. Forklift Systems, Inc., 510 U.S. 17, 21 (1993) ("Conduct that is not severe or pervasive enough to create an objectively hostile or abusive work environment—an environment that a reasonable person would find hostile or abusive—is beyond Title VII's purview."); Saxton v. American Tel. & Tel. Co., 10 F.3d 526, 533 (7th Cir. 1993) (observing that "'relatively isolated' instances of non-severe misconduct will not support a hostile environment claim") (quoting Weiss v. Coca-Cola Bottling Co. of Chicago, 990 F.2d 333, 337 (7th Cir. 1993); Martinelli v. Bancroft Chophouse, LLC, 357 F. Supp. 3d 95, 102 (D. Mass. 2019) (finding that "[a] single, isolated incident of harassment . . . is ordinarily insufficient to establish a claim for hostile work environment unless the incident was particularly egregious and the employee must demonstrate how his or her ability to work was negatively affected").

14. Whether discipline is imposed for any particular violation of Rule 8.4(g) will depend on a variety of factors, including, for example: (1) severity of the violation; (2) prior record of discipline or lack thereof; (3) level of cooperation with disciplinary counsel; (4) character or reputation; and (5) whether or not remorse is expressed. For a full discussion of factors that influence the imposition of discipline imposed, see ANNOTATED ABA STANDARDS FOR IMPOSING LAWYER SANCTIONS (2d ed. 2019).

15. The most noteworthy example is Rule 8.4(c). Indeed, the misconduct addressed in that rule—dishonesty, fraud, deceit, and misrepresentation—has traditionally been viewed as unacceptable by the legal profession, whether it occurs in the courtroom or on the street. Other Model Rules that subject lawyers to discipline for conduct not necessarily connected with the practice of law include Model Rules 8.2.(a) (prohibiting statements by lawyers about judges or other legal officials known to be false or in reckless disregard as to their truth), and 8.4(b) (misconduct for a lawyer to commit a criminal act that reflects adversely on the lawyer's honesty, trustworthiness, or fitness). *See also* Rebecca Aviel, *Rule 8.4(g) and*

pose a higher standard on lawyers than that expected of the general public.[16] As the Preamble to the Model Rules states, "A lawyer, as a member of the legal profession, is a representative of clients, an officer of the legal system and a public citizen having special responsibility for the quality of justice."[17] Harassment and discrimination damage the public's confidence in the legal system and its trust in the profession.

Section II of this opinion elaborates further on the scope of Rule 8.4(g) and explains in more detail how it safeguards the integrity of the legal system and the profession. Section III contains hypotheticals that illustrate the Rule's application.

II. Analysis

Rule 8.4(g) provides:

> It is professional misconduct for a lawyer to . . . engage in conduct that the lawyer knows or reasonably should know is harassment or discrimination on the basis of race, sex, religion, national origin, ethnicity, disability, age, sexual orientation, gender identity, marital status or socioeconomic status in conduct related to the practice of law. This paragraph does not limit the ability of a lawyer to accept, decline or withdraw from a representation in accordance with Rule 1.16. This paragraph does not preclude legitimate advice or advocacy consistent with these Rules.[18]

Comment [3] to Rule 8.4(g) addresses the meaning of "discrimination" and "harassment" and emphasizes that such conduct "undermine[s] confidence in the legal profession and the legal system."[19] It defines "discrimina-

---

the First Amendment: Distinguishing Between Discrimination and Free Speech, 31 GEO. J. LEGAL ETHICS 31, 67 (2018) (noting that "the bar readily considers conduct completely unconnected to the practice of law when such conduct is either deceptive or otherwise reflective on fitness, with some jurisdictions requiring and others omitting the element that the conduct in question be criminal").

16. See, e.g., MODEL RULES R. 3.6(a) ("A lawyer who is participating or has participated in the investigation or litigation of a matter shall not make an extrajudicial statement that the lawyer knows or reasonably should know will be disseminated by means of public communication and will have a substantial likelihood of materially prejudicing an adjudicative proceeding in the matter."); MODEL RULES R. 4.1(a) ("In the course of representing a client a lawyer shall not knowingly make a false statement of material fact or law to a third person . . . ."); MODEL RULES R. 8.4(c) ("It is professional misconduct for a lawyer to engage in conduct involving dishonesty, fraud, deceit or misrepresentation . . . ."). See also Hess, supra note 10, at 596 ("Rather than having lawyers escape accountability for their sexually harassing conduct that might not meet Title VII's high bar, the legal profession can instead take the opportunity to hold itself to a higher standard of professionalism.").

17. MODEL RULES Preamble [1].

18. MODEL RULES R. 8.4(g).

19. Id. cmt. [3].

tion" to include "harmful verbal or physical conduct that manifests bias or prejudice towards others."[20] Harassment includes "derogatory or demeaning verbal or physical conduct."[21] "Sexual harassment" is more specifically described as "unwelcome sexual advances, requests for sexual favors, and other unwelcome verbal or physical conduct of a sexual nature."[22] The Comment also indicates that "[t]he substantive law of antidiscrimination and anti-harassment statutes and case law may guide application of paragraph (g)."[23]

The existence of the requisite harm is assessed using a standard of objective reasonableness. In addition, a lawyer need only know or reasonably should know that the conduct in question constitutes discrimination or harassment.[24] Even so, the most common violations will likely involve conduct that is intentionally discriminatory or harassing.

Comment [4] identifies the scope of "conduct related to the practice of law," listing such activities as: "representing clients; interacting with witnesses, coworkers, court personnel, lawyers and others while engaged in the practice of law; operating or managing a law firm or law practice; and participating in bar association, business or social activities in connection with the practice of law."[25]

Comment [5] describes specific circumstances that do not violate paragraph (g). For example, a judge's determination that a lawyer has utilized peremptory challenges in a discriminatory manner, alone, will not subject the lawyer to discipline.[26] Furthermore, limiting one's practice to providing representation to underserved populations, consistent with the rules of professional conduct and other law, will not constitute a violation.[27]

---

20. *Id.*

21. *Id.*

22. *Id. See also* MODEL CODE OF JUDICIAL CONDUCT R. 2.3 cmt. [4] (noting that "[s]exual harassment includes but is not limited to sexual advances, requests for sexual favors, and other verbal or physical conduct of a sexual nature that is unwelcome").

23. MODEL RULES R. 8.4(g) cmt. [3].

24. "Knows" and "reasonably should know" are defined terms in the Model Rules. *See* MODEL RULES R. 1.0(f) & (j).

25. MODEL RULES R. 8.4 cmt. [4].

26. *See id.* cmt. [5].

27. *See id.* The balance of the Comment notes some additional actions that will not violate Rule 8.4(g):

A lawyer may charge and collect reasonable fees and expenses for a representation. . . . Lawyers also should be mindful of their professional obligations under Rule 6.1 to provide legal services to those who are unable to pay, and their obligation under Rule 6.2 not to avoid appointments from a tribunal except for good cause. . . . A lawyer's representation of a client does not constitute an endorsement by the lawyer of the client's views or activities.

Id. (citations omitted).

Finally, Rule 8.4(g) specifically excludes from its scope "[l]egitimate advice or advocacy consistent with these Rules." Thus, the Rule covers only conduct for which there is no reasonable justification. Common usage and Rule 8.4(g)'s Comments reinforce this point by elucidating the type of harassing or discriminatory conduct that is disciplinable.

A. "Harassment"

Harassment is a term of common meaning and usage under the Model Rules.[28] It refers to conduct that is aggressively invasive, pressuring, or intimidating.[29] Rule 8.4(g) addresses harassment in relation to the practice of law that targets others on the basis of their membership in one or more of the identified categories.[30]

Preventing sexual harassment is a particular objective of Rule 8.4(g).[31] As Comment [3] makes clear, sexual harassment encompasses "unwelcome sexual advances, requests for sexual favors, and other unwelcome verbal or physical conduct of a sexual nature."[32] This type of behavior falls squarely within the broader, plain meaning of harassment and is consistent with the term's application throughout the Model Rules.

Model Rule 3.5(c)(3), for example, prohibits lawyers from communicating with jurors or prospective jurors following their discharge if "the communication involves misrepresentation, coercion, duress or *harassment*."[33] Here,

---

28. *See, e.g.*, MODEL RULES R. 3.5(c)(3) & 7.3(c)(2) (both discussed in the text). *See also* MODEL RULES Preamble [5] ("A lawyer should use the law's procedures only for legitimate purposes and not to harass or intimidate others.").

29. *See, e.g.*, NEW OXFORD AMERICAN DICTIONARY 790 (3d ed. 2010) (defining "harassment" as "aggressive pressure or intimidation"); MERRIAM-WEBSTER DICTIONARY (defining "harass" as meaning "to annoy persistently"; "to create an unpleasant or hostile situation for, especially by uninvited and unwelcome verbal or physical conduct"), https://www.merriam-webster.com/dictionary/harass (last visited June 23, 2020).

30. Consistent with the guiding principle that the Model Rules are rules of reason and "should be interpreted with reference to the purposes of legal representation and of the law itself," the term "harassment" in Rule 8.4(g) must be construed and applied in a reasonable manner. *See* MODEL RULES Scope [14].

31. *See* Gillers, *supra* note 4, at 200 (noting that decisions and surveys cited overwhelmingly "disclose that the targets [of bias and harassment] are predominantly women"); Hess, *supra* note 10, at 582 (noting conservatively that an estimated "25% of women in the legal workplace have reported unwanted sexual harassment"); Chuck Lundberg, *#MeToo in the Law Firm*, BENCH & BAR MINN., Vol. 75, No. 3, at 16, 17 (Mar. 2018) (noting that in speaking to many male and female "bar leaders, judges, present and former ethics partners and managing partners at large law firms," the author learned from the men that they had observed or heard about a "broad spectrum of workplace conduct" of a sexual nature, including "some pretty egregious sexual misconduct"; as for the women with whom the author spoke, "[t]o a person, they were able to relate multiple instances of such behaviors—in law firms, law schools, court chambers, and other legal workplaces").

32. MODEL RULES R. 8.4(g) cmt. [3].

33. MODEL RULES R. 3.5(c)(3) (emphasis added).

the term "harassment," as in Rule 8.4(g), refers to conduct that is aggressively invasive, pressuring, or intimidating, including that which is reasonably perceived to be demeaning or derogatory, as demonstrated in *In re Panetta*.[34] In *Panetta*, the respondent was disciplined for sending an email to another lawyer who had served as the jury foreperson in a trial the respondent had lost several years earlier. The message was insulting, badgering, and threatening. Its subject line read, "ALL THESE YEARS LATER I WILL NEVER FORGET . . . THE LIAR" and went on to state, among other things: "After numerous multi-million dollar verdicts and success beyond anything you will attain in your lifetime, I will never forget you: the bloated Jury [Foreperson] that I couldn't get rid of and that misled and hijacked my jury." He ended the message with "Well you should get attacked you A-hole. Good Luck in Hell."[35] The court easily found that this conduct was intended to harass the former jury foreperson and adversely reflected on the respondent's fitness as a lawyer.[36]

Model Rule 7.3(c)(2) also prohibits "harassment." It forbids "solicitation that involves coercion, duress or *harassment*."[37] As with other uses of "harassment" in the Model Rules, a rational reading of the term includes badgering or invasive behavior, as well as conduct that is demeaning or derogatory. Similarly, Model Rule 4.4(a) subjects lawyers to discipline for using "means that have no substantial purpose other than to embarrass, delay, or burden a third person."[38] While it does not expressly use the word "harassment," the conduct prohibited is clearly of the same sort that comes within that word's definition.

B. "Discrimination"

Discrimination "includes harmful verbal or physical conduct that manifests bias or prejudice towards others."[39] Bias or prejudice can be exhibited in any number of ways, some overlapping with conduct that also constitutes harassment. Use of a racist or sexist epithet with the intent to disparage an individual or group of individuals demonstrates bias or prejudice.

For example, in *In re McCarthy*,[40] a lawyer was suspended for a minimum of thirty days for sending an email message that was deeply offensive and

---

34. 127 A.D.3d 99 (N.Y. 2d Dept. 2015).

35. *Id.* at 101.

36. *Id.* at 102. *See also* Pa. Bar Ass'n Legal Ethics & Prof'l Responsibility Comm., Advisory Op. 91-52 (1991) (finding that it was permissible for a lawyer's paralegal to conduct post-trial interviews of jurors, provided that no intimidation or pressure was used).

37. MODEL RULES R. 7.3(c)(2) (emphasis added).

38. MODEL RULES R. 4.4(a).

39. MODEL RULES R. 8.4(g), cmt. [3] (emphasis added). In addition, "[t]he substantive law of antidiscrimination and anti-harassment statutes and case law" may serve as a guide in applying paragraph (g). *Id.*

40. 938 N.E.2d 698 (Ind. 2010).

undoubtedly evinced racial bias. In connection with a real estate title dispute, the secretary of the seller's agent sent a message to the lawyer demanding that he take certain action. The lawyer responded, by stating, among other things, that "I am here to tell you that I am neither you [sic] or [your boss's] n****r."[41] The Indiana Supreme Court found that such remarks "serve only to fester wounds caused by past discrimination and encourage future intolerance."[42] Similarly, the same court found that a lawyer engaged in conduct manifesting bias or prejudice in relation to a personal bankruptcy proceeding by distributing flyers that referred to other counsel in the matter as "'bloodsucking shylocks' who were part of a 'heavily Jewish [sic] . . . reorganization cartel.'"[43]

As many courts have emphasized, such behavior is unacceptable generally but especially when engaged in by members of the bar. In *In re Charges of Unprofessional Conduct*,[44] for instance, the Minnesota Supreme Court expressed this general judicial perspective: "When any individual engages in race-based misconduct it undermines the ideals of society founded on the belief that all people are created equal. When the person who engages in this misconduct is an officer of the court, the misconduct is especially troubling."[45] Rule 8.4(g) embodies this principle.

C. Rule 8.4(g) and the First Amendment

The Committee does not address constitutional issues, but analysis of Rule 8.4(g), as with our analysis of other rules, is aided by constitutional context.[46] For Rule 8.4(g), two important constitutional principles guide and constrain its application. First, an ethical duty that can result in discipline must

---

41. *Id.*

42. *Id.* (quoting *In re* Thomsen, 837 N.E.2d 1011, 1012 (Ind. 2005)).

43. *In re* Dempsey, 986 N.E.2d 816 (Ind. 2013). *See also In re* Thomsen, 837 N.E.2d 1011 (Ind. 2005) (publicly reprimanding lawyer for filing a petition in a divorce action arguing that couple's children were put in "harm's way" by wife's association with an African-American man); *In re* Charges of Unprofessional Conduct, 597 N.W.2d 563 (Minn. 1999) (prosecutor disciplined for filing motion seeking to prohibit defendant's counsel from including a lawyer of color as part of the defense team "for the sole purpose of playing upon the emotions of the jury"); People v. Sharpe, 781 P.2d 659, 660, 661 (1989) (prosecutor disciplined for exhibiting racial prejudice against Latinos by stating, in reference to two Latino defendants, that he did not "believe either one of those chili-eating bastards").

44. 597 N.W.2d 563 (Minn. 1999).

45. *Id.* at 567-68.

46. *See, e.g.*, ABA Comm. on Ethics & Prof'l Responsibility, Formal Op. 490 (2020) (discussing ability-to-pay inquiries required by the due process and equal protection clauses, as interpreted in *Bearden v. Georgia*, 461 U.S. 669 (1983) and its progeny); ABA Comm. on Ethics & Prof'l Responsibility, Formal Op. 486, at 9 (2019) (discussing Sixth Amendment Right to Counsel rooted "[i]n a series of cases beginning with Argersinger v. Hamlin," 407 U.S. 25 (1972)); ABA Comm. on Ethics & Prof'l Responsibility, Formal Op. 09-454 (2009) (discussing obligations based on Brady v. Maryland, 373 U.S. 83 (1963)).

be sufficiently clear to give notice of the conduct that is required or forbidden. Second, the rule must not be overbroad such that it sweeps within its prohibition conduct that the law protects. Identifying the proper balance between freedom of speech or religion and laws against discrimination or harassment is not a new problem, however. The scope of Rule 8.4(g) is no more or less reducible to a precise verbal formula than any number of regulations of lawyer speech or workplace speech that have been upheld and applied by courts.[47]

Courts have consistently upheld professional conduct rules similar to Rule 8.4(g) against First Amendment challenge. For example, in addressing the constitutional authority of a court of appeals to discipline a lawyer for "conduct unbecoming a member of the bar of the court," the Supreme Court observed that a lawyer's court-granted license "requires members of the bar to conduct themselves in a manner compatible with the role of courts in the administration of justice."[48] More recently, the Kentucky Supreme Court echoed this message in an opinion concerning Rule 8.2(a), which generally prohibits a lawyer from making a false or reckless statement concerning the qualifications or integrity of a judicial or other legal official, stating that regulation of lawyer speech "is appropriate in order to maintain the public confidence and credibility of the judiciary and as a condition of '[t]he license granted by the court.'"[49]

Rule 8.4(d)'s prohibition of conduct that is prejudicial to the administration of justice has likewise withstood constitutional challenges based on vagueness and overbreadth arguments, with one court observing that: "The language of a rule setting guidelines for members of the bar need not meet

---

47. For a discussion of workplace speech limitations upheld against a First Amendment challenge, see Aviel, *supra* note 15, at 48-50. For a discussion of lawyers' speech and Rule 8.4(g), see Robert N. Weiner, *"Nothing to See Here": Model Rule of Professional Conduct 8.4(g) and the First Amendment*, 41 HARV. J.L. & PUBLIC POLICY 125 (2018). *See also infra* note 49.

48. *In re Snyder*, 472 U.S. 634, 644-45 (1985).

49. Ky. Bar Ass'n v. Blum, 404 S.W.3d 841, 855 (Ky. 2013) (*quoting In re* Snyder) (observing that while a lawyer does not surrender First Amendment rights in exchange for a law license, once admitted, "he must temper his criticisms in accordance with professional standards of conduct") (quoting *In re* Sandlin, 12 F.3d 861, 866 (9th Cir. 1993)). There are also other Model Rules that curtail attorney speech but are uniformly understood as proper regulatory measures, including, for example, the following: Rule 1.6 (generally prohibiting disclosure of "information relating to the representation of a client"); Rule 3.5(d) (prohibiting a lawyer from "engag[ing] in conduct intended to disrupt a tribunal"); Rule 3.6 (restricting a lawyer's ability to comment publicly about an investigation or litigation matter in which the lawyer is participating or has participated when the lawyer knows or reasonably should know that the comments "have a substantial likelihood of materially prejudicing an adjudicative proceeding"); Rule 4.1 (prohibiting a lawyer from "knowingly mak[ing] a false statement of material fact or law to a third person"); and Rule 7.1 (limiting communications about a lawyer or a lawyer's services to those that are truthful and not otherwise misleading).

the precise standards of clarity that might be required of rules of conduct for laymen."[50] Similarly, in rejecting a vagueness challenge to the prohibition against conduct prejudicial to the administration of justice, the Fifth Circuit stated:

> The traditional test for vagueness in regulatory prohibitions is whether "they are set out in terms that the ordinary person exercising ordinary common sense can sufficiently understand and comply with, without sacrifice to the public interest." . . . The particular context in which a regulation is promulgated therefore is all important. . . . *The regulation at issue herein only applies to lawyers, who are professionals and have the benefit of guidance provided by case law, court rules and the "lore of the profession."*[51]

There is wide and longstanding acceptance of these principles, given lawyers' status as members of the bar. For example, in upholding the constitutionality of DR 1-102(A)(6), which prohibited a lawyer from engaging "in any other conduct that adversely reflects on [the lawyer's] fitness to practice law," the New York Court of Appeals noted: "As far back as 1856, the Supreme Court acknowledged that 'it is difficult if not impossible, to enumerate and define, with legal precision, every offense for which an attorney or counsellor ought to be removed'. . . . Broad standards governing professional conduct are permissible and indeed often necessary."[52]

Furthermore, the fact that it is possible to construe a rule's language to reach conduct protected by the First Amendment is not fatal to its application to unprotected conduct. As observed by Justice Scalia in *Virginia v. Hicks*:

> [T]here comes a point at which the chilling effect of an overbroad law, significant though it may be, cannot justify prohibiting all enforcement of that law—particularly a law that reflects "legitimate state interests in maintaining comprehensive controls over harmful, constitutionally unprotected conduct". . . . For there are substantial social costs *created* by the overbreadth doctrine when it blocks appli-

---

50. *In re* Keiler, 380 A.2d 119, 126 (D.C. 1977), *overruled on other grounds, by In re* Hutchinson, 534 A.2d 919 (D.C. 1987) (upholding against a vagueness challenge DR 1-102(A)(5), Rule 8.4(d)'s predecessor).

51. Howell v. State Bar of Texas, 843 F.2d 205, 208 (5th Cir. 1988) (emphasis added); *see also* Attorney Grievance Comm'n of Maryland v. Korotki, 569 A.2d 1224, 1235 (1990) (observing that a professional conduct rule for lawyers need not "meet the standards of clarity that might be required for rules governing the conduct of laypersons") (citations omitted).

52. *In re* Holtzman, 577 N.E.2d 30, 33 (N.Y. 1991) (quoting *Ex Parte* Secombe, 60 U.S. [19 How.] 9, 14 (1857) (citing *In re* Charges of Unprofessional Conduct Against N.P., 361 N.W.2d 386, 395 (Minn. 1985), appeal dismissed, 474 U.S. 976 (1985)); *see also In re* Knutson, 405 N.W.2d 234, 238 (Minn. 1987).

cation of a law to constitutionally unprotected speech, or especially to constitutionally unprotected conduct. To ensure that these costs do not swallow the social benefits of declaring a law "overbroad," we have insisted that a law's application to protected speech be "substantial," not only in an absolute sense, but also relative to the scope of the law's plainly legitimate applications . . . before applying the "strong medicine" of overbreadth invalidation.[53]

Rule 8.4(g) promotes a well-established state interest by prohibiting conduct that reflects adversely on the profession and diminishes the public's confidence in the legal system and its trust in lawyers.[54]

Numerous judicial opinions confirm the significance and legitimacy of a state's regulatory interest in this area. For instance, the Minnesota Supreme Court has noted that "racially-biased actions" engaged in by lawyers "not only undermine confidence in our system of justice, but also erode the very foundation upon which justice is based."[55] Similarly, in affirming the public reprimand of a lawyer who made racially disparaging accusations in a court filing, the Indiana Supreme Court stressed that "[i]nterjecting race into proceedings where it is not relevant is offensive, unprofessional and tarnishes the image of the profession as a whole."[56] The New Jersey Supreme Court expressed the same opinion in *Matter of Vincenti*, observing that:

> Any kind of conduct or verbal oppression or intimidation that projects offensive and invidious discriminatory distinctions, be it based on race or color, . . . or . . . on gender, or ethnic or national background or handicap, is especially offensive. In the context of either the practice of law or the administration of justice, prejudice both to the standing of this profession and the administration of justice will be virtually conclusive if intimidation, abuse, harassment, or threats focus or dwell on invidious discriminatory distinctions.[57]

Rule 8.4(g) protects specific categories of victims from identified harm, and a violation can only take place when the offending conduct engaged in is

---

53. 539 U.S. 113, 119-20 (2003) (emphasis in original) (citations omitted); *see also* Howell v. State Bar of Texas, 843 F.2d 205, 208 (5th Cir. 1988) ("Assuming for the argument that [the rule prohibiting conduct prejudicial to the administration of justice] might be considered vague in some hypothetical, peripheral application, this does not, as this Court [has] observed, . . . warrant throwing the baby out with the bathwater. To invalidate the regulation in toto, . . . we would have to hold that it is impermissibly vague in all of its applications.") (citations omitted).

54. *See supra* note 6 and accompanying text.

55. *In re* Charges of Unprofessional Conduct, 597 N.W.2d 563, 568 (Minn. 1999).

56. *In re* Thomsen, 837 N.E.2d 1011, 1012 (Ind. 2005).

57. 554 A.2d 470, 474 (N.J. 1989).

"related to the practice of law" and the lawyer knows or reasonably should know that it constitutes harassment or discrimination.

Using these various interpretative principles and applying them in an objectively reasonable manner, a lawyer would clearly violate Rule 8.4(g) by directing a hostile racial, ethnic, or gender-based epithet toward another individual, in circumstances related to the practice of law. For example, in a case referenced earlier, under Indiana's version of Rule 8.4(g), a lawyer received a three-year suspension for distributing flyers in relation to personal litigation depicting his adversaries as "slumlords," calling their counsel "bloodsucking shylocks," and making various derogatory remarks about Jews generally.[58] Another Indiana lawyer representing a husband in a custody dispute violated that state's version of Rule 8.4(g) by filing a petition in which he alleged that the wife associated herself "in the presence of a black male, and such association [caused] and [placed] the children in harm's way."[59] Similarly, a Colorado lawyer was disciplined for disparagingly referring to a female judge as a "c**t" in the course of negotiating a plea deal with prosecutors.[60]

Each of these examples would likewise violate Model Rule 8.4(g), even if the conduct occurred outside of a court-related setting. It need only take place in a context related to the practice of law, as Comment [4] explains.

III. Application of Rule 8.4(g) to Hypotheticals

To further illustrate the scope and application of Rule 8.4(g), this section discusses several representative situations.

(1) A religious organization challenges on First Amendment grounds a local ordinance that requires all schools to provide gender-neutral restroom and locker room facilities.[61] Would a lawyer who accepted representation of the organization violate Rule 8.4(g)?

No. This situation does not involve the type of conduct covered by Rule 8.4(g). The blackletter text underscores this by explaining that the "paragraph does not limit the ability of a lawyer to *accept,* **decline or withdraw from a representation in accordance with Rule 1.16."[62] In addition, the provision's next sentence further emphasizes that it "does not preclude legitimate advice or advocacy consistent with these Rules." Though individuals may disagree with**

---

58. *In re* Dempsey, 986 N.E.2d 816, 817 (Ind. 2013) (court specifically found that "none of these violations are based on any communication that falls within Respondent's broad constitutional right to freedom of speech and expression").

59. *Thomsen*, 837 N.E.2d at 1012.

60. People v. Gilbert, 2011 WL 10PDJ067, *10-11 (Colo. O.P.D.J. Jan. 14, 2011).

61. *Cf.* Texas Att'y Gen. Op. KP-0123 (Dec. 20, 2016).

62. MODEL RULES R. 8.4(g) (emphasis added).

the position the lawyer in the hypothetical would be defending, that would not affect the legitimacy of the representation.

(2) A lawyer participating as a speaker at a CLE program on affirmative action in higher education expresses the view that rather than using a race-conscious process in admitting African-American students to highly-ranked colleges and universities, those students would be better off attending lower-ranked schools where they would be more likely to excel. Would the lawyer's remarks violate Rule 8.4(g)?

No. While a CLE program would fall within Comment [3]'s description of what constitutes "conduct related to the practice of law," the viewpoint expressed by the lawyer would not violate Rule 8.4(g). Specifically, the lawyer's remarks, without more, would not constitute "conduct that the lawyer knows or reasonably should know is harassment or discrimination on the basis of . . . race." A general point of view, even a controversial one, cannot reasonably be understood as harassment or discrimination contemplated by Rule 8.4(g). The fact that others may find a lawyer's expression of social or political views to be inaccurate, offensive, or upsetting is not the type of "harm" required for a violation.

(3) A lawyer is a member of a religious legal organization, which advocates, on religious grounds, for the ability of private employers to terminate or refuse to employ individuals based on their sexual orientation or gender identity.[63] Will the lawyer's membership in this legal organization constitute a violation of Rule 8.4(g)?

No. As with the prior hypothetical, Rule 8.4(g) does not forbid a lawyer's expression of his or her political or social views, whether through membership in an organization or through oral or written commentary. Furthermore, to the extent that such conduct takes the form of pure advocacy it would not qualify as sufficiently "harmful" or targeted. Moreover, even though the Supreme Court has now recognized that discrimination based on sexual orientation and gender identity violates Title VII,[64] it is not a violation of Rule 8.4(g) to express the view that the decision is wrong.

(4) A lawyer serving as an adjunct professor supervising a law student in a law school clinic made repeated comments about the student's appearance and also made unwelcome, nonconsensual physical contact of a sexual nature with the student. Would this conduct violate Rule 8.4(g)?

Yes. This is an obvious violation and demonstrates the importance of making the scope of the provision broad enough to en-

---

63. *See Cf.* Texas Att'y Gen. Op. KP-0123 (Dec. 20, 2016).
64. *See* Bostock v. Clayton County, 590 U.S.__ (2020); *see also supra* note 11.

compass conduct that may not necessarily fall directly within the context of the representation of a client.[65]

(5) A partner and a senior associate in a law firm have been tasked with organizing an orientation program for newly-hired associates to familiarize them with firm policies and procedures. During a planning session, the partner remarked that: "Rule #1 should be never trust a Muslim lawyer. Rule #2 should be never represent a Muslim client. But, of course, we are not allowed to speak the truth around here." Do the partner's remarks violate Rule 8.4(g)?

Yes. Even if one assumes that the associate was not Muslim, the comments violate Rule 8.4(g).[66] The partner's remarks are discriminatory in so far as they are harmful and manifest bias and prejudice against Muslims. Furthermore, the partner surely knew or reasonably should have known this. In addition, the fact that the comments may not have been directed at a specific individual would not insulate the lawyer from discipline; though, in many instances, the offending conduct will be targeted towards someone who falls within a protected category. Because the remarks were made within the law firm setting, they were "related to the practice of law." Moreover, given the supervisory-subordinate nature of the partner's relationship to the associate, the remarks may influence how similarly-situated firm lawyers treat clients, opposing counsel, and others at the firm who are Muslim.

IV. Conclusion

Model Rule 8.4(g) prohibits a lawyer from engaging in conduct related to the practice of law that the lawyer knows or reasonably should know is harassing or discriminatory. Whether conduct violates the Rule must be assessed using a standard of objective reasonableness, and only conduct that is found harmful will be grounds for discipline.

Rule 8.4(g) covers conduct that occurs outside the representation of a client or beyond the confines of a courtroom. In addition, it is not restricted to conduct that is severe or pervasive, a standard utilized in the employment context. However, and as this opinion explains, conduct that violates paragraph (g) will often be intentional and typically targeted at a particular individual or group of individuals, such as directing a racist or sexist epithet

---

65. *See In re* Griffith, 838 N.W.2d 792 (Minn. 2013) (lawyer suspended for ninety days and required to petition for reinstatement for engaging in unwelcome verbal and physical sexual advances towards a student the lawyer was supervising in a law school clinic); *see also id.* at 793-96 (Lillenhaug, J., dissenting) (maintaining that more severe discipline was warranted in light of the egregious nature of the misconduct).

66. *Cf. In re* McCarthy, 938 N.E.2d 698 (Ind. 2010); *see also supra* text accompanying notes 40-42.

towards others or engaging in unwelcome, nonconsensual physical conduct of a sexual nature.

The Rule does not prevent a lawyer from freely expressing opinions and ideas on matters of public concern, nor does it limit in any way a lawyer's speech or conduct in settings unrelated to the practice of law. The fact that others may personally disagree with or be offended by a lawyer's expression does not establish a violation. The Model Rules are rules of reason, and whether conduct violates Rule 8.4(g) must necessarily be judged, in context, from an objectively reasonable perspective.

Besides being advocates and counselors, lawyers also serve a broader public role. Lawyers "should further the public's understanding of and confidence in the rule of law and the justice system because legal institutions in a constitutional democracy depend on popular participation and support to maintain their authority."[67] Discriminatory and harassing conduct, when engaged in by lawyers in connection with the practice of law, engenders skepticism and distrust of those charged with ensuring justice and fairness. Enforcement of Rule 8.4(g) is therefore critical to maintaining the public's confidence in the impartiality of the legal system and its trust in the legal profession as a whole.

Abstaining: Hon. Goodwin Liu.

---

67. MODEL RULES Preamble [6].

AMERICAN BAR ASSOCIATION
STANDING COMMITTEE ON ETHICS AND PROFESSIONAL RESPONSIBILITY
321 N. Clark Street, Chicago, Illinois 60654-4714 Telephone (312) 988-5328
CHAIR: Barbara S. Gillers, New York, NY
■ Lonnie T. Brown, Athens, GA ■ Robert Hirshon, Ann Arbor, MI ■ Hon. Goodwin Liu, San Francisco, CA
■ Thomas B. Mason, Washington, DC ■ Michael H. Rubin, Baton Rouge, LA
■ Lynda Shely, Scottsdale, AZ ■ Norman W. Spaulding, Stanford, CA
■ Elizabeth Clark Tarbert, Tallahassee, FL ■ Lisa D. Taylor, Parsippany, NJ

CENTER FOR PROFESSIONAL RESPONSIBILITY
©2020 by the American Bar Association. All rights reserved.

Formal Opinion 494   **July 29, 2020**

Conflicts Arising Out of a Lawyer's Personal Relationship with Opposing Counsel

Model Rule 1.7(a)(2) prohibits a lawyer from representing a client without informed consent if there is a significant risk that the representation of the client will be materially limited by a personal interest of the lawyer. A personal interest conflict may arise out of a lawyer's relationship with opposing counsel. Lawyers must examine the nature of the relationship to determine if it creates a Rule 1.7(a)(2) conflict and, if so, whether the lawyer reasonably believes the lawyer will be able to provide competent and diligent representation to each affected client who must then give informed consent, confirmed in writing.

To assist lawyers in applying Rule 1.7(a)(2), this opinion identifies three categories of personal relationships that might affect a lawyer's representation of a client: (i) intimate relationships, (ii) friendships, and (iii) acquaintances. Intimate relationships with opposing counsel involve, e.g. cohabiting, engagement to, or an exclusive intimate relationship. These relationships must be disclosed to clients, and the lawyers ordinarily may not represent opposing clients in the matter, unless each client gives informed consent confirmed in writing. Because friendships exist in a wide variety of contexts, friendships need to be examined carefully. Close friendships with opposing counsel should be disclosed to clients, and, where required as described in this opinion, their informed consent obtained. By contrast, some friendships and most relationships that fall into the category of acquaintances need not be disclosed, nor must clients' informed consent be obtained. Regardless of whether disclosure is required, however, the lawyer may choose to disclose the relationship to maintain good client relations.[1]

I. Introduction

The ABA Model Rules of Professional Conduct address conflicts arising when lawyers "closely related by blood or marriage" represent "different cli-

---

1. This opinion is based on the ABA Model Rules of Professional Conduct as amended by the ABA House of Delegates through August 2020. The laws, court rules, regulations, rules of professional conduct, and opinions promulgated in individual jurisdictions are controlling.

ents in the same matter or in substantially related matters." This guidance appears in Comment [11] to Model Rule 1.7, which reads:

> When lawyers representing different clients in the same matter or in substantially related matters are closely related by blood or marriage, there may be a significant risk that client confidences will be revealed and that the lawyer's family relationship will interfere with both loyalty and independent professional judgment. . . . . [A] lawyer related to another lawyer, e.g., *as parent, child, sibling or spouse,* ordinarily may not represent a client in a matter where that lawyer is representing another party, unless each client gives informed consent. . . .[2]

The Model Rules do not address other types of personal relationships with opposing counsel.[3] But these other personal relationships may also cre-

---

2. MODEL RULES OF PROF'L CONDUCT R. 1.7 cmt. 11 (2020) (emphasis added) [hereinafter MODEL RULES].

3. By contrast, there is significant authority, from the ABA and elsewhere, addressing business relationships with opposing counsel. For opinions on a lawyer's obligations when negotiating or seeking employment with the opposing firm. *See, e.g.,* ABA Comm. on Ethics & Prof'l Responsibility Formal Op. 96-400 (1996); N.C. State Bar Formal Op. 3 (2016); D.C. Bar Op. 367 (2014); N.Y.C. Bar Ass'n Comm. on Prof'l Ethics, Formal Op. 1991-1 (1991); Pa. Bar Ass'n Legal Ethics & Prof'l Responsibility Comm. Advisory Op. 2007-300 (2007); Ky. Bar Ass'n Formal Op. E-399 (1998). There is also significant authority addressing a lawyer's obligations when the lawyer represents or has represented opposing counsel in an unrelated matter. *See, e.g.,* ABA Comm. on Ethics & Prof'l Responsibility Formal Op. 97-406 (1997) ("lawyers cannot simultaneously have a lawyer-client relationship and represent third party clients whose interest are adverse if a reasonable lawyer would conclude that his relationship as a lawyer for or client of opposing counsel may materially limit and would adversely affect the lawyer's representation of his 'third-party' client"; opinion discusses when disclosure and consent will permit the representation; "imputation analysis differs for the representing lawyer and the represented lawyer"); Utah State Bar Ethics Advisory Comm. Op. 14-05 (2014) (both affected clients may consent to conflict caused by one's lawyer representing opposing counsel in unrelated malpractice or discipline case); Conn. Bar Ass'n Informal Op. 2012-10 (2012) (personal injury lawyer and insurance defense counsel who are opponents in many cases and one represents the other in unrelated litigation must determine if the representation would materially limit the representation of each lawyer's clients and, if so, must obtain the affected clients' informed consent, confirmed in writing); Me. Prof'l Ethics Comm'n Opinion 205 (2011) (lawyer who is representing opposing counsel in an unrelated matter must determine if there is a significant risk of materially limiting his ability to represent either client and may seek informed consent to continued representation of each client if the lawyer reasonably believes the lawyer can give competent diligent representation to each); N.J. Advisory Comm. on Prof'l Ethics Op. 679 (1995) (conflict of interest caused by lawyer's representation of opposing counsel in unrelated matter may be waived with informed consent); Iowa State Bar Ass'n Ethics & Practice Guidelines Comm. Advisory Op. 92-28 (1993) (lawyer may represent a frequent opposing counsel in an unrelated matter); N.Y. State Bar Ass'n Comm. on Prof'l Ethics Op. 579 (1987) (lawyer may represent opposing counsel in unrelated litigation with client's informed consent if no effect on their independent professional judgment); Ill. State Bar Ass'n Advisory Op. 724 (1981) (no conflict for opposing counsel where one previously represented the other).

ate conflicts of interest. Because changing living patterns suggest that more people are living in households and arrangements that do not correspond to traditional categories,[4] this opinion offers guidance on conflicts that may arise from personal relationships with opposing counsel that fall within the Rules but are not specifically addressed by the Comments. In explaining these obligations, this opinion relies heavily on ABA Formal Opinion 488, issued in September 2019, which addresses judges' personal relationships with lawyers or parties that may require disqualification or disclosure."[5]

Section II below sets out the framework for analysis and identifies three categories of potential relationships between opposing counsel, drawing on the analysis in ABA Formal Opinion 488. The categories here are: (i) "intimate relationships," (ii) "friendships," and (iii) "acquaintances."[6] This opinion explains the relevant considerations in these circumstances.

II. Analysis

Model Rule 1.7(a)(2) provides that in the absence of informed consent confirmed in writing a lawyer may not represent a client if "there is a significant risk that the representation of one or more clients will be materially limited by the lawyer's responsibilities to another client, a former client or a third person or by a personal interest of the lawyer." Comment [11] explains that when opposing counsel are related by blood or marriage "there may be a significant risk that client confidences will be revealed and that the lawyer's family relationship will interfere with both loyalty and independent professional judgment."[7] The Committee concludes that these risks also arise when there are close personal or intimate relationships between lawyers who rep-

---

4. For example, according to U.S. Census Bureau data from November 2018, "[t]he median age at first marriage in the United States has continued to rise in recent years." The number of young adults living with an unmarried partner has also increased. For example, "[a]mong young adults 18 to 24, cohabitation is now more prevalent than living with a spouse." *See* U.S. Census Bureau Releases 2018 Families and Living Arrangements Tables, https://www.census.gov/newsroom/press-releases/2018/families.html (Nov. 14, 2018).

5. ABA Comm. on Ethics & Prof'l Responsibility Formal Op. 488 (2019) [hereinafter ABA Formal Op. 488].

6. *See id.* at 1, 2, 4-6. Some different considerations affect judicial disclosure and disqualification, e.g. judges must appear to be impartial as well as be impartial in fact, but the categories and considerations set forth in Formal Opinion 488 are useful for lawyers when analyzing their personal relationships with opposing counsel, as described in this opinion.

7. By contrast, some jurisdiction's rules explicitly address the types of personal relationships discussed in this opinion. *See, e.g.*, Cal. Rules of Prof'l Conduct R. 1.7(c)(2) (2018) (addressing "intimate personal relationship"); Iowa Rules of Prof'l Conduct R. 1.8(i) (2012) (including cohabiting lawyers and lawyers in any "romantic capacity"); Or. Rules of Prof'l Conduct R. 1.7 (2020) (including "domestic partner"); Va. Rules of Prof'l Conduct R. 1.8(i) (2020) (including a lawyer "intimately involved with another lawyer"); Wash. Rules of Prof'l Conduct R. 1.8(k)(1) (2015) (including "intimate relationship with another lawyer"); and W. Va. Rules of Prof'l Conduct R. 1.7 cmt. [11] addressing "sharing living quarters with another lawyer").

resent opposing clients. How lawyers should analyze these relationships for purposes of Rule 1.7(a)(2) is discussed below in Sections A, B, and C. There are general principles, however, that apply to all of them.

First, not all personal relationships with opposing counsel create a conflict that would require client informed consent or even disclosure. Some relationships with opposing counsel are so casual that they would not affect a lawyer's independent professional judgment. For other relationships, a lawyer's duty of communication under Rule 1.4 might obligate the lawyer to disclose a relationship, even if the lawyer believes that the relationship would not create a conflict under Rule 1.7. For still other relationships, a conflict based on personal relationships with opposing counsel exists and may be waived if the lawyer "reasonably believes that the lawyer will be able to provide competent and diligent representation to [the client]" and the lawyer obtains the affected client's informed consent, confirmed in writing.[8]

The reasonableness of the lawyer's belief will depend on the circumstances. "Reasonable" is defined in Model Rule 1.0(h).[9] For instance, a lawyer's independent judgment is likely to be materially limited if due to the personal relationship with opposing counsel the lawyer would refrain from filing a well-founded motion for sanctions against opposing counsel. In that circumstance, the conflict may not be waivable. In addition, if the lawyer's personal relationship is one that is not known to others and the lawyer is therefore hesitant to disclose it to the client, the lawyer may not be in a position to seek the client's informed consent. For example, if the personal relationship with opposing counsel is an affair that the lawyer wishes to keep secret, the lawyer may be unable to comply with the rule's requirements of disclosure and informed consent. In that situation the lawyer is unlikely to be able to commence or continue the client-lawyer relationship.

Second, in determining whether a personal interest conflict exists, the lawyer should consider the lawyer's role in the matter. A lawyer who is sole or lead counsel in a matter is more likely to have a disqualifying conflict than

---

8. MODEL RULES R. 1.7(b)(1). If a lawyer believes that informed consent of a client due to the lawyer's relationship with opposing counsel is required, the lawyer should confer with opposing counsel. If opposing counsel disagrees that informed consent is required, the lawyer should consider whether the issue should be raised with the court if the matter is in litigation, and whether the lawyer has an obligation pursuant to Model Rule 8.3(a) to report opposing counsel. Model Rule 8.3(a) reads: "A lawyer who knows that another lawyer has committed a violation of the Rules of Professional Conduct that raises a substantial question as to that lawyer's honesty, trustworthiness or fitness as a lawyer in other respects, shall inform the appropriate professional authority."

9. Model Rule 1.0(h) reads: "'Reasonable' or 'reasonably' when used in relation to conduct by a lawyer denotes the conduct of a reasonably prudent and competent lawyer." *See also* Model Rule 1.0(i) which reads: "'Reasonable belief' or 'reasonably believes' when used in reference to a lawyer denotes that the lawyer believes the matter in question and that the circumstances are such that the belief is reasonable."

a lawyer who has a subordinate or tangential role, such as researching discrete issues or drafting sections of papers to be filed, where that lawyer has little or no direct decision-making authority in the matter and minimal contact with the opposing counsel.[10]

Third, even when the lawyer has obtained informed consent confirmed in writing from the affected client, the lawyer must not reveal information relating to the representation unless permitted by one of the exceptions in Model Rule 1.6(b). Additionally, such a lawyer must take reasonable measures to assure that no confidential information is inadvertently disclosed to the opposing counsel with whom the lawyer has the personal relationship.[11] Inadvertent disclosure could occur, for example, if papers relating to the representation are left in view or telephone conversations are overheard.

Fourth, if a lawyer undertakes representation in which the lawyer has a personal relationship with opposing counsel and later determines that the lawyer will no longer be able to provide competent and diligent representation to the client because of the personal relationship, the lawyer must withdraw from the representation.[12]

Finally, personal interest conflicts ordinarily are not imputed. As Rule 1.10(a)(1) provides:

> While lawyers are associated in a firm, none of them shall knowingly represent a client when any one of them practicing alone would be prohibited from doing so by Rules 1.7 or 1.9, unless (1) the prohibition is based on a personal interest of the disqualified lawyer and does not present a significant risk of materially limiting the representation of the client by the remaining lawyers in the firm.

For close family relationships, Rule 1.7, cmt. [11] explains: "[t]he disqualification arising from a close family relationship is personal and ordinarily is not imputed to members of firms with whom the lawyers are associated."[13] Similarly, a conflict arising when a lawyer seeks employment with an oppos-

---

10. Subordinate lawyers may have to consult with supervisory lawyers in order to withdraw or move to withdraw. A subordinate lawyer, or any other lawyer who is not lead counsel, should disclose the relationship to a supervisor and seek advice on how to proceed in the circumstances, consistent with this opinion. *See also* MODEL RULES R. 5.1 & 5.2.

11. *See* MODEL RULE R. 1.6(c): "A lawyer shall make reasonable efforts to prevent the inadvertent or unauthorized disclosure of, or unauthorized access to, information relating to the representation of a client." *See also* MODEL RULE R. 1.6 cmt. [18].

12. *See, e.g.*, MODEL RULE R. 1.16(a), which provides in relevant part, "[a] lawyer shall not represent a client or, where representation has commenced, shall withdraw from the representation of a client if: (1) the representation will result in violation of the Rules of Professional Conduct . . . ". This obligation to withdraw may arise if a personal relationship develops during the course of a representation.

13. MODEL RULE R. 1.7 cmt. [11].

ing law firm is not ordinarily imputed.[14] The Committee concludes, as have other ethics committees, that conflicts arising out of the types of personal relationships discussed in this opinion also are not ordinarily imputed under Rule 1.10.[15] Imputation would be appropriate, for example, when other lawyers at either firm also have personal relationships with the opposing counsel or where the personal relationships involve managing partners. In such circumstances, the broader ties to the opposing counsel's firm may influence the lawyer's independent judgment.

A. Intimate Relationships

Lawyers who cohabit in an intimate relationship should be treated similarly to married couples for conflicts purposes. The same is true for couples who are engaged to be married or in exclusive intimate relationships. These lawyers must disclose the relationship to their respective clients and ordinarily may not represent the clients in the matter, unless each client gives informed consent confirmed in writing, assuming the lawyers reasonably believe that they will be able to provide competent and diligent representation to each client.[16]

---

14. ABA Comm. on Ethics & Prof'l Responsibility Formal Op. 96-400, at 8 (1996). For situations where the negotiating lawyer's conflict might be imputed, *see id.* at note 12. *See also* D.C. Bar Ethics Op. 367 (2014).

15. *See, e.g.*, State Bar of Ariz. Advisory Op. 01-12 (2001) (finding that a conflict created by "romantic relationship" between a public defender and a police officer is not imputed to the entire public defender's office); State Bar of Mich. Op. R-3 (1989) (regarding lawyer spouses (or their firms) representing opposing clients; no imputation unless the lawyer spouses or the lawyers litigating the cases have a personal interest in the outcome of the litigation); N.C. State Bar Formal Op. 2019-3 (2019) (stating that where there is an "ongoing" and "sexually intimate relationship" between a public defender and a prosecutor there is no imputation "so long as the conflict 'does not present a significant risk of materially limiting the representation of the client by the remaining lawyers in the firm [or office]'").

16. Comment [11] to Rule 1.7 provides in relevant part: "[A] lawyer related to another lawyer, e.g. as parent, child, sibling *or spouse, ordinarily* may not represent a client in a matter where that lawyer is representing another party, unless each client gives informed consent." (Emphasis added.) Opinions from several jurisdictions agree that intimate and cohabiting relationships should be treated like spousal ones. *See, e.g.*, State Bar of Ariz. Advisory Op. 01-10 (2001) (stating that attorney in Legal Defender's Office who is cohabiting with an attorney in the County Attorney's Office may work opposite each other on the same case only if: (i) both attorneys believe that the representation will not be materially limited by their relationship and (ii) both obtain informed consent by the clients; "[t]he conflict created by the cohabiting relationship is not imputed to other members of the offices"); State Bar of Mich. Op. R-3 (1989) (finding cohabiting lawyers must follow the same rule as lawyer spouses; they may not represent clients who are adverse unless the clients are informed of the relationship and give their consent to the representation; dating lawyers representing adverse parties also have obligations: they should "disclose the relationship to the clients if their relationship is sufficiently close that it could raise questions in the minds of the clients as to whether their interests would be zealously served"; "[l]awyers should err on the side of caution and should disclose such relationships or decline representation . . . if there is any possibility that the clients would consider the existence of the lawyers' dating relationship to be detrimental to the

Opposing counsel who are in some type of intimate relationship, but are not exclusive, engaged to be married or cohabiting, must carefully consider whether the relationship creates a significant risk that the representation of either client will be materially limited by the lawyers' personal relationships.[17] The prudent course would be to disclose to the affected clients and obtain their informed consent.[18]

---

lawyer-client relationship."); N.C. State Bar Formal Op. 2019-3 (2019) (noting that assistant district attorney and criminal defense lawyer in an intimate relationship may not be adversaries in a case unless they disclose the relationship to and obtain written informed consent from the affected clients and the appropriate governmental official).

Failure to disclose intimate relationships and secure adequate consents can result in discipline, disqualification or other significant consequences. A conviction may be reversed. *See* People v. Jackson, 213 Cal. Rptr. 521, 522 (3d Dist. Ct. App. 1985) (reversing conviction; defense counsel failed to inform defendant of his "dating" relationship with the prosecutor; the two "appeared as counsel in directly adverse roles representing defendant and the People respectively at the preliminary examination, at the pretrial settlement conferences, and at trial"); Commonwealth v. Stote, 922 N.E.2d 768, 778 (Mass. 2010) (Marshall, C.J.) (denying reversal after evidentiary hearing, and noting, "[w]e remind members of the bar of their professional obligation under rule 1.7(b) [analogous to M.R. 1.7(a)(2) and (b)(1)&(4)] to disclose to their clients any intimate personal relationship that might impair their ability to provide untrammeled and unimpaired assistance of counsel."). Fees may be forfeited. *See* DeBolt v. Parker, 560 A.2d 1323 (N.J. 1988) (finding lawyer spouses represented adverse interests; fees allowed but only after finding adequate disclosure and consent under then NJ RPC 1.8(i): "[a] lawyer related to another lawyer as parent child, sibling or spouse shall not represent a client in a representation directly adverse to a person who the lawyer knows is represented by the other lawyer except upon consent by the client after consultation regarding the relationship").

17. *See, e.g.*, State Bar of Mich. Op. R-3 (1989) (opposing counsel who are dating but not cohabiting or engaged must determine whether the relationship is sufficiently close to require disclosure to and informed consent of affected clients); N.Y. State Bar Ass'n Comm. on Prof'l Ethics Op. 660 (1993) ("a couple who date frequently" may not appear opposite one another in a criminal case; "a dating relationship between adversaries is inconsistent with the independence of professional judgement required by [the New York Rules]"; "whether other lawyers [in defense counsel's firm] will be disqualified depends on the facts and circumstances"). *See also* ABA Formal Op. 488, *supra* note 5, at 6-7 (discussing judges' close personal relationships).

18. This opinion does not address personal relationships involving previous marriages or cohabitations, engagements, and exclusive dating arrangements that have ended. Adversaries in such situations, however, must also determine pursuant to Rule 1.7(a)(2) whether there is "a significant risk that the representation of one or more clients will be materially limited" by the lawyer's prior relationship with opposing counsel and act accordingly. *See also* ABA Formal Opinion 488, *supra* note 5, at 6 (stating that "close personal relationships" include "an amicable divorce" and being a "godparent" of a lawyer's or party's child). This opinion also does not address when an existing relationship between opposing counsel ends during the course of the representation. The lawyer whose relationship ends while the representation continues must analyze whether the lawyer's new circumstances create a significant risk that the representation of the client will be materially limited by the change in the relationship and, if so, whether the lawyer must disclose the new circumstances to the affected client and obtain the client's informed consent to continued representation. A factor to be considered would be whether the breakup is amicable or hostile.

B. Friendships

Friendships may be the most difficult category to navigate. On the one hand, an adversary may be a dear and longtime friend or someone with whom the lawyer regularly socializes. On the other hand, an adversary may be considered a "friend" even though contact is occasional, brief, or superficial. As noted in ABA Formal Opinion 488:

> 'Friendship' implies a degree of affinity greater than being acquainted with a person . . . the term connotes some degree of mutual affection. Yet, not all friendships are the same; some may be professional, while others may be social. Some friends are closer than others.[19]

Close friendships with opposing counsel should be disclosed to each affected client and, when circumstances require as described further below, their informed consent obtained. ABA Formal Opinion 488 provides guidance here, too. The following are indicia of friendships that would require disclosure and, ordinarily, informed consent:

> [Lawyers who] exchange gifts at holidays and special occasions; regularly socialize together; regularly communicate and coordinate activities because their children are close friends and routinely spend time at each other's homes; vacation together with their families; share a mentor-protégé relationship developed while colleagues . . . [or] share confidences and intimate details of their lives.[20]

By contrast, friendships that might require disclosure to the affected clients but will not ordinarily require consent from clients include lawyers who "once practiced law together [and] may periodically meet for a meal when their busy schedules permit or, if they live in different cities, try to meet when one is in the other's hometown."[21] Similarly, adversaries who "were law school classmates or were colleagues years before [and] may stay in touch through occasional calls or correspondence, but not regularly see one another"[22] will typically not require the consent of affected clients and may not even require disclosure. Whether either consent or disclosure is required depends on the lawyer's considered judgment as to whether Model Rule 1.7(a)(2) applies and,

---

19. ABA Formal Op. 488, *supra* note 5, at 4. In addition, as noted in footnote 11 of Formal Opinion 488, "[s]ocial media, which is simply a form of communication, uses terminology that is distinct from that used in this opinion. Interaction on social media does not itself indicate the type of relationships participants have with one another either generally or for purposes of this opinion. . . . The proper characterization of a person's relationship with an opposing counsel depends on the definitions and examples used in this opinion."

20. ABA Formal Op. 488, *supra* note 5, at 4.

21. *Id.*

22. *Id.*

if so, whether the lawyer reasonably believes the lawyer can competently and diligently carry out the representation notwithstanding the conflict.

In sum, opposing lawyers who are friends are not *for that reason* alone prohibited from representing adverse clients. The analysis turns on the closeness of the friendship. If there is a significant risk that the representation of one or more clients will be materially limited by a lawyer's relationships, the lawyers must disclose the relationship to each affected client and obtain that client's informed consent, confirmed in writing, assuming the lawyers reasonably believe they will be able to provide competent and diligent representation to each affected client. If the lawyers cannot do so, one or both of the lawyers must decline or withdraw from the affected representations, consistent with Model Rule 1.16.

C. Acquaintances

Acquaintances are relationships that do not carry the familiarity, affinity or attachment of friendships. Lawyers, like judges, "should be considered acquaintances when their interactions . . . are coincidental or relatively superficial, such as being members of the same place of worship, professional or civil organizations, or the like."[23] Lawyers who are "acquaintances" may see each other at such gatherings, even frequently, without feeling a close personal bond. They might regularly meet at bar association or other business events, present continuing education programs together, or serve on bar association committees or boards together where their relationships may be collegial but not necessarily fall into the category of a "friend" that could materially limit the lawyer's independent professional judgment on behalf of a client. Similarly, lawyers who regularly see each other at civic or social events but do not make any particular effort to seek each other's company do not have the type of close personal friendship requiring disclosure and informed consent. Again, as described in ABA Formal Opinion 488, the following without out more do not create a close personal relationship:

> [Lawyers] might both attend bar association or other professional meetings; they may have represented co-parties in litigation. . .; they may meet each other at school or other events involving their children or spouses; they may see each other when socializing with mutual friends; they may belong to the same country club or gym; they may patronize the same businesses and periodically encounter one another there; they may live in the same area or neighborhood and run into one another at neighborhood or area events, or at homeowners' meetings; or they might attend the same religious services. . . . Generally, neither . . . seeks contact with the other, but they greet each other amicably and are cordial when their lives intersect.[24]

---

23. *Id.* at 4.
24. *Id.*

Lawyers who are acquaintances of opposing counsel need not disclose the relationship to clients, although the lawyer may choose to do so. Disclosure may be advisable to maintain good client relations. It may be helpful to inform a client that the lawyer has a professional connection with opposing counsel and then explain how that will not materially limit the lawyer's objectivity but may, in fact, assist in the representation because the lawyers can work collegially.

III. Conclusion

A lawyer's personal relationship with opposing counsel may create a conflict under Model Rule 1.7(a)(2). Lawyers must examine the nature of the relationship to determine if there is a significant risk that lawyer's representation of the client will be materially limited by the lawyer's personal relationship and, if so, whether the lawyer reasonably believes the lawyer will be able to provide competent and diligent representation to each affected client and each affected, who must then give informed consent, confirmed in writing.

Using the guidelines in this opinion, lawyers should evaluate whether the relationship is a close personal or intimate relationship, a friendship, or the adversary is merely an acquaintance. Cohabiting, intimate and similar relationships with opposing counsel must be disclosed, and the lawyers ordinarily may not represent clients in the matter, unless each client gives informed consent confirmed in writing. Because friendships exist in a wide variety of contexts, friendships need to be examined closely. Close friendships with opposing counsel should be disclosed to clients and, where appropriate, as discussed in Part IIB, their informed consent, confirmed in writing, obtained. By contrast, some friendships and most relationships that fall into the category of acquaintances need not be disclosed, nor is clients' informed consent required. Regardless of whether disclosure is mandated, however, the lawyer may choose to disclose the relationship. Disclosure may even be advisable to maintain good client relations.

AMERICAN BAR ASSOCIATION
STANDING COMMITTEE ON ETHICS AND PROFESSIONAL RESPONSIBILITY
321 N. Clark Street, Chicago, Illinois 60654-4714 Telephone (312) 988-5328
CHAIR: Barbara S. Gillers, New York, NY
■ Lonnie T. Brown, Athens, GA ■ Robert Hirshon, Ann Arbor, MI ■ Hon. Goodwin Liu, San Francisco, CA
■ Thomas B. Mason, Washington, DC ■ Michael H. Rubin, Baton Rouge, LA
■ Lynda Shely, Scottsdale, AZ ■ Norman W. Spaulding, Stanford, CA
■ Elizabeth Clark Tarbert, Tallahassee, FL ■ Lisa D. Taylor, Parsippany, NJ

CENTER FOR PROFESSIONAL RESPONSIBILITY